PROGRAMME EVALUATION IN ELT

D.T. Crystal

Applied Language Studies
Edited by David Crystal and Keith Johnson

This new series aims to deal with key topics within the main branches of applied language studies – initially in the fields of foreign language teaching and learning, child language acquisition and clinical or remedial language studies. The series will provide students with a research perspective in a particular topic, at the same time containing an original slant which will make each volume a genuine contribution to the development of ideas in the subject.

Series List

EVALUATION IN ELT

Cyril Weir and Jon Roberts

BLACKWELL
Oxford UK & Cambridge USA

Copyright © C. J. Weir and J. Roberts 1994

The right of C. J. Weir and J. Roberts to be identified as authors of this work has been asserted in accordance with the Copyright, Designs and Patents Act 1988.

First published 1994

Blackwell Publishers
108 Cowley Road
Oxford   OX4 1JF
UK

238 Main Street
Cambridge, Massachusetts 02142
USA

British Library Cataloguing in Publication Data

A CIP catalogue record for this book is available from the British Library.

Library of Congress Cataloging-in-Publication Data

Weir, Cyril J.
     Evaluation in ELT / Cyril Weir and Jon Roberts.
          p.   cm. — (Applied language studies)
     Includes bibliographical references and index.
     ISBN 0–631–16571–1. — ISBN 0–631–16572–X (pbk.)
     1. English language—Study and teaching—Foreign speakers—
—Evaluation.   2. English language—Ability testing—Evaluation.
I. Roberts, Jon.   II. Title.   III. Series.
PE1128.A2W3953   1994
428′.0076—dc20   93–43243
                                                              CIP

Typeset in 10 on 12 pt Ehrhardt
by Graphicraft Typesetters Ltd, Hong Kong
Printed in Great Britain by T.J. Press (Padstow) Ltd, Padstow, Cornwall.

This book is printed on acid-free paper

Contents

Figures

Tables

Acknowledgements

The authors would like to thank colleagues whose comments on earlier drafts of this book helped greatly to improve its final form. Special thanks are due to Pauline Rea-Dickins, Ron Mackay, Carew Treffgarne, Keith Johnson, and Eddie Williams. Our thanks are also due to MATEFL students taking the Evaluation course in CALS who offered comments and criticisms on earlier versions of the book; in particular we are grateful to Ester Jansen-Strasser, Paul Maw, and Simon Sergeant.

The authors would like to acknowledge the debt they owe to the work of Charles Alderson (1985, 1986, 1992), Judith Bell (Bell 1987, Bell et al. 1984), Alan Beretta (1986a, 1986b, 1986c, 1987, 1990), Cohen and Manion (1980) and most of all to the contributors to the Program Evaluation Kit developed by Sage publications (particularly King et al. 1987 and Patton 1987b) in developing their ideas on collecting data reported below. These works influenced us greatly in the early evaluations we conducted and our work owes much to the ideas they contain. We recommend them strongly to all would be evaluators.

We have learnt about evaluation from a range of sources: from various authorities in the field (such as Cronbach, Fullan, the Joint Committee on Standards for Educational Evaluation, MacKay, ODA staff); from the teachers we have worked with; from the students on our MA programme and from our own experience. We are grateful for their contribution to this book.

The publisher would like to thank the following for their permission to reproduce material that falls within their copyright:

The British Council for extracts from *Managing ELT Aid Projects, Dunford House Seminar Report, 1989* (1990); a figure from *Statistics of Overseas Students in the United Kingdom, 1978/9* (1980); and a passage from *Testing English for University Study*, ELT Documents 127. The British Association of Lecturers in English for Academic Purposes for *Guidelines for the Code of Practice* (June 1989). Cambridge University Press for a figure from *Training Foreign Language Teachers* (1991) by M. J. Wallace. The Centre for Applied Language Studies, Don McGovern, and John Trzeciak for pre-sessional course evaluation instruments. Croom Helm for a figure from *Research Methods in Education* (1980) by L. Cohen and L. Manion

Deakin University Press for ten figures from *Studying Classrooms* (1981) by Colin Hook. The Department of Psychology, University of London for an extract from *Effective In-service Training: A Learning Resource Pack*. A table in *Inservice Education for Content Area Teachers* (1985) edited by M. D. Siedow, D. Memory, and P. S. Bristow. Reprinted with permission of the International Reading Association. Longman Group UK for an extract from *English for Special Purposes* (1978) edited by R. Mackay. Macmillan ELT for appendix 2 and appendix 5 from *Testing English for University Study*, ELT Documents 127 (1988) edited by A Hughes. David Middleton for his mimeo on nominal group technique. The Open University Press for a figure from *A Teacher's Guide to Classroom Research* (1985) by David Hopkins. The Overseas Development Administration for permission to refer to the authors' reports to them (Nepal and Paraguay). Four figures from A. Malamah-Thomas: *Classroom Interaction* (1987). © Oxford University Press. Reprinted by permission of Oxford University Press. Pergamon Press for an extract from *Professional Standards for Educational Evaluation* (1990) by D. Stufflebeam. RELC SEAMEO Singapore for permission to use extracts from Weir and Roberts (1991). A figure from *How to Design a Programme Evaluation* (1987) by Carol Taylor Fitz-Gibbon and Lynn Lyons Morris and figures from *Utilization-focused Evaluation* (1986) by M. Q. Patton. Reprinted by permission of Sage Publications Inc. The Teachers College Press for a checklist from *The Classroom Observer: A Guide for Developing Observation Skills* (1977) by Ann E. Boehm and Richard A. Weinberg. The University of Cambridge Local Examinations Syndicate for the summary of criteria for RSA/UCLES Dip TEFLA assessors.

Acronyms

ARELS–FELCO	Association of Recognized English Language Schools Federation of English Language Course Organizers
BALEAP	British Association for Lecturers in English for Academic Purposes
CALS	Centre for Applied Language Studies, University of Reading
DipTEFLA	Diploma in Teaching English as a Foreign Language to Adults
EAP	English for Academic Purposes
EFL	English as a Foreign Language
ELT	English Language Teaching
ELTO	English Language Teaching Officer
IELTS	International English Language Testing Service
ESP	English for Specific Purposes
INSET	In-service Education and Training
MATEFL	MA in Teaching English as a Foreign Language
ODA	Overseas Development Administration
RSA	Royal Society of Arts
SAS	Statistical Analysis System
SEPELT	Science Education Project English Language Teaching
SLC	School Leaving Certificate
TALOS	Target Language Observation Scheme
TEEP	Test in English for Educational Purposes
TEU	Testing and Evaluation Unit, University of Reading
UCLES	University of Cambridge Local Examinations Syndicate

Part I Overview

1 Evaluation of Second Language Projects and Programmes: An Overview

1.1 Introductory

This book is for readers who may be subject to an evaluation or who may do one. If you are *subject* to an evaluation, you will need an understanding of evaluation approaches and techniques because you will then be able to assess the worth of the evaluation and, if necessary, defend your rights. This book is intended to help equip you to be a better critic of evaluations in their planning, execution, and product. If you act as an *evaluator*, you will need a sound grasp of evaluation principles and techniques married to curricular expertise and experience in areas such as teaching, materials writing, syllabus design, test writing, teacher training, and management. We hope that this book can contribute to the preparation of ELT programme and project evaluators.

We refer in this book to the evaluation of programmes and projects. The term *'programme'* applies to any organized educational activity offered on a continuing basis. 'Programme' therefore embraces both individual language programmes or training courses as well as a wider range of ELT-related operations at one or more locations within a single country. It might be an institutional offering, an innovative syllabus, a teacher-upgrading course, or any of a variety of applied linguistics related activities.[1] However, once educational activities are subjected to contractual definition and finite time-scales, they are normally referred to as projects (Joint Committee 1981). The term *'project'* therefore refers to activities funded to achieve a particular task, usually based on a formal contract in which staff duties are defined and measurable outcomes or products are specified, all within a stated timescale. Overseas Development Administration (ODA) aid project frameworks are a case of this.[2] The key distinction lies in expectations: in the case of a programme, that it will be ongoing, whereas projects are normally expected to have a limited lifespan (Joint Committee 1981: 12–13).

This chapter was originally conceived in collaboration with Professor Ron MacKay of Concordia University, Canada.

The purpose of evaluation is to collect information systematically in order to indicate the worth or merit of a programme or project (from certain aspects or as a whole) and to inform decision making. Decisions may be made by staff who are 'insiders' in order to improve their programme or project, or they may be made by 'outsiders' (e.g. employees of the bureaucracy or of a funding body) in order to determine educational policy and spending. The differing nature of these decisions has tended to lead insiders to focus on development and outsiders on end products. The central thesis of this book, arrived at from the personal experience of the writers, is that while both sides have their distinctive needs, the most constructive approach to evaluation would seek to integrate and synthesize their respective contributions to curriculum improvement through evaluation (see sections 1.3 and 1.5).

A good working definition of evaluation suitable for this book might therefore be: 'the systematic collection and analysis of all relevant information necessary to promote the improvement of the curriculum, and assess its effectiveness and efficiency, as well as the participants' attitudes within a context of particular institutions involved' (Brown 1989: 223), since it can apply to programme or project design, implementation and outcomes, and can relate evaluation to participants' reactions and also to educational contexts.

In the rest of this chapter, we present a framework for considering ELT programme or project evaluation and end by discussing standards by which to 'evaluate evaluations'.

1.2   Evaluation: Accountability and development

We first distinguish between evaluation for purposes of *accountability* and evaluation for purposes of programme or project *development*. These two purposes have often been assumed to be in conflict. However, as a result of our experiences reported in the case studies below (see chapters 3–5), we feel that in the future it would be more productive to incorporate both dimensions into ELT programme or project evaluation.

In general, *accountability* refers to the answerability of staff to others for the quality of their work. 'Others' in this case could be bureaucrats, employers, senior school staff, parents, students, the community, or the taxpayer. We should distinguish between *contractual accountability*, where job descriptions and planned outcomes are clearly specified in formal contracts and project frameworks (as for Overseas Development Administration project staff – see Coleman 1987, British Council 1990, chapter 3, and appendix 1.1) and more general *professional accountability*, where there may be an expectation that staff and administrators should be answerable for their work as it affects others, for example in the use of resources, in their professional practice, or in programme outcomes. This is often less formally defined than contractual accountability; also, the term may be interpreted differently by different interest groups. The most formal and explicit expression of professional accountability is met where practitioners submit themselves to external inspection or assessment by a regulatory body (see section 4.5 and appendix 4.1).

It is characteristic of the nineties, as state and private resources shrink, that in many sectors professional responsibility is seen to include public accountability both to clients and to resource providers. An aspect of this greater accountability is that budgetary responsibility is often devolved to those who previously were merely spenders: this is currently the situation in the United Kingdom in the business sector and in the state sector, such as in health care and in state schools in England and Wales, which now have to manage their own annual budgets ('Local Management of Schools'). Accountability-oriented evaluation is intended to assess the degree to which staff have met contractual or professional accountability demands. It is usually *summative* in focus, in that it examines the effects of a programme or project at significant end points of an educational cycle (in the case of programmes) or at its completion date (in the case of projects). It is usually conducted for the benefit of an external audience or decision maker.

In comparison, development-oriented evaluation is intended to bring about programme or project improvement and will normally be *formative* in nature; it 'regards the program as fluid and seeks ways to better it' (Cronbach 1982: 12); 'Formative evaluators . . . aim . . . to ensure that the program be implemented as effectively as possible. The formative evaluator watches over the program, alert both for problems and good ideas that can be shared' (Morris and Fitz-Gibbon 1978: 24). It may be carried out by internal or external evaluators but is generally held to be more effective when carried out by a combination of both (see chapters 4 and 5, Day et al. 1987).

It is important to note, however, that the data generated by such formative evaluations can *also* contribute to meeting both professional and contractual accountability demands. Furthermore, in the case of the pre-sessional language programme reported in chapter 4, though much of the evaluation is formative in that it is conducted during the course to facilitate improvement, summative test and questionnaire data are also generated at the end of the course. These data are used summatively to examine the value of the course from a bureaucratic perspective but additionally are used by the course director and teachers for taking educational decisions which relate formatively to subsequent programmes. Thus, labelling evaluation data as formative or summative must relate closely to the purpose for which it has been collected. Where data are used to evaluate effectiveness against specified criteria, it is summative, and where it is used to influence change, it is formative. Data can serve both formative and summative purposes in both developmental and accountability-oriented evaluations.

1.2.1 Evaluation for external accountability

An accountability-oriented evaluation is often motivated by the bureaucracy's need to monitor programmes or projects for which it is responsible. Much of the data may be collected on a routine basis by management (e.g. a project manager, head teacher, or a director of studies). Periodic checks may also be made by an external evaluator, possibly from within the bureaucracy. The focus of evaluation for accountability is likely to be upon planned events: whether they occurred on schedule and made use of resources within the budget as planned, and whether they eventually produced intended effects.

Such an *extrinsically* motivated evaluation conforms to the traditional model of bureaucratic inspection. Within this approach, what is to be inspected, how the inspection is undertaken, and what action, if any, must be taken as a result of the inspection have conventionally been determined at the bureaucratic level outside the programme or project itself, external to the staff concerned with implementation (teachers, project staff, and so on).

The advantages of extrinsically motivated accountability evaluation are several. The bureaucracy (funding agency, government department) can compare plans (for example, the time-line of events, expenditures, personnel hired, materials prepared, training sessions delivered, or numbers of students provided for) with actual events and assess the achievement of objectives. However, unless data have been collected relating to the actual implementation of the project or programme, they are unlikely to provide reasons for success or failure (see sections 1.3 and 1.5).

In the financial climate of the nineties, in which all spending (public and private) is subject to rigorous review, there is a danger of educational evaluation being driven by the need to demonstrate cost-effectiveness through the comparison of quantified, verifiable inputs and outputs. Typifying this view, one educator has likened educational processes to industrial production: 'Like the makers of hamburgers or automobiles, we must be able to weigh our product, measure it, engineer it for effectiveness and efficiency, and market it' (Holcomb quoted in Mackay forthcoming).

It is understandable that this trend should be particularly strong in the case of project evaluation. The ODA has stressed that:

> projects must be planned in relation to the contribution they make to the social and economic development of a country, with a focus on the alleviation of poverty. It is against this criterion that they will be assessed. . . . Moreover, this 'value' must not just be demonstrable but measurable, since without measurement the relationship of value-of-output to cost-of-input cannot be demonstrated. (British Council 1989: 11)

There are, however, limitations to and potential dangers in the bureaucratic, extrinsic inspection approach. The most obvious limitation is that only readily observed or measured phenomena (e.g. events and expenditures) may be applied as criteria of success, whereas less readily measured phenomena (such as staff morale and attitudes, staff reactions or institutional ethos) may be ignored or regarded as insufficiently reliable evidence with which to justify spending decisions. However, these less reliably described features may in fact be of crucial importance to the sustained quality of the programme or project.

1.2.2 Evaluation for development

Development-oriented evaluation is intended to improve the educational quality of a programme or project, normally while it is in progress. This form of evaluation may be carried out cooperatively between an external evaluator and the insider staff (see chapter 5 for a proposed framework and also Alderson and Scott 1992, Bachman 1987) or by insiders only (chapter 4 and, for example, Easen 1985). In either case, evaluation for development should be guided by the intrinsic concerns of insiders: by the identification of strengths which can be built upon (for example, parts of the course, materials or teaching which are working well) as well as by the identification of obstacles to progress and the introduction of more effective means to achieve desired objectives. It can be both formative and summative in focus, with a tendency for the former to be foregrounded by those concerned with implementation – that is, the teaching staff – while the latter may be of greater priority to project managers and programme administrators.

Cronbach (1982: chapter 1) makes a strong case for the formative dimension in all evaluation studies. He sees it as making a greater contribution to education than merely evaluating a finished product at an end point in a programme or project when it is often too late to take any action. For example, in the Nepal study described in chapter 3, the summative evaluation threw up a number of problems in the design of the teacher training project but by then the project was over. These problems could have been sorted out earlier if resources and conditions of service had allowed for formative monitoring through follow-up visits to trainees after the training courses. Similarly, modifying new materials in the language programme (see the case study in chapter 4) was better carried out formatively on a week-to-week basis rather than if we had waited until the end of the course to make important changes or provide additional exercises for certain of the units in the course materials. In the same way, on such programmes it is better to identify *at an early stage* students whose progress is slow rather than to wait until the end of the course, possibly failing them and sending them back to face disgrace in their own country. (The timing of formative and summative evaluation is discussed further in section 1.4.2.)

Furthermore, it should be recognized that involvement in self-directed formative evaluation is *a form of teacher development*, arguably one of the most effective forms if done consistently, collaboratively, and with relevant external help if and when it is needed (Cohen and Manion 1984, Day et al. 1987, Edge and Richards 1993, Kemmis and McTaggart 1982a, 1982b, McNiff 1988: chapter 4; see also chapters 5 and 8). The benefits for teachers of involvement in self-directed formative evaluation are considerable, including as they do a deepening and development of teachers' perceptions of classroom events, developments in practice, improved professional dialogue with peers, and improved skills and confidence in exploring and presenting issues of professional concern (Linder 1991, Roberts 1993). These benefits of active and collaborative self-evaluation are probably maximized if teachers are able to participate in systematic action research into their own practice (Edge and Richards 1993, McNiff 1988, Somekh 1993). However, though action research may not suit all contexts nor all teachers, it still seems that there is a potential professional development spin-off in all formative evaluation activity (Easen 1985, Roberts 1993).

In terms of methods, it is most important that formative/development-oriented evaluation plans take into account the workload upon teachers. Burton and Mickan (1993: 115) are right to refer to teaching as 'a practical and hectic activity' and so the benefits of involvement in programme or project development must not be lost by overloading teachers with impractical evaluation tasks. The best general principle is to try to incorporate formative evaluation into the normal work of the teacher (through interpretation of formal test results, study of students' written work, and well-focused and systematic observation of their classroom behaviour) rather than tacked on to it (such as in recording classroom events or administering open item questionnaires). It is also very important that timetables build in opportunities for collaborative development work, for example through regular staff meetings (see section 1.4.6 and chapters 4 and 5).

1.3   A broader approach to evaluation

A more comprehensive approach to evaluation would seek to embrace both the accountability and development dimensions discussed briefly above: it would not only measure educational products but also help to throw light on the reasons why things are turning out the way they are. It would satisfy contractual or bureaucratic demands and produce information for programme or project improvement as well. It would encourage the greater professional accountability of staff to the receivers of teaching or training, to their colleagues, to the institutions where they work, and to the community. This approach suggests that insiders can collect information to meet external (both contractual and formal professional) accountability demands as well as for the more usual developmental purposes (chapters 4 and 5).

One benefit of insider involvement is that working through staff concerns can have a highly positive effect on a programme or project as it encourages active participation in identifying and collecting information which all parties recognize as useful. It enables cooperative evaluation in which both client and staff concerns are addressed. In our experience, this type of evaluation (possessing characteristics of both extrinsically and intrinsically motivated approaches) can forge stronger and more trusting relations between the bureaucracy, staff, and external evaluators. Furthermore, since most changes recommended by an external evaluation study must be implemented by insiders, it is more likely that they will address them actively if they have been party to the process that identifies them (Alderson and Scott 1992, Patton 1986; also section 1.4.7, on the use of evaluation data, and chapter 8, on the issue of ownership).

Conversely, external evaluators for accountability can themselves contribute to formative study in at least two ways.

1 They could help formulate evaluation designs which are clearly structured to provide a positive role for insider data collection.
2 They could be involved in collecting formative information, other than that required for extrinsic accountability purposes (as in the Nepal example reported in chapter 3 and as suggested in chapter 4).

Of course both contributions are potentially subject to constraint. First, there are situations where the role of an external evaluator would be compromised by any prior involvement in formative studies. This is especially true where a consideration of product outcomes is the valid basis for decisions, as in the case of a summative evaluation of a project to determine the merit of a project extension in terms of its socio-economic value to the host community – for example, whether the project delivered an adequate number of trained personnel who have remained in the system as planned. Second, the extent to which information resulting from accountability-oriented evaluation can be made available to staff for formative purposes will of course depend on the body contracting the evaluation, in two ways: by virtue of its power to control the amount of funds dedicated to the evaluation activity; and by virtue of its authority to withhold or make available information of various kinds about the operation of the project.

1.3.1 A broader approach: Focus on projects

In most ELT projects to date, there has been a tendency not to integrate the development and accountability-oriented dimensions to evaluation, because they are carried out by different parties serving different interests. As external evaluators in Nepal, we were acutely aware of the strong accountability orientation of the baseline study which the external funding agency had contracted us to carry out for summative purposes. We were equally aware of the valuable formative contribution we could have made had our terms of reference been different. The tensions involved in conducting such baseline measures are discussed more fully in chapter 2 below and in the Nepal case study discussed in chapter 3.

Our experiences in conducting evaluations in Nepal and subsequently in Guinea and Paraguay (see chapters 3 and 5 and Burton and Weir forthcoming) have convinced us of the need for a broader approach to evaluation which would involve project staff (both local and expatriate) as active participants in ongoing data collection for both formative *and* summative purposes, rather than merely as suspicious objects of contractual accountability (Alderson and Scott 1992). This would integrate evaluation into the whole life-cycle of the project. As Brown (1989) has argued, evaluation is the crucial element for success in all stages of a project's life. The process of active monitoring (evaluation during the implementation stage) could be of great benefit to both staff and project in that it would maintain and develop staff awareness of goals and objectives. After the initial enthusiasm of a project launch, staff can fall into routines so that their energies go into 'keeping things going', rather than reflecting on why certain things are done or to what effect. We would argue that active involvement in project monitoring and data collection could lead to a heightened awareness of the long-term purpose of projects. This awareness would provide staff with a yardstick against which to measure the value and the effect of their day-to-day activities, and to consider alternative lines of action. It should enable all concerned to better reflect upon, understand, and assess what they are doing, why they are doing it, and how to improve upon it. We therefore suggest that as a result of active involvement in evaluation, project staff could be led to reappraise learning objectives, prepare or adapt materials in response to unfolding student needs, and develop techniques to monitor performance and progress – both theirs and their students'. Indeed, integrated evaluation activity can be seen as crucial to the development of insiders' professional competence and to the capability of local staff to sustain a project when expatriates leave. (See chapters 3 and 5 where the sustainability of both projects would have been enhanced by involving local staff in the evaluation process.)

However, the involvement of staff in evaluation does have certain prerequisites: conditions of service which give them the time and resources to carry out the activities; the devolution of genuine responsibility to monitor and modify a project; the readiness of more senior staff to share significant information; the acquisition of necessary skills by insider staff.

We therefore suggest that a product-oriented, contractual model of accountability should not be assumed to be the only viable basis for programme and project evaluation. It is a necessary but not sufficient contribution to the more comprehensive approach to evaluation proposed, which views evaluation as contributing to understanding and thereby to general professional accountability and development, as well as satisfying any contractual accountability requirements.

We summarize our position on evaluation design in section 1.6 and discuss its relation to the case studies in the introduction to part 2.

This approach to programme and project evaluation is now discussed further under the traditional 'Wh' question headings: *Why, When, How long, What, Who,* and *How.* We have found it useful to consider an evaluation from these different perspectives at the planning stage.

1.4 Aspects of evaluation

1.4.1 Why?

Professional information

A major reason for programme and project evaluation is that a wider audience can benefit from the educational experience than those immediately involved (on condition that there are effective information channels for disseminating this information). Evaluations of programmes and projects can provide:

1 evidence which can inform theoretical disputes about directions to be followed in language teaching or in teacher education, and
2 context-sensitive information on implementation: for example, to indicate whether particular approaches or techniques are suitable under given conditions; whether they meet the claims made for them; whether certain textbooks or materials are appropriate or inappropriate, effective or not for various contexts, purposes, and groups of learners.

The value of a broader approach to evaluation is suggested by the case of the Bangalore project, also known as the Communicative Teaching Project (CTP; Beretta and Davies 1985, Beretta 1992). Here there was disappointment in some quarters at the limited extent to which it provided insights for a wider audience about the project and how it achieved its results. Greenwood (1985: 272) expressed the implementation concerns of the professional audience by framing four questions, which he expected to be answered by such an evaluation:

1 How much language-based rehearsal is needed for students in the Communicative Teaching Project (C.T.P.) to succeed in carrying out the tasks?
2 What does experience with the C.T.P. have to say about the role of a linguistic syllabus?
3 How well do C.T.P. students transfer their classroom learning to the street?
4 In what ways is the C.T.P. methodology innovative?

As his implementation concerns were not addressed because of its limited attention to the formative dimension, he dismissed the evaluation, as follows: 'as their account deals with an evaluation of the project in terms of comparing the performance of experimental and control groups taught by the communicative method and the structural method, the article has little direct bearing on the points I raise here (see questions 1–4 above)'.

A further example of the value of comprehensive evaluation data can be found in the field of teacher training. Professional standards require that training be reported in a way that enables the audience to evaluate the knowledge base used, the approach to training that determines activities used, and the outcomes of the training in terms of teachers' attitudes and practice. Therefore, evaluation methods and findings are routinely included in accounts of training in education (e.g. Ashton et al. 1989 and Martin and Norwich 1991). Remarkably, no equivalent, adequate accounts in the field of ELT are known to the authors at the time of writing (but see some detail in Alderson and Beretta 1992) and are frequently glaring in their omission (e.g. Dubin and Wong 1990).

A broader approach to evaluation would make a wide range of information available to help and inform others interested in the same sort of activities or involved in similar programmes or projects. This would enable them to learn from these experiences and improve upon them. One shudders to think how many times the wheel has been re-invented in ELT programmes and projects round the world. Where is the collective memory of decades of projects? Where does one go to learn from the mistakes and successes of similar projects in the past? Even from one course to the next there is often no documentation as to what was done last time; what worked and what did not. There is sometimes even no permanent record available for those who teach the course the next time round. The main reason for the absence of such evaluation data is often the lack of any infrastructure to ensure its collection. Furthermore, systems are required to ensure the follow-through of the evaluation process: that information is acted on and made publicly available (Rudduck 1981 and section 1.4.7). As such there is often a clear need for managers to take an active role in setting up such systems, and ensuring that the resources for carrying them out are available (see chapter 4). The logistics of collecting such implementation data in a systematic fashion cannot be ignored; we understand that it is demanding and time consuming but we are also aware that it is valuable and viable if resources and terms of employment allow it.

There may also be some resistance among staff to recognizing the relevance of other evaluation findings to their own context. This may be a result of a lack of awareness or insight into the evaluation process; or simply that they have never encountered these data or that these data are not available in the professional literature.

Professionals in other spheres such as engineering or sport would find it strange to fail to analyse their performance so that they could improve next time, or to fail to provide fellow professionals with accounts of practice that enable improvement in their work. A concern for professionalism in language teaching might urge us to do the same in a similarly systematic fashion. As Davies (1992) points out, it is important for those writing evaluation accounts for their peers to identify and interpret the key issues and potentially generalizable lessons contained in their findings.

Focus on projectization

In the past, aid projects were sometimes started with insufficient attention to a host of important issues such as:

- aims and objectives
- the inputs necessary to achieve specified outputs
- the means of verification of this achievement
- viability of intended courses of action in particular contexts
- the adequacy of available means (human and material) for success
- the hoped-for impact of the project on the host country
- whether it was really worth doing anyway
- the commitment of the host country to the project
- how the project was to be managed both from the home base and locally
- other lines of responsibility of both the expatriates and counterparts

If one (or more) of these key elements is overlooked before the start of a project or during its implementation, project staff may only become aware of problems after something has begun to go wrong. By the time these unforeseen problems display themselves with sufficient severity to warrant attention, it is often too late to correct the situation without major compromises being made, compromises which can endanger the entire project.

Recently, ELT and other projects both at home and overseas have become subject to economic constraints as the educational sector has had to compete with other bids for government funding (see section 1.2). By insisting that they take into consideration, *inter alia*, cost-effectiveness as a criterion for judging merit, funding agencies are able to determine whether their money is being well spent. Effectiveness and value for money are criteria which must now be adequately met and demonstrated by project mangers (see Horngren 1977 and Levin 1983). In fact, financial accountability is increasingly a priority for all managers, both in programmes (e.g. private language schools) or in projects.

In this respect, the value of a project framework approach, such as that used by the ODA (see appendix 1.1), is particularly apparent both at the appraisal stage (assessing a project's feasibility prior to any funding; see chapter 2) and at the summative, end-of-project stages (to assess how successful it has been; see chapter 3). Key players submitting a proposal, having referred to other stakeholders (people who potentially have a stake in the evaluation – i.e. who it may affect to varying degrees; see Case et al. 1985: 6–7), are better able to specify clear and reasonable goals for the project, objectives to be accomplished at various key stages, the quantity and quality of resources required for each objective or cluster of objectives, the results expected from the management of these resources, and the quantity and quality of outputs to be produced during the project period. The purpose of completing such a framework is to provide for proof of achievement by indicating clearly the criteria for success. Means of verification have to be clearly specified so as to show what and how data will be gathered to assess the achievement of objectives. The project stakeholders also have to consider and document assumptions and conditions already known to affect the progress or success of the project, but over which they may have little or no control. (See British Council 1989, 1990 and 1991 and Coleman 1986, 1987 for details of the project framework approach; for examples of actual frameworks, see British Council 1990 and appendix 1.1).

The project framework is the medium for contractual accountability, spelt out for key stakeholders including the host government, and as such is a valuable stimulus to project effectiveness. As argued above, it is not in itself, however, sufficient as a basis for evaluation because it limits its attention to an external accountability and virtually not at all to internally motivated development concerns.

A development orientation requires monitoring – that is, the description and explanation of events occurring in the life of a project in order to permit the fine-tuning of project work on a short-term basis and to provide an understanding of the dynamics of how results are related to actions. A comprehensive picture of what has happened in a project implementation is needed before explanations can be offered. Therefore the role of development evaluation is to understand how a programme or project produces its effects and what factors and processes influence its effectiveness. The purpose of a comprehensive and adequate evaluation should not just be to determine whether a project has produced successful 'outputs' but also to provide stakeholders with as detailed a description as possible of all implementation factors and how the interaction of these factors contributed to the project's degree of success.

In the case of some ELT programmes, the highly structured framework of projectization may be less appropriate (see Rea-Dickens and Germaine 1992). The increasing demand for value for money and accountability, however, are likely to require a similar systematicity in the work of programme staff (*mutatis mutandis*). Furthermore, with the increasing privatization of ELT project work by UK funding agencies, in which bids are invited through open tendering, commercial language teaching organizations are increasingly accepting contractual responsibility for projects. This means that their employees are now required to function as insider project staff who have to meet the demands of contractual accountability. For many this will constitute the adoption of a new professional role and a different orientation to evaluation activity.

1.4.2   When?

The timing of evaluation: Formative and summative dimensions

We have briefly considered reasons for carrying out evaluation activities at a number of stages: to assess the feasibility of a project or programme before the start (appraisal); to evaluate events during its life (monitoring); and to assess its worth as it ends (summative evaluation). All are important parts of the evaluation process. We now consider in more detail at what points in the life of a programme or project interventions by insider or outsider evaluators are appropriate. As suggested above, systematic evaluation *throughout* a programme or project for improvement (formative evaluation), should be integrated with summative evaluation.

Systematic formative evaluation can operate as a form of quality control, the monitoring of progress and the provision of immediately useful information for decision making and change, at managerial and staff level. It is used to help guide the programme or project in the light of regular feedback on the way it is developing, through gathering information which might enable corrections to be made (for example, to pedagogical approach or overall weighting of components). It is important that evaluation conducted for this purpose is explicit and systematic and is fed back to bureaucrats as well as insider staff. A further benefit is that it could arm insiders with evidence to justify changes that may be questioned by the bureaucracy. Such formative data may of course contribute to effective summative evaluation (see discussion in section 1.2 above).

For evaluation to be comprehensive, data need to be generated which not only provide a full account of what has taken place but which also contribute to an understanding of the reasons behind the practices that affect success. Summative data collected on the results obtained at the end of a programme or project (e.g. student test scores) are unlikely to help us understand the processes that gave rise to them. (See chapters 2 and 3 for a discussion of the need for observational data on teacher take-up of training in an accountability-oriented evaluation in order to interpret the impact of the training process on student language performance as measured by summative tests.) In this case summative data are of little use on their own in deciding how improvements might be made.

Evaluation could usefully integrate formative and summative dimensions and be concerned both with the results of a programme or project as well as an understanding of how these results came about – that is, with *processes* and activities during implementation as well as with end *products*.

Formative evaluation during a programme or project (preferably throughout its life) can help those involved to negotiate its direction with a deeper understanding of its internal and external dynamics. In many ways this 'middle period' is the most important time to be getting information, as it will enable staff to take any steps necessary in terms of readjustment and to justify their actions to the bureaucracy. In-house mid-term feedback sessions are invaluable in this respect in most courses. Regular feedback sessions with students and lesson pro forma sheets filled out by teachers provide a valuable permanent record of a course and allow for ongoing modification (see chapter 4 for further discussion of formative evaluation in relation to a language course).

When evaluation is conducted only at the end of programmes or projects, it frequently means that crucial information for the evaluation is no longer available. Beretta (1987, 1992) gives an interesting account of the problems this created for the evaluation of an experimental teaching project, more commonly known as the Communicative Teaching Project (also in section 1.4.1).

If there is no commitment to documentation during implementation, then any summative evaluation is likely to be less informative or effective since so much data would be lost, for example regarding what's been done in lessons, feedback on this from staff and students, comments on materials and methodology, test data, continuous assessment data, time allotted, attendance records, classroom observations, etc. Thus a commitment to ongoing professional accountability in no way conflicts with, and indeed can only serve to improve, the more summatively oriented contractual or external accountability.

Baseline measures in language projects

As a result of the projectization of ELT aid work, there has also been much recent interest in collecting *baseline* evaluation data. Baseline measures can be made at two stages.

1   At the appraisal stage (before implementation), the feasibility and potential value of a project can be established.
2   To determine gains made as an effect of instruction, it is advisable to take relevant measures on entry to and on exit from a project.

Thus, at the very start of the implementation stage, measurements of criterial features can be determined (e.g. pupil language data or teachers' classroom behaviour) to allow later comparisons with project outcomes. Chapter 2 discusses fully baseline data collection at both these stages.

Our experiences in setting up a baseline evaluation study in Nepal (see chapters 2 and 3) convinced us of the additional need for a development orientation in short in-service teacher training projects. Our original brief as outside evaluators was to establish the language level of students in the classes of trained teachers who had been through one of the project's one-month training courses and in those of untrained teachers. This was done at the start of the study (the baseline data point) and at the end of the study. What became evident very early on in the study was the additional need to collect data on process variables relating to the take-up of training by the trained teachers when they left the short one-month training course and returned to their classrooms. Without these data it would not have been possible to interpret the impact of the project through test data alone: if there had been no significant difference in performance between pupils in trained and untrained teachers' classes, we would not have known why this was so. The teachers may not have put into practice essential elements of the training and we would not have been aware of this.

Retrospectively we feel that formative monitoring through follow-up activities should be built into any teacher training project from the outset (and allowance made for this in the conditions of service of the officers employed) and the results fed back on a regular basis to improve the subsequent training courses. In this way some of the problems brought up by the baseline study (see chapter 3) could have been avoided, such as the fact that though a number of days were spent on writing activities in the training, the Nepalese teachers had no time to try these out on return to their schools because of time pressure and the low value accorded to writing in the School Leaving Certificate.

If a summatively oriented baseline study had been more harmoniously integrated with insider-driven formative evaluation, then a more powerful picture could have emerged concerning any improvement in pupil performance resulting from increasingly effective one-month training courses. Our baseline measures might usefully have been staggered to determine whether the increasingly improved one-month training courses resulted in increasingly improved impact on student language performance.

1.4.3   How long?

The duration of external evaluator involvement is related to the timing of evaluations in the life-cycle of a project or programme. Although the situation is improving, in some cases a visiting outside evaluator still comes, gathers a necessarily limited amount of date (usually rapidly and in a matter of days), and leaves, often to examine the data and draw conclusions far from the project or programme and its participants and without the benefit of their comments or insights. Indeed, the brief, data-gathering visit may be the end of any direct connection they may have and the external evaluator may not even receive any feedback how the report, conclusions, and recommendations were received by staff, if indeed they actually see the report (see chapter 5 for an example of this).

Such a state of affairs is obviously inadequate for the conduct of cooperative comprehensive evaluations. The duration of an evaluation, including the length of contact time any external evaluator or evaluation facilitator needs to have with the project or programme and its staff, would need to be considered very carefully at the planning stage. Programmes and projects evolve over time. Where the focus is on language improvement, mastery is a slow and incremental process and so it is appropriate for this to be matched by the evaluation design. In mounting, managing, and evaluating second language projects or programmes, we are dealing with the long-term effects of whole 'treatments' quite different from short 'laboratory-style' experiments (Beretta 1986a, 1986c, 1987). If evaluation is to be valid and reliable, and to have credibility with an outside audience and with insider staff, it needs to cover a representative period or periods. This argues for longer time-scales, perhaps lasting the whole life of a project or programme, or for meaningful episodes. More crucially, it necessitates that those involved in the day-to-day running of the programme have a prime responsibility for collecting the data that enable comprehensive evaluations. The implications of this for job descriptions and professional development opportunities have been discussed above.

1.4.4   What?

The choice of focus

The scope of evaluations can vary greatly because an educational evaluation may have a number of possible focal points, according to the decisions it is designed to inform and the assumptions of participants. The object of evaluation therefore may include, for example, teaching materials, staff, student needs, or student performance. As an example, Sanders (1992: 5–6) summarizes the foci (in terms of school programmes in the United States) as:

1   *Program needs assessment*: to establish goals and objectives
2   *Individual needs assessment*: to provide insights about the instructional needs of individual learners
3   *Resource allotment*: to provide guidance in setting priorities for budgeting
4   *Processes or strategies for providing services to learners*: to provide insights about how best to organize a school to facilitate learning

    a   *Curriculum design*: to provide insights about the quality of program planning and organization
    b   *Classroom processes*: to provide insights about the extent to which educational programmes are being implemented
    c   *Materials of instruction*: to provide insights about whether specific materials are indeed aiding student learning
    d   *Monitoring of pupil progress*: to conduct formative (in-progress) evaluations of student learning
    e   *Learner motivation*: to provide insights about the effectiveness of teachers in aiding students to achieve goals and objectives of the school
    f   *Learning environment*: to provide insights about the extent to which students are provided with a responsive environment in terms of their educational needs
    g   *Staff development*: to provide insights about the extent to which the school system provides the staff opportunities to increase their effectiveness
    h   *Decision making*: to provide insights about how well a school staff – principals, teachers and others – makes decisions that result in learner benefits

5   *Outcomes of instruction*: to provide insights about the extent to which students are achieving the goals and objectives set for them

Consideration of such taxonomies of potential focal points raises a number of important general issues which affect all evaluations.

First, Sanders' list is perhaps broader than some might expect. This is because the scope for an evaluation is not decided in objective or technical terms. A value decision is required in order to determine what aspects of a programme are significant, are capable of development, and should be made open to scrutiny. These assumptions will vary between participants within one context and between different contexts, a point illustrated in our discussion of the Bangalore project evaluation

(Beretta and Davies 1985) above, where serious differences in expectations emerged. Such differences in perspective may also characterize insider and outsider approaches to evaluation of some language programmes. (See chapter 4 for an extended discussion of this.)

Second, it would be naive to expect all those concerned, generally referred to as *stakeholders*, to agree upon all the criteria that might be used to decide the worth of the programme purposes and school characteristics listed above. There is therefore a great potential for personal and ideological conflict when approaching evaluations. Furthermore, as Case et al. (1985: 7) point out:

> There are no easy formulas for identification of and adjudication among stakeholders. However, if there are no obvious principal stakeholders, it is wise to solicit concerns about the programme from as broad a base as possible. To these may be added some of the particular concerns of individual stakeholders . . . The point of identifying the groups and agencies who are the stakeholders is to increase the likelihood that the evaluation provides answers to significant and pressing questions.

Third, the methods by which these different foci may be described must be chosen according to their characteristics as objects of description and not some ideological commitment to a particular paradigm of enquiry. In short, quantified data (numbers from structured and standard measures) and qualitative data (accounts of the values, plans and purposes which affect behaviour) can both be relevant in answering evaluation questions. These and other methodological issues are explored in the following sections. (See also chapters 6 and 7 for a detailed discussion of self-report methods and observation.)

Fourth, both evaluators and subjects of evaluation need a clear awareness of the structural conditions of the context they are in; of their own and others' assumptions, frames of reference, and criteria; and of the purpose, scope, and *usefulness* of the particular evaluation in which they are involved. Appropriate evaluation practice results from an interaction between awareness of context, respect for participants' perspectives, a clear evaluation purpose, and a concern for usefulness and relevance. (See Patton 1986 for a discussion of 'utilization-focused evaluation'.)

Finally, the list above is largely framed in terms of *development*, characterized by formative, educational motivation for understanding and improvement. Where summative, *contractual* accountability concerns apply, for example in language project contexts in which participants are employed by an outside funding agency (see chapters 2 and 3), one would expect a greater concern for proof and the demonstration of efficiency and value for money. (Scriven 1967 provides the first clear discussion of these two approaches. See also Levin 1983.) For example, fund providers might wish to replace the word 'insight' with the word 'evidence', with strong implications for data collection goals and methods. Economic pressures in the 1980s have encouraged many educational sectors to pay more attention to the latter extrinsically motivated form of accountability. Clearly, the manager of a private language school has an important responsibility for financial accountability (see Horngren 1977, Levin 1983 and White et al. 1991: part 3). Lewy (1990) notes that both developmental and contractual accountability approaches have important roles and despite the primacy often given to formative studies in the field (the arguments for this are developed in Cronbach et al. 1980: 27), he points out that: 'Summative evaluation is an inescapable obligation of the project director, an obvious requirement of the sponsoring agency and a desideratum for schools.'

Dependence on measurable objectives?

It is a common practice in accountability-oriented evaluation to compare intended outputs and objectives against their actual achievement (Alderson 1986, 1992). This is especially the case for projects where there is a strong dependence on measurable objectives. These projects are judged as successful by the extent to which outputs coincide with objectives, and how far one can demonstrate 'added value' as a result of the commitment of resources as inputs.

However, basing evaluation on objectives too slavishly can be problematic. Smith (1989a, 1989c) has recently raised some doubts about the attempt to impose a project culture premised on the achievement of preplanned objectives within a specific time-scale, using preplanned resources to produce outputs that can be quantifiably assessed. (Alderson 1986 was one of the first British evaluators to draw attention to this problem.) Smith argues for more flexibility in the structure of projects than is presently allowed for under project framework, with the project directors allowed to deal with the unpredictable and to lead the project in the direction that they rather than planners see fit. Smith argues that human, educational projects are more unpredictable than physical or technical projects (such as road building), the latter's success being more dependent on predictable physical laws. As a consequence, he considers project framework as it is presently constituted as being too rigid an instrument for use in human projects.

While we accept the case for flexibility, we would still maintain that the specification of objectives in the project framework approach is an important and valuable exercise. It demands anticipation of viability, benefits and adequacy of resourcing in the light of intended outcomes. (See further discussion on the need for a clear direction for projects and monitoring of attainment in section 2.3, which deals with the measurement of the effect of projects and their impact on the host country. See also Brumfit 1983, Oxfam 1988.) Similarly, such specification demands the analysis of contextual constraints and opportunities which might mean the difference between success and failure, particularly those affecting outcomes (e.g. that jobs should actually be available for teacher trainees on completing training). In framing precise and potentially measurable objectives, applicants for project funding will be led to think through the indicators by which the success of a project will be judged and the factors in the local situation that might work for or against that success. Finally, a further benefit is that both donors and recipients should know exactly what is expected in terms of time, resources, finance and personnel, etc. (Brumfit 1983). To plan a route, it is important to know the destination and be aware of hazards along the way.

Therefore, while we agree with Smith on the need for flexibility and realism in the management of projects, one must also recognize the value of objectives framed at the outset according to a wider perspective of social and economic needs. As Fullan (1982) has argued, unless significant change is envisaged through the setting of initial objectives, there is a danger that little progress may result. There is a need for forward vision if the status quo is ever to change and the wider perspectives of 'outsiders' such as funding agency personnel should contribute to the setting of worthwhile objectives (Patton 1990).

However, taking measurable, behavioral objectives alone to be an adequate specification of what it is that programmes or projects can and should achieve is not without limitations, as Alderson (1986) has clearly pointed out (also Barrow 1984, Patton 1986).

Objectives can change

An obvious problem in measuring performance against initial objectives is that learning situations are dynamic and objectives might need to be altered to some degree during implementation (Alderson 1986). The priority of certain objectives might change, and some may prove to have been misconceived and so require reformulation. Also, new, more desirable objectives may well emerge during implementation. It is right to ask whether educational objectives are indeed totally predictable or whether one should expect them to be modified or altered in certain respects as programmes and projects unfold. An evaluation should be capable of monitoring or tracing the development of objectives at least as much as their fulfilment. What happens *during* implementation can be just as important as the outcomes.

In evaluations where objectives-driven methods are used (such as restricted response questionnaires, or certain test formats), there is a danger that pre-specification of the content to be focused on as a basis for evaluation decisions might lead to the exclusion of data on unpredicted or unintended outcomes (Parlett and Hamilton 1977). It is therefore important to allow for evaluations to take account of unpredictable outcomes or effects even if they may be hard to define in quantitative terms and for these also to be documented.

Objectives can be conceived differently

Patton (1986) points out that there is a second problem with measuring performance against objectives, namely the issue of the origin of objectives selected for scrutiny. There is no necessary consensus as to which objectives should be seen as a relevant basis for evaluation criteria. In the case of learning outcomes, there is a whole range of possible dimensions which we might investigate: learner change in terms of knowledge, understanding, skill, interest, motivation, self-esteem, autonomy, social development, etc. Decisions on which of these to examine may be difficult to take at the start of a programme or project. The relative importance of these dimensions is a matter of their relative perceived worth according to conflicting ethical and ideological positions. Each stakeholder will know what learning outcomes matter, but unfortunately they may well not agree.

There is a further problem in projects where funding agencies are concerned that the broader social and economic effects of second language projects be used as evaluation criteria. A former Chief Education Advisor of the ODA has suggested that ELT activity must be seen within a broader socio-economic framework: 'We wanted to place ELT within an economic context, examine how it contributes to overall manpower development in the recipient country, and how it is organised and managed' (British Council 1989: 7). This may raise a real difficulty for ELT personnel to have to think in terms of economic or social objectives. It may be difficult for ELT practitioners to specify the economic and social impact of ELT aid until the descriptive categories for detailing such objectives and the means for collecting such data efficiently are established. Economists need to talk to language specialists and vice versa to identify the parameters of ELT related impacts. (See British Council 1992 for an account of one of the first ELT seminars in Britain to address these matters directly.) A colloquium on 'Language and Aid Projects: Towards the Year 2000' was held at Lancaster University in September 1992 to initiate a dialogue in this area in the full knowledge that lack of concern for dialogue on either side might have unfortunate consequences for the ELT sector. Further initiatives are necessary.

However, any attempt to attribute an increase in the gross national product of a country or the per capita income of its inhabitants to the success of an ELT or teacher training project is likely to require a lengthy time frame for appropriate data collection and may not be easy to accomplish. It must also be noted that any claim of cause and effect may have little credibility, given the complexity of intervening variables.

1.4.5 Who?

'Experts', outsiders, and insiders

For many years, ELT project evaluations were carried out by external, 'fly-in, fly-out' ELT specialists. (Alderson 1992 provides a useful discussion of who is to evaluate.) It was assumed that these specialists, because of the years they had spent teaching, running projects or training, possessed the expertise to conduct an evaluation of an ELT project. However, whereas many training courses (often Master's degrees in TESL/TEFL/Applied Linguistics) have been specifically developed to prepare personnel to shoulder the responsibilities of syllabus design, test preparation, materials development, teacher training, etc., parallel preparation for the role of evaluation in curriculum planning and development has been conspicuous by its absence from many university and college calendars. The assumption has continued to be held in the ELT field (though not in general education: see Open

University 1980 for an early example) that evaluation skills cannot be imparted through training and that subject specialization is in itself sufficient. As discussed above, subject expertise alone is hardly sufficient, though necessary. The standards for evaluator practice summarized later in this chapter could hardly be met by an evaluator armed with ELT experience alone.

Frequently, outsiders are brought in on the grounds that they have no vested interest and are more objective than insiders and so provide a more credible evaluation report. Unlike insiders, they have no personal investment in the successful achievement of project or programme outcomes and are therefore less likely to be biased towards particular interpretations of events (King et al. 1987). Also, crucially, they can address aspects of a programme or project which are affected by insiders' 'blind spots' or by insiders' often tacit agreement not to bring uncomfortable or controversial issues into the open.

Nevertheless, they must come to a project or programme with their own previous experiences, perspectives, and views of the world. This raises a key question: can outsiders evaluate effectively without the cooperation and indeed the collaboration of insider staff? It is doubtful whether short-stay visitors can understand the full complexity of an educational programme or project. It is certainly unlikely they would be able to gather the evidence that would be required in order to do this.

Insiders have far greater experience of the situation, and are aware of the history behind developments. Collectively and sometimes individually, they have considerably more insight into the workings of a programme or project than any short-stay outsider can possibly be expected to possess. In particular, they will understand the human predispositions and relationships that affect implementation. Insiders can help evaluators trace developments because they will be involved in those developments and will have particular understandings or recollections of reasons for decisions taken. The insiders can thus provide a far more detailed understanding of developments than an outsider would gather in a short visit.

In short, what we need in evaluation is an acceptable mix of outsider and insider perspectives and contributions. (See chapters 4 and 5 for further discussion of the need for this, and also Alderson and Scott 1992 and Love 1991.) This may necessitate that the contracting body for the evaluation (usually the bureaucracy or funding agency) secures early agreement on the formative and summative data that are to be collected by insiders in the programme or project team and the role the outside evaluator will be called on to play. Issues relating to ownership and 'freedom of information' would also need to be clarified at the outset. (See chapter 8 for a discussion of these issues.)

1.4.6 How?

Summative evaluation methods: Is testing sufficient?

How should evaluation be carried out in accountability-oriented summative evaluation? There can be a mistaken view that it comprises the collection of student test results and their statistical analysis and interpretation. A broader approach suggests that summative evaluation should not necessarily be restricted to obtaining test data which can be quantified or subjected to psychometric manipulation. Tests are an important, possibly an essential part, but nevertheless only one part, of language programme or project evaluation. They are merely one of the many instruments which may be employed in accountability-oriented evaluations, one of a number of means to a general end. In certain circumstances other means may be equally appropriate.

Initiators of evaluation for contractual accountability tend to favour the use of test data because they are measurable and have the veneer of quantifiable objectivity. Unfortunately, using test data is not as simple, 'clean', or conclusive as its advocates might wish to believe. In chapter 3 we comment critically on the use of test data in the baseline evaluation for accountability purposes of a teacher training project in Nepal. In section 3.6 we note the limitations of test data if used without reference to data on implementation. We also refer specifically to the problems of developing parallel tests to measure learning gains and the need to interpret the worth of any differences that are recorded.

In this particular evaluation design we worked on the premise that if we had a control group of classes taught by teachers who had not received training and an experimental group of the classes of trained teachers, then it should be possible to administer and re-administer relevant tests to these two groups of students over a period of time and examine whether significant differences emerged. (Baseline enquiries would ensure the comparability of the groups.) In designs of this type, if improvements in the scores of the students in the trained group are recorded, then it might be inferred that it was worth continuing the training of teachers, though one might not be able to comment meaningfully on the size of the differences resulting in tests of students' general proficiency or in tests of their receptive skills. (See section 3.6 for a discussion of this.) More crucially, if no differences were observed between the test scores of the two groups, then one might want to examine carefully the nature of the training and, possibly, ponder the continuation of the funding.

Unfortunately, though such information might satisfy in its elegant simplicity and its psychometric qualities, it does not necessarily give us a valid picture of the impact of training. In evaluating the success of a teacher training project if no differences emerge in the summative test performances of students in control and experimental groups the information does not tell us why this is the case. We would need to monitor the classroom practice of both trained and untrained teachers to interpret the test data. In section 3.7 we report on how *observation* of trained and untrained teachers provided such data concerning the faithful implementation of the training programme (see also chapter 7).

In those circumstances where a reasonable number of observations is not possible, then *self-report* data might be useful (see chapters 3 and 6). This might involve asking teachers to introspect in *interviews* or getting teachers to provide written accounts (e.g. through *questionnaires*) of their post-training experiences. (Self-report methods are discussed in chapter 6.) The concept of *levels of use* (Beretta 1987, 1992, Hall et al. 1977, Loucks et al. 1975) may also be of value here. Beretta's investigation employed, in a *post hoc* analysis, a scheme of three teacher implementation levels in the Bangalore study and his use of Hall et al.'s (1977) Stages of Concern Questionnaire indicates how systematic this can be.

The three key evaluation methods of interview, questionnaire, and observation will be considered in part III of this book. This arises from our experience of using these methods in the accountability and developmental evaluations reported in part II. These methods were appropriate to the evaluations we have carried out and are the most frequently used in both developmental and accountability-oriented evaluations. We describe below a number of other methods which we do not deal with in any depth. We provide a brief survey of these and give references to helpful practical guides (see appendix 1.2 and the references at the end of this chapter). We do not intend this to downgrade the importance of any of the methods not dealt with in part III of this book. They may well be relevant in other contexts, for other evaluation purposes. There is no inherent superiority of one method over another. The choice of method depends on relevance to the evaluation questions being posed and the constraints affecting their use.

Evaluation methods: Developmental purposes

Formative evaluation by 'insiders' (teaching and administrative staff) has both product and process dimensions. The product lies in practical curriculum improvement; the process in teachers' related professional development. Since the work of Stenhouse (1975), the link between curriculum development and teacher development has been recognized. Formative evaluation can support teacher development in that it can promote the revised and deepened perception of classroom realities, obtained through monitoring (Vulliamy and Webb 1992); it can develop a better understanding of pedagogic issues and problems; it can enable the critical application of pedagogic strategies; and it can entail critical problem focused discourse with peers and visiting specialists. (See McNiff 1988: chapter 4 for fuller discussion in relation to action research.)

Methods for formative, insider-led evaluation are designed to explore issues and problems, monitor classroom events, and assess the relative success of teaching remedies that have been adopted. They should be informative, useful, accessible, economic, flexible (in order to adapt to each teacher's particular circumstances), and as explicit and systematic as possible.

There are a number of helpful references available for formative and self-directed evaluation by teachers. These are included at the end of this chapter.[3] The reader is referred to them for details of useful procedures. However, *no guide can anticipate the particular circumstances a teacher works in: there can be no absolute blueprints.*

The goal of the formative evaluator [is] to collect and share with planners and staff information that will lead to improvement in a developing programme. The diversified nature of formative evaluation might make providing a step-by-step guide seem a little silly or arbitrary. In truth there is no step-by-step way to perform the tasks involved with the role. (Morris and Fitz-Gibbon 1978c: 35)

Each teacher/evaluator will have to work out the most effective methods to suit his or her own situation. We outline below some of the methods reported in the literature on developmental evaluation. A reflective planning stage addressing all the aspects of evaluation discussed (sections 1.4.1–5) should precede choice of method. Choices must be made in the situation on the ground as to which method(s) are the most appropriate and the most useful for the purposes involved (*Why*), for the particular focus(es) for data collection (*What*), and for the people carrying out the evaluation (*Who*). The duration and timing of the evaluation (*When* and *How long*) also need to be considered at the planning stage as do, crucially, the additional factors summarized in section 1.4.7 which determine the extent to which evaluation activity leads to effective change.

Methods for developmental evaluation: An outline

Tests

These can include:

- Achievement tests
- Proficiency tests
- Existing internationally recognized tests such as IELTS
- Course book tests (unit, exit)
- Student records, continuous assessment, profiles of achievement, etc.

The key considerations in collecting and using test data are:

- What should be tested? What constitutes an acceptable cut-off point/pass score in terms of these tests?
- How far can the key principles of reliability, validity and practicality be satisfied and where might some compromise be necessary? For example, double marking of essays would be desirable for reasons of reliability but there are strong practical obstacles to it.

For a detailed examination of principles and practice in the collection of language test data, see Weir (1993), where a principled way of describing target level behaviour in terms of a three-part framework of test operations, performance conditions, and quality of output is mapped out. This framework enables course directors to specify levels of acceptable performance in terms of the four skills, and the 'success' of the course can be judged in terms of whether students who entered the course at an appropriate level have reached the desired level of exit behaviour (for example, in the three hundred hours available over the twelve-week course). See also chapter 3 for a critical discussion of the use of test data in a baseline evaluation of a teacher training project.

Course statistics

Factual information can be gathered on such aspects as intake numbers, attendance patterns, and use of resources such as self-access facilities, etc. This type of quantitative information can have a qualitative dimension in the sense that patterns, contrasts or significant changes in these numbers can be interpreted in terms of programme quality and the reactions of participants. It can also serve as unambiguous information which can either confirm or challenge insiders' perceptions of the programme, in a depersonalized manner.

Classroom description – Narrative

Methods can include:

- Field notes (unstructured written descriptions including critical incidents: significant single events)
- Shadowing reports (of one student through a day; Laaksonen 1987)

Field notes are often the most practical means to record impressions of lessons, and have a valuable place in giving a global view of classroom events. However, they risk selectivity and personal bias (see section 7.1). Shadowing entails 'tracking' a student through a whole day, recording information by either taking field notes or using more structured methods when relevant. It provides a more rounded description than could be provided by any one teacher, or an observer in a single class. It can provide staff with new perspectives on a pedagogic issue.

Classroom description – Recorded

Methods can include:

- Video taping
- Audio taping
- Slide/tape photography

These methods provide a direct record of classroom events (Walker and Adelman 1975). However, the recordings may be analysed by a range of procedures (see chapter 7 and Patton 1987b) which will determine the nature of the data available to others.

Classroom description – Structured observation methods

Methods can include:

- Checklists
- Interaction analysis schedules
- Rating scales

Observation is the only way to get direct data about the classroom. However, it is time consuming, requires a systematic and explicit approach, and must be done in a way acceptable to teachers and students. The collection of observational data is discussed in chapter 7 (also see Hook 1981, King et al. 1987, Malamah-Thomas 1987, Rea-Dickins and Germaine 1992).

Document analysis

Sources can include:

- Programme descriptions (aims and objectives, criterial features of teacher training courses)
- Minutes of meetings, circulars, newsletters, etc.
- Teaching records: lesson plans, lesson pro forma, self-report sheets, student workbooks, displays of work, syllabuses, teaching materials, teachers' guides, etc. Morris and Fitz-Gibbon (1978c) and Patton (1987b) provide helpful guidelines for collection and analysis.

Diaries and logs

These may be kept by teachers and, in some cases, by students (perhaps more commonly by student teachers than language students). They provide a personal record of a course over time, which can be most useful as a memory aid when asked to provide self-report data, and can also offer feedback to diary keepers on developments in their perceptions and experience as a course progresses (Bailey 1983, Jarvis 1992, Murphy-O'Dwyer 1985, Thornbury 1991).

Questionnaires

These can elicit reactions to both course content (aims, objectives, materials) and methodology. They can also provide information through self-assessments and attitude measurement (see appendices 4.4, 4.5, 6.2.1, 6.2.2 for examples). They can be administered to students, directors of studies, teachers, school principals, and other stakeholders. The value of the questionnaire is that it enables course providers to distinguish a generally held point of view from purely idiosyncratic or individual reactions and opinions. Quite often teachers can form a false impression of student reactions by attending only to a vocal minority. Data from an adequately large and representative sample are needed to justify changes in the content or methodology of a programme. Normally no changes would be contemplated in course design unless a sizeable minority, perhaps a fifth, appeared to be having problems with a particular element. This of course is a subjective figure and ideally one would like to say that all areas of concern would be examined and any improvements that could be made would, however small the level of dissatisfaction. However, the staff must use their professional judgement before making significant changes to the programme as views on a course may differ from one intake to the next. The reader is referred to chapter 6 for a discussion of the use of questionnaires and also the excellent practical discussions of questionnaire design in published methodology guides and a number of critical reviews in the area (Bell 1987, Cohen and Manion 1980, Fink and Kosecoff 1985, Gibbs and Haigh 1983, 1984, Labaw 1980, Low 1988, 1991 and Oppenheim 1992).

Delphi technique

The Delphi technique (appendix 8.1.2) allows a respondent to see how his/her views compare with those of all fellow respondents. It can distinguish general trends from individual standpoints.

Interviews

Rich and detailed explanatory information on informants' experiences, perceptions and opinions is best obtained by interviewing, which may be done individually or in groups. It makes it possible to pursue specific issues of interest and is generally more flexible than the questionnaire approach for gathering formative data. However, it is time consuming to do and its results can be questioned unless systematic procedures are used to minimize bias. (We are aware of the need for time to be allocated for the training of evaluators in this area: see chapter 6, Bell 1987, Millar et al. 1992, Molenaar 1982 and Powney and Watts 1987 for more detailed discussion.)

Structured discussion and feedback

There are a number of ways in which group discussions can be structured, of which the authors have found the *nominal group technique* the most helpful in small-scale evaluations (not discussed in this book but see the example provided in appendix 8.1a). It is a method designed to elicit and prioritize the responses of a group to any problem statement, and is structured so as to ensure equal participation and equal rights for all. It is in this respect greatly superior to unstructured group or class discussion, in which vocal individuals can dominate discussion and present a false picture of the responses of the whole group.

Self-assessment checklists

These are a means for teachers to apply criteria to their own teaching (see Rea-Dickins and Germaine 1992: 39–40) by ticking off items on a standard checklist.

They can be helpful in raising awareness and providing a common focus for discussion. However, it is essential that teachers have a clear and shared understanding of the concepts and assumptions underlying the criteria in these checklists. Also, if checklists are imposed on teachers without adequate negotiation, it contradicts the principle of ownership (see chapter 8) and the move towards more cooperative evaluation proposed in this book. Simply providing such checklists will not, in itself, ensure constructive self-evaluation.

Materials evaluation checklists

These are most helpful in saving teachers from 'reinventing the wheel' when evaluating materials. Their use is discussed in Candlin and Breen (1979), Cunningsworth (1984), Hutchinson and Waters (1987), and Rea-Dickins and Germaine (1992).

Case study

Case study has been proposed as an evaluation method for teachers (e.g. Hopkins 1985), but is only likely to be used by teachers engaged in evaluation as part of their higher education studies (Vulliamy and Webb 1992) since it requires a great deal of time to collect, analyse, and interpret data. It is a common misconception that case studying is easy, perhaps because it presents in a familiar narrative form. It is not. We cannot devote attention to case study in this book and refer the reader to Nisbet and Watt (1984), Patton (1987b), and Yin (1989).

What can a busy teacher do?

There is likely to be a difference in approach to method between the full-time evaluator and a teacher or administrator who is combining evaluation with other duties. The 'full-timer' may be an outside 'expert', or an insider with full-time commitment. Much effective teacher self-evaluation and formative evaluation has been done where circumstances allow teachers time to do it systematically, and with support (for example, see Burton and Mickan 1993). In the case of the full-timer (outsider or insider), stakeholders have the right to expect high standards of accuracy, systematicity, and detailed reporting (see section 1.5).

The starting point for formative evaluation by hard-pressed teachers or administrators when it is done on top of other duties is one single but difficult question: what can be achieved in the time available? In the case of this 'part-timer', workload and practical deadlines will enforce *adaptation* and *compromise* in the methods used, *but this does not mean that they thereby have 'permission' to produce poor quality, questionable information or, even worse, not to bother to evaluate their work at all*. Just like the full-time (or external summative) evaluator, the part-timer needs the best possible quality of data upon which to make decisions (see Introduction to part III).

Adaptation to circumstances suggests that methods should be chosen that are realistic and economical, and are as far as possible integrated with teachers' normal duties. Too many methodology guides ignore this principle; for example, by proposing the use of complex systems of observation and interaction analysis for teachers to use, when they cannot possibly devote the time to it (e.g. Rea-Dickins and Germaine 1992: 62–4, Walker 1985). Since testing and observation are part and parcel of daily classroom life, two realistic means by which to integrate teaching and evaluation would be the sensible use of achievement tests, and the development of structured observational systems for formative self-evaluation applied in peer discussion of pedagogic issues (Linder 1991, Roberts 1993, Weir 1993 and appendix 7.1.)

Compromise may limit the scale of data collection (e.g. by reducing time spent getting and analysing the data) but not the systematicity of the approach, nor the accuracy or quality of the information obtained. Methods suggested for formative evaluation and self-evaluation (see above) should therefore combine realism with the principle of 'best quality'. A good test of quality would be the amount another teacher can learn about students or the classroom from the information you provide ('transmissibility'). The transmissibility of data is a key criterion to be met in conducting all evaluations. In conclusion, we would endorse the principle of best possible quality of data, obtained as economically as possible and, where possible, integrated with the normal work processes of the 'part-timer'.

1.4.7 But . . . will it be used?

In certain cases, after data collection and reporting, evaluators may take no further responsibility for the use of their findings. This may be because they prefer to remain detached from utilization concerns and merely 'write and run' (Rutman and Mowbray 1983: 97); or it may be that their terms of reference restrict the availability of findings since they remain solely under the control of a funding agency that is concerned with policy issues and may not be prepared to 'share power' with an evaluator in future programme plans (as in the Nepal evaluation, chapter 3). Weiss (1984: 160) describes cases where the funding agency has little or no interest in acting on evaluation findings from the outset; for example, it may merely be using evaluations to paper over cracks, as ammunition in bureaucratic contests to support a particular position, to document success to secure additional funding or for use in public relations, or because it merely requires evaluation as a condition of programme support. Dodd (1986) cites some similar cases where there was no intention to seek answers to neutral and open-ended questions – for example, where the purpose of the evaluations had been to seek evidence to give credibility to what had already been decided, to praise what the sponsoring body wanted praised, and to avoid or postpone unwanted action. Involvement by professionals in such activities is questionable.

Evaluation is only worthwhile in projects where there is an informational intent on the part of the funding agency at least to *consider* results in taking decisions (see

Weiss 1984: 161), or in programme evaluations where there is a commitment to use the information developmentally. *There is no value in collecting data unless they are to be considered in decision making or they lead to action* (see appendix 1.3).

In order to achieve this, those managing the evaluation should be aware of potential *barriers* to the practical use of their findings from the outset, so that they can produce what Rutman and Mowbray (1983: 97) refer to as 'actionable results'. Rutman and Mowbray argue that in any programme or project there should be a management structure which identifies the staff responsible for following through on an evaluation. The key task for these staff will be to resolve resistance to the change process at organizational and individual levels (see Love 1991: 40–1 for a useful and detailed discussion of the internal evaluation consulting process). Rutman and Mowbray argue further (1983: 98–9) that an essential task for evaluators/ management is to identify and negotiate responses to these obstacles at the planning stage:

> Problems such as these should be faced early in the evaluation planning process so that they do not spring up unexpectedly at the end and negate much of the value of the evaluation effort . . . implementation problems of an institutional and practical nature need to be ventilated before decisions are made about how and when evaluation results will be used.

Weiss argues in a similar vein (1984: 161):

> The time to begin planning for utility is in the planning phase of the study. It is part of the process of choosing the appropriate evaluation questions, focusing on salient issues, developing measures that make sense to people in practice, and designing appropriate comparisons . . . it should be grounded in a realistic appreciation of the dynamics of the program context.

In developmental evaluations this indicates the importance of early, active and sympathetic involvement of key insiders and the unambiguous identification of the stakeholders who will have the responsibility and also the *authority* to manage the evaluation and act upon findings. (Harrison 1987 offers useful advice on how to identify key players.) Patton (1987a: 255) similarly suggests that there are two fundamental requirements for an approach emphasizing the *use* of evaluation findings: 'First, the intended evaluation users must be identified – real, visible, specific . . . human beings, not ephemeral, general, and abstract "audiences", organizations, or agencies. Second, evaluators must work actively, reactively and adaptively with these specific stakeholders.'

Mackay (1991) also advocates the value of insiders' becoming active participants in an evaluation of their programme and demonstrates procedures by which they might become 'respected partners' in such evaluations. Case et al. (1985: 8–16) also argue for the inclusion of stakeholders in the setting of evaluation aims.

In those cases where decisions are taken at a level above those directly involved in carrying out the evaluation, then it would be politic to take into account the interests and wishes of those further up in the hierarchy to make it more likely that findings will be considered when decisions are made. In the case of external agency funded project evaluations, Weiss (1984: 162–6) argues for close consideration of the institutional arrangements/worlds of the external decision makers and funding agencies as against the evaluators. She points out that they respond to the settings in which they work and that the motivations and rewards of evaluators, pro- gramme decision makers, and funding agencies are likely to differ: different gods, different mountain tops. She concludes (Weiss 1984: 166): 'When the major actors in the evaluation-to-decision process have such disparate concerns and motivations, small wonder that the fit between research and decision is often poor. Each set of actors may be playing in the same game, but they are likely to be playing by different sets of rules.'

In evaluations where there is a clearer developmental purpose and a bigger stake and clearer role for insider involvement, there is potentially a closer match between evaluation activity and decision making involving change. Insiders (often working cooperatively with outsiders) can more readily translate information into action. Where evaluation is conducted in intellectual and structural conditions which permit the possibility of a reasonable level of action (see Weiss 1984: 173–4), the path between the planning stage of the evaluation and the application of results to decision making may be smoother. The management of innovation is a major issue in the curriculum studies literature. This literature (see source references at the foot of table 1.1) identifies a complex of factors which *link evaluation to effective planned change* (table 1.1).

Our experience confirms that to carry through evaluation findings it is highly important that there should be an infrastructure within the institution which enables the collection, dissemination, and *use* of data. It is essential to identify who is responsible for introducing changes. (See section 4.4 for a discussion of staff responsibilities for evaluation and change in a language programme.) Additionally, those responsible for managing the evaluation process should ensure from the start that all stakeholders are aware of the purpose and scope of the evaluation and the decisions which it is intended to inform. By means of effective communication, stakeholders need a clear awareness of their personal involvement in the evaluation in terms of their contribution to the identification of strengths and weaknesses, making decisions and following through agreed changes. A few specific examples from our own experience of effective and less effective utilization of postgraduate course evaluation may illuminate some of the points referred to above. In some cases in the past, our institutional practice was less than effective, in that student feedback was obtained but (in our view) insufficient concerted decision making or action resulted, for two probable reasons. First, staff would be presented with evaluation findings at the end of a course without having previously discussed the purpose and function of these data, nor their own place in contributing to the issues they raised or in acting on them. There was insufficient 'ownership' of the evaluation process, so that when findings appeared in the in-trays, staff might not

Table 1.1 Factors linking evaluation to effective change

- Relevance of information generated on evaluation questions to the decisions that will be made in the future
- Selecting research methods which best fit the issues, not vice versa
- Engaging in high quality research: quality makes a difference to use, evaluation needs to be taken seriously
- Effective communication between evaluators and key personnel and maintenance of close contact with the programme or project
- Involvement of prospective users in planning (and as co-investigators where possible, especially when there is a formative dimension)
- Involvement of insiders in discussing findings
- Credibility of results, making links with other studies done in similar areas; 'evaluation synthesis'
- Effective dissemination of results to appropriate audiences
- Accessibility of findings to the intended readership through appropriate language and presentation
- Timeliness and availability of findings when they are needed by decision makers
- Early warning of any findings requiring action (especially where things are going seriously wrong)
- Identification of positive benefits from the proposed change
- Structures supporting the implementation of change (including the availability of adequate resources)
- The central importance of positive leadership

We acknowledge our debt to the following for the factors listed above: Fullan (1982), Kennedy (1987, 1988), Nicholls (1983), Rea-Dickins and Germaine (1992: 8–19), Rossi and Freeman (1985), Rutman and Mowbray (1983), Scriven (1991: 369–71), Weiss (1984), White (1988), White et al. (1991).

have had a sense of commitment or engagement sufficient to encourage concerted action. Second, attempts to safeguard a time for discussion of results were often frustrated by time management problems and staff over-loading.

A more recent case of a postgraduate course evaluation illustrates a positive attempt by course leaders to improve this aspect of our practice. We circulated a paper summarizing issues for consideration and possible changes to course content and structure, at the beginning of the third term in the academic year, where any agreed changes would be implemented in the following academic year. To encourage good communication, staff were invited to respond in writing, and in due course all their responses were circulated to all teaching staff. At the same time, a meeting was convened for the end of the term, with a clear indication that its purpose was to make binding decisions concerning the next year's course. The timing of the meeting was important because we had to ensure that all staff would be available and free of other commitments. In addition, the timing made it possible for a systematic and detailed end-of-course student report on the course (based on a twenty-hour practical course component on evaluation) to be circulated to all staff in advance of the meeting. Thus, good quality information from both staff and students was made available for consideration beforehand, with a clear awareness of what the meeting was for and with time beforehand for staff to think through the implications for their own work in the institution. As a result, in the meeting we were able to identify a clear agenda for utilization with a common understanding of the purpose, benefits, and rationale of the proposed changes. We also agreed and minuted who would be accountable for implementation.

To make such involvement in evaluation positive, advance planning, and consideration of strategies to maximize ownership (e.g. timeliness and availability of findings) are crucial (see table 1.1 and also chapter 8 for further discussion). All this is of course normally dependent on a commitment to improvement within the institution concerned.

We are aware that many teachers find themselves in situations where there is no system for collaborative development, and management has little concern for programme improvement. We would argue, however, that even where change is limited to an individual teacher's own classes, he/she still benefits from considering the impact upon others (students, colleagues, school management) of conducting formative studies, in particular how to carry through any resulting change in terms of possible obstacles within the institution. Teachers should try to develop strategies both to minimize or by-pass obstacles and to maximize helping factors (e.g. to enlist the support of colleagues).

In this section we have considered the implementation of evaluation findings and have summarized factors affecting successful utilization (an issue discussed in some detail in Patton 1986, Rea-Dickins and Germaine 1992: section 1.4, and Weiss 1984). In conclusion, we would agree with Rossi and Freeman (1985: 392–4) that in evaluations with a developmental focus, 'Utilization and dissemination plans should be part of the evaluation design . . . Evaluations should include an assessment of utilization. Evaluators and decision makers must not only share an understanding of the purposes for which a study is undertaken, but also agree on the criteria by which its successful utilization may be judged.'

As indicated at the beginning of this chapter, this book is intended both for potential evaluators and for those subject to evaluation. In either role, ELT professionals should be able to judge the merit of an evaluation (though, unfortunately, published criticism of evaluation reports is quite uncommon). For them to do so requires explicit and well-grounded criteria to apply to evaluations of concern to them. In the section below, two sets of standards for the *evaluation of evaluations* are presented and discussed (Harlen and Elliot 1982, Joint Committee 1981). Apart from standards of practicality, accuracy and propriety, these standards of evaluation 'mandate a focus on utility' (Patton 1986: 333), i.e. 'focusing on use and working with intended users is important and can increase evaluation use'.

1.5 Evaluating evaluations

This section presents two sets of standards, proposed by authoritative sources, which merit close attention for anyone involved in evaluation. We should note first that some criteria to apply to evaluations will be relatively objective and widely acceptable, while others will reflect an ideological stance, in particular as regards the rights of stakeholders. Objective criteria are endorsed by Fitz-Gibbon and Morris (1987b: 13–14): 'The critical characteristic of any evaluation study is that it provide the best possible information that could have been collected under the circumstances, and that this information meet the credibility requirements of its evaluation audience'.

Both objective and also more ideologically based criteria appear in both sets of standards offered below, and the reader should be alert to the distinction throughout. One set of standards is provided by the Joint Committee (1981) recommendations summarized by Stufflebeam (1990), the other is directly reprinted from Harlen and Elliott (1982).

Ultimately, the readers of this book should develop their own standards for evaluations, according to their own needs and circumstances. However, to do this they should profit from attention to the standards summarized below. In general, explicit and agreed evaluation standards can serve to help define the scope of evaluations; can bring into the open the ethical aspect to any controversies about evaluation method; can suggest principles to plan evaluations or to tackle evaluation problems; can help judgement of evaluation plans and reports; and, finally, can suggest a framework for training or academic study (Stufflebeam 1990).

1.5.1   The Joint Committee on Standards for Educational Evaluation

In the United States there has been a long-term attempt to develop and control the quality of educational evaluation. This is reflected in an extensive professional literature, in detailed practical guides (e.g. the Sage Programme Evaluation Kit, an extremely valuable source for all would-be evaluators), and in the publication of professional standards drawn up by practitioners of wide experience and good standing: The Joint Committee on Standards for Educational Evaluation, which consisted of seventeen members appointed by twelve organizations with an interest in educational evaluation. The Committee published their standards to maintain good practice in the evaluation of educational programmes and projects: a summary of the standards with a most helpful and authoritative commentary appears in Stufflebeam (1990). As he indicates (1990: 95), the thirty standards were grouped under headings of utility (responsive to information needs), feasibility (cost-effectiveness and workability), propriety (issues of ethics and individual rights), and accuracy (validity, reliability and objectivity). Table 1.2 is based on the standards published by the Joint Committee, as summarized in Stufflebeam (1990).

These criteria combine a concern for objective technical adequacy (to provide data of good integrity, as in sections B and D) with an ideologically grounded emphasis upon the availability of information and upon protecting the rights of the audience and/or those subject to evaluation. In this respect, the criteria

Table 1.2 Summary of the standards

(A)   Utility Standards

The utility standards are intended to ensure that an evaluation will serve the practical information needs of given audiences. These standards are:

(A1)   Audience Identification
Audiences involved in or affected by the evaluation should be identified, so that their needs can be addressed.

(A2)   Evaluator Credibility
The persons conducting the evaluation should be both trustworthy and competent to perform the evaluation, so that their findings achieve maximum credibility and acceptance.

(A3)   Information Scope and Selection
Information collected should be of such scope and selected in such ways as to address pertinent questions about the object of the evaluation and be responsive to the needs and interests of specified audiences.

(A4)   Valuation Interpretation
The perspectives, procedures, and rationale used to interpret the findings should be carefully described, so that the bases for value judgments are clear.

(A5)   Report Clarity
The evaluation report should describe the object being evaluated and its context, and the purposes, procedures, and findings of the evaluation, so that the audiences will readily understand what was done, why it was done, what information was obtained, what conclusions were drawn, and what recommendations were made.

(A6)   Report Dissemination
Evaluation findings should be disseminated to clients and other right-to-know audiences, so that they can assess and use the findings.

(A7)   Report Timeliness
Release of reports should be timely, so that audiences can best use the reported information.

(A8)   Evaluation Impact
Evaluations should be planned and conducted in ways that encourage follow-through by members of the audiences.

(B)   Feasibility Standards

The feasibility standards are intended to ensure that an evaluation will be realistic, prudent, diplomatic, and frugal. These standards are:

(B1)   Practical Procedures
The evaluation procedures should be practical, so that disruption is kept to a minimum, and that needed information can be obtained.

(B2)   Political Viability
The evaluation should be planned and conducted with anticipation of the different positions of various interest groups, so that their cooperation may be obtained, and so that possible attempts by any of these groups to curtail evaluation operations or to bias or misapply the results can be averted or counteracted.

(B3)   Cost Effectiveness
The evaluation should produce information of sufficient value to justify the resources expended.

Table 1.2   (cont.)

(C)   Propriety Standards
The propriety standards are intended to ensure that an evaluation will be conducted legally, ethically, and with due regard for the welfare of those involved in the evaluation, as well as those affected by its results. These standards are:

(C1)   Formal Obligation
Obligations of the formal parties to an evaluation (what is to be done, how, by whom, when) should be agreed to in writing, so that these parties are obligated to adhere to all conditions of the agreement or formally to renegotiate it.

(C2)   Conflict of Interest
Conflict of interest, frequently unavoidable, should be dealt with openly and honestly, so that it does not compromise the evaluation processes and results.

(C3)   Full and Frank Disclosure
Oral and written evaluation reports should be open, direct, and honest in their disclosure of pertinent findings, including the limitations of the evaluation.

(C4)   Public's Right to Know
The formal parties to an evaluation should respect and assure the public's right to know, within the limits of other related principles and statutes, such as those dealing with public safety and the right to privacy.

(C5)   Rights of Human Subjects
Evaluations should be designed and conducted so that the rights and welfare of the human subjects are respected and protected.

(C6)   Human Interactions
Evaluators should respect human dignity and worth in their interactions with other persons associated with an evaluation.

(C7)   Balanced Reporting
The evaluation should be complete and fair in its presentation of strengths and weaknesses of the object under investigation, so that strengths can be built upon and problem areas addressed.

(C8)   Fiscal Responsibility
The evaluator's allocation and expenditure of resources should reflect sound accountability procedures and otherwise be prudent and ethically responsible.

(D)   Accuracy Standards
The accuracy standards are intended to ensure that an evaluation will reveal and convey technically adequate information about the features of the object being studied that determine its worth or merit. These standards are:

(D1)   Object Identification
The object of the evaluation (program, project, material) should be sufficiently examined, so that the form(s) of the object being considered in the evaluation can be clearly identified.

(D2)   Context Analysis
The context in which the program, project, or material exists should be examined in enough detail, so that its likely influences on the object can be identified.

(D3)   Described Purposes and Procedures
The purposes and procedures of the evaluation should be monitored and described in enough detail, so that they can be identified and assessed.

Table 1.2 (cont.)

(D4) Defensible Information Sources
The sources of information should be described in enough detail, so that the adequacy of the information can be assessed.

(D5) Valid Measurement
The information-gathering instruments and procedures should be chosen or developed and then implemented in ways that will assure that the interpretation arrived at is valid for the given use.

(D6) Reliable Measurement
The information-gathering instruments and procedures should be chosen or developed and then implemented in ways that will assure that the information obtained is sufficiently reliable for the intended use.

(D7) Systematic Data Control
The data collected, processed, and reported in an evaluation should be reviewed and corrected, so that the results of the evaluation will not be flawed.

(D8) Analysis of Quantitative Information
Quantitative information in an evaluation should be appropriately and systematically analyzed to ensure supportable interpretations.

(D9) Analysis of Qualitative Information
Qualitative information in an evaluation should be appropriately and systematically analyzed to ensure supportable interpretations.

(D10) Justified Conclusions
The conclusions reached in an evaluation should be explicitly justified, so that the audiences can assess them.

(D11) Objective Reporting
The evaluation procedures should provide safeguards to protect the evaluation findings and reports against distortion by the personal feelings and biases of any party to the evaluation.

pre-suppose a democratic context (institutional or national) for the evaluation, where individual and communal rights will be respected, and in which information can be readily obtained. It also implies that negotiation can take place between evaluation sponsors, evaluators and stakeholders without challenging political structures, and also seems to assume that some form of redress might be available should any of these criteria not be met. The values underpinning these criteria are reflected in Simons' (1982c, 1984b) model of democratic evaluation. These are standards suited to democratic contexts where there is an ethos of open information. Indeed, Stufflebeam (1990: 95) comments: 'The Joint Committee's standards are distinctly American and may not reflect the values, experiences, political realities, and practical constraints in some other countries'.

In other contexts, these criteria may seem utopian or dangerously radical. It could also be argued that these criteria pre-suppose a formative or developmental dimension to any evaluation, and that in a bureaucratically oriented evaluation designed to inform policy, one could not reasonably expect negotiation and release of evaluation data to be thrown openly into the public arena of competing interest groups. However, while one may debate certain aspects of their content, these standards set a benchmark for evaluators in their rigour, explicitness and presentation.

1.5.2   Harlen and Elliott

Another set of standards, proposed by Harlen and Elliott (1982), are rather more general in nature, and are posed as a set of questions:

Questions for reviewing (evaluating) evaluations

1 Did the evaluation serve to inform the decisions or judgements for which it was originally intended?
2 What decisions have been taken as a consequence of the evaluation?
3 Was the evaluation task interpreted and carried through consistently as intended?
4 Was the information which was gathered appropriate to the purpose of the evaluation?
5 What steps were taken to allow for bias, unrepresentativeness, and low reliability in the information gathered?
6 Were the actual evaluators in the best position to carry out the evaluation?
7 Were the methods used appropriate to the kind of information which was required?
8 Were the methods systematic and explicit?
9 Did those involved in supplying the information approve of the methods used for collecting it?
10 Was there sufficient time allowed in the evaluation for the necessary data to be collected?
11 Was the evaluation carried out at the best time to serve its purpose?
12 What were the side-effects, positive and negative, of the evaluation process?
13 Were satisfactory procedures used to protect the interests of those who supplied information?
14 Were the criteria by which judgement or decisions were made appropriately drawn and explicitly stated?
15 Was the evaluation reported in a way which communicated effectively with the intended audience?
16 What reactions did the report provoke in the participants and in the decision makers?

These questions emphasize the consistency of the evaluation to its purpose, the credibility of evaluators, the integrity of methods, the identification of consequences (planned and unplanned), and the 'readability' of the final report. The rights of informants are considered in questions 9 and 13, which deal with the approval of data collection methods and the protection of informants' interests (for example, through confidentiality). Harlen and Elliott's set of standards, written from the British experience, therefore does not emphasize community and stakeholder rights quite to the extent of the first set of criteria (though in their paper they emphasize the need to understand the political and tactical features of any evaluation that affects you). In two of their questions, however, there is concern for evaluator accountability: that the report should be 'readable' (question 15) and, crucially, that evaluators should state the criteria they use to make judgements (question 14). Harlen and Elliott's criteria are not as explicitly based on as powerfully democratic a model as the Joint Committee's, and yet questions 9 and 13 do assume the protection of programme and project staff interests, and questions 14 and 15 do anticipate that evaluators and evaluation-based decisions should be *potentially* open to critique. As is argued in chapter 8 and elsewhere in this book, evaluations tend to reveal the true political nature of institutions. A failure to meet the criteria proposed by Harlen and Elliott (questions 9, 13, 14, 15) would justify the interpretation of an evaluation as infringing the rights of stakeholders.

Harlen and Elliot give particular emphasis to the *utility* of evaluations, by focusing on the relevance and impact of the evaluation on decisions to be made (questions 1 and 2). This is in common with Patton's (1986: 172) view on evaluating evaluations, in which criteria should apply to a hierarchy of steps in an evaluation leading to the most important: 'to improve programs and increase the quality of decisions made'.

In common with Patton and Harlen and Elliott (viz. question 2), we would wish to make the ultimate test of an evaluation the extent to which it improves educational decisions and leads to action (see also Patton's hierarchy of evaluation criteria in appendix 1.3). To this end, Patton (1986: 183) argues that the information collected should be relevant, understandable, and useful to the stakeholders and the methods and measurements used should be appropriate to the problem under study. Additionally, the best evaluation practice, in our view, is also led by principles of ethical propriety, and the constructive integration of 'insider' and 'outsider' contributions.

1.6 Endnote

The design used for an evaluation must be appropriate to the questions being addressed and be capable of providing useful information to inform decision making. (See Patton 1986, Fitz-Gibbon and Morris 1987b and Walberg and Haertel 1990: 61–81 for informed and thorough surveys of the manifold design options which lie within the parameters of the accountability–developmental approaches we have outlined in section 1.2).

There is no single 'best' or 'correct' method of evaluating a project or programme.

Hence the strategies used in any evaluation must represent appropriate and defensible choices from a range of options, not simply the only or the preferred *modus operandi* of the evaluator. Also, the evaluator should have a wide repertoire of skills to implement these strategies. In terms of our central questions – *Why, When, Who, What* and *How?* – our experience suggests a broad view of evaluation design and implementation. This would draw upon both external accountability-oriented evaluation and internally motivated evaluation for development. This broad view is characterized by:

1   A need for both insider and outsider commitment and involvement to ensure adequate evaluation (see chapters 3–5)
2   A central interest in improvement, as well as the demonstration of the 'product value' of a programme or project or their components (see chapters 4–5)
3   An associated commitment to a deeper professional understanding of the process of educational change, as well as the results of that change (see chapters 2–5)
4   Systematic documentation for evaluation purposes both during implementation and at the beginning and end of a programme or project's life (see chapter 4).
5   A willingness to embrace both qualitative and quantitative methodologies as appropriate to the purpose of the evaluation and the characteristics of the context under review (see chapters 6–7)

The reader will note that the evaluation conducted by the writers reported in chapter 3 largely followed a strictly summative and external paradigm, as was required by the terms of reference set by the ODA. Our sense that this form of evaluation was missing some potentially fruitful opportunities (in tapping insiders' potential for contribution to the evaluation, and in the external evaluator's possible contribution to improvement in the training) led us to seek a more integrated approach in further work. The same realization can be seen in chapter 4 (regarding an EAP programme) in that some positive opportunities for more integrated and cooperative evaluation work were felt to have been missed. In chapter 5, we present a framework which could enable a subsequent genuine integration of internal and external perspectives.

The systematic pursuit of deeper understanding of how second language programmes and projects produce the results that they do, makes a dual contribution to the field of applied linguistics. It enhances the professional accountability of evaluators and insider staff both to the client-bureaucracy and to those with an immediate interest in the success of a particular programme or project. In addition, it contributes to the wider professional community whose interest lies in acquiring a broader data base and in learning from the carefully documented experience of others.

In the next chapter we provide a more detailed discussion of current baseline studies being carried out by the ODA in British-funded aid projects. While supporting the rigour and systematicity they bring to project design, implementation, and evaluation, we also suggest the value of involving insiders professionally committed to project improvement in such accountability-oriented evaluations for reasons of economy, usefulness, balance, depth, and project sustainability. In the subsequent chapters we turn to practical cases (chapters 3 to 5) and principles of methodology (chapters 6 and 7) before returning to the political and personal meaning of evaluations in the final chapter.

NOTES

1   For useful general discussion of programme evaluation see Bachman (1981, 1987), BALEAP (1993), Bell (1982), Beretta (1986a, 1986b), Brown (1989), Elley (1989), Long (1984), Lynch (1990, 1992), McGinley (1986), MacKay (1981, 1988, 1991), Madaus et al. (1983), and Rowntree (1982: chapter 6).
2   For further discussion of the nature of projects and the evaluation of projects, see Asian Development Bank (1986), British Council (1989, 1990, 1991), Brumfit (1983), Clarke (1988), Coleman (1986, 1987), Cracknell (1984), Dodd (1986), Fullan (1982), Hayes (1983: 16–22), Iredale (1990), Kennedy (1988), Lecomte (1986), ODA (1987, 1988), Oxfam (1988), Plomp et al. (1992), Thompson (1985), Wiggins (1985), and chapter 3.
3   There are a number of helpful references available for formative and self-directed evaluation by teachers. These include Altrichter et al. (1993), Easen (1985), Harlen and Elliot (1982), Herman et al. (1987), Hopkins (1985), Kemmis and McTaggart (1982a), Merritt et al. (1980), Murphy and Torrance (1987), and Siedow et al. (1985). Alderson and Beretta (1992), Nunan (1989), and Rea-Dickins and Germaine (1992) provide help specifically for ELT teachers; see also appendix 1.2, the Introduction to part III and chapter 4. The reader is referred to them for details of useful procedures.

2 Recent Developments in Project Evaluation: The Issue of Baseline Design

2.1 Introductory

We have already referred briefly to the use of baseline measures in the preceding chapter (1.4.2) and in this chapter we discuss the role of baseline design in project evaluation in greater depth. We focus on projects for three reasons: it reflects our experience (see chapters 3 and 5); we are concerned to bring out the systematic nature of effective evaluation; and because accountability to external agencies (be they project funding agencies, Ministries, employers or professional bodies) is sure to be a matter of concern for many ELT professionals.

Since the 1985 Overseas Development Administration (ODA) decision to projectize British technical assistance, i.e. impose fixed objectives and time and cost limits on all projects, the nature of ELT aid work has changed. Efforts are being made to try to ensure that ELT is more closely integrated with other sectors into a coherent aid scheme and ELT has become subject to economic criteria such as cost-effectiveness as it competes with applicants from other sectors for government funding.

There is now an increasing demand from sponsoring agencies that project staff should be contractually accountable for what occurs in the implementation phase, i.e. during the life of a project from the granting of funds to the end of the external involvement of the donor country. Therefore projects now tend to be evaluated to provide answers to a range of questions:

- Did they achieve what they set out to achieve in terms of original objectives?
- Has the funding agency received value for money?
- Has the programme shown a sensible allocation of people and money?
- Has it been worthwhile?
- Has it had the desired impact on the infrastructure of the host country?
- Could the results have been achieved more cost-effectively?
- Could a better job have been done, and if so, how?
  (See also sections 1.2, 1.4.1, 1.4.4.)

Educational innovation and curriculum change consume valuable resources, money, time, and energy. The allocation of these resources between competing projects can be a contentious matter. The effectiveness, both potential and actual, of projects needs to be demonstrated in order to help decision makers make choices. There is an irrefutable case for confirming whether or not scarce resources have been sensibly and efficiently deployed. Valid and reliable data are needed to inform future decisions about resource allocation and to suggest appropriate remedies for securing improvements in similar projects that follow.

British government (ODA) projects are now drawn up according to a matrix which relates wider national goals, immediate objectives, project outputs and inputs to indicators of achievement, to how these indicators can be quantified and assessed, and to important assumptions upon which successful outcomes are founded (identifying in advance the possible risks and the prior conditions that should be made explicit and binding). This is now commonly referred to as the project framework approach (see Coleman 1987, and also discussion in section 1.4.1 and appendix 1.1).

Those submitting project proposals for funding purposes are now obliged to specify detailed objectives in as precise, comprehensive, quantified, and time-specific a form as possible. They need to detail the results expected from the management of inputs in terms of outputs (for example, number of staff trained) and the socio-economic benefits resulting from these outputs. They have to specify objectively verifiable indicators which will demonstrate proof of achievement by clearly indicating the criteria for success. They also have to take into account the conditions and the important assumptions which might affect the progress or success of the project but over which they may have no control. Any commitments necessary from the host government need to be made explicit and funding will normally be conditional on these being fulfilled.

The limitations inherent in the 'traditional' approach to project management (prior to the framework approach) were apparent in its reliance on 'fixing the machine while it was in motion'. The more systematic approach demanded by the introduction of project frameworks necessitates a feasibility/appraisal type of study *before a project gets off the ground* (see section 1.4.2 for discussion of evaluation at each stage in the life of a project: appraisal before it starts, monitoring during implementation, and summative evaluation at the end). So, even prior to a project submission for funding purposes data are collected to permit an analysis of the project's viability in the particular target system; the degree of fit between the proposed innovation and the problem identified; and soundings taken on the prevailing societal environment, appropriate management systems, and requirements and availability of resources (Smith 1989a, 1989c). A pre-project feasibility study is thus one important way in which the *baseline* concept might be utilized.

As part of a more systematic approach to project design and implementation, the ODA is also currently investigating the parameters for gathering baseline data at the start of the *implementation* phase when funding has been authorized and the project team is in place (see Burton et al. forthcoming). It is felt that if we are to determine what effect or impact a project has, we need to establish what certain conditions are before 'treatment', i.e. before the implementation stage. In other words we might need to establish baseline data at the start of a project which will help us to monitor any effects that occur during or after 'treatment'. For example, if an objective were to improve the English language proficiency of students in universities in country X, it might be useful to determine precisely what the proficiency level of students is before they experience a new programme of language instruction. Considerable resources might need to be allocated for this data collection.

Rational planning approaches to management normally assume an information-gathering stage which includes establishing relevant knowledge, evidence, experience, and ideas and assessing the risks involved. Gathering baseline data at the start of a project or even before a project is submitted for approval should not be seen as deviant in any way but what good management principles and practice advocate (White et al. 1991).

A suggested sequence in project design and implementation and the place of evaluation within it might be as follows:

- Problem recognized in host country
- Baseline feasibility study
- Objectives clarified
- Project framework proposal drawn up and submitted
- Project approved and implementation begins
- Benchmark baseline data collected for measuring effects of implementation
- Monitoring
- Summative evaluation

Following Fullan (1982) and Smith (1989a), we recognize that real life may well deviate from this tidy linear pattern. We argue below that evaluation of the actual implementation of projects will need to take account of this, and systematically document and justify any changes, remodelling of objectives, redefinition of solutions, and emergence of unanticipated outcomes. In terms of the decision basis for funding at the pre-project stage, however, a loose approach to programme objectives (colloquially known as a 'let's suck it and see' approach) is no longer acceptable. We need to be as clear as we can about what we hope to achieve from the outset whilst developing the mechanisms for documenting and justifying any essential changes that might need to be made *en route*.

In this chapter we examine baseline data collection for the two purposes described above. First we discuss the concept in relation to the appraisal (pre-project) stage where a problem has been recognized and baseline data is needed to clarify objectives in preparation for a project proposal. In section 2.3 we take it up more specifically in relation to the implementation stage. In chapter 3 we use as an illustration a baseline study to assess the impact of a teacher training project in

Nepal and make reference to the use of test data and observation as the indicators of achievement and means of verification used in that study.

2.2 Baseline studies at the appraisal (pre-project) stage

Financing a baseline feasibility study at the appraisal stage is not without its difficulties. Service organizations unused to the idea of funding front-end planning studies may be, initially at least, unwilling to put money up front to determine the appropriateness, viability, and sustainability of a project before they have secured a contractual guarantee of funding. The major question, however, is whether any funding should be allocated in the absence of such front-end planning. Indeed, evidence of such front-end planning can be a very powerful persuasive factor in encouraging a funding agency to finance a new project. Any prospective business-man or entrepreneur knows the importance of a carefully thought out business plan in attracting potential investment partners. No bank manager will lend money for a project 'to see how it goes' without first having been persuaded of the project's viability.

It may well turn out that the funding body itself is prepared to support a feasibility study prior to a major investment and a current feasibility study of ELT materials design and teacher training in Bangladesh would seem to be an example of this. It may be that this type of study could form the first short phase of a project and the manager apparent or equivalent made responsible for conducting it. Funding for the major part of the project would then be contingent on a satisfactory outcome.

The problems inherent in a full-scale target situation analysis are well docu-mented (Weir 1983). The particular problem is that such analyses face the danger of taking on a life of their own and *consuming inordinate amounts of money and time*. The crucial factor is conducting them at the right level of delicacy.

As yet there are no British Council/ODA guidelines on the decision-making process to be adopted in obtaining the information for a project framework for a particular type of project, or the categories of information it would be useful to have information in for the various ELT projects undertaken. In principle it would seem useful to have a checklist for each cell in the project framework matrix, ideally cross-referenced to a procedural column for how this data might best be generated (see appendix 1.1). Empirical efforts to follow this approach would demonstrate its viability and a useful body of information concerning criteria and procedural means could result.

Our concern in advocating this first use of baseline data collection is to establish what the situation will be at the start of a project. We are interested in whether the inputs and outputs specified are reasonable. Are they likely to achieve the imme-diate objectives as specified? Will the indicators of achievement specified give us necessary and sufficient information to make judgements on whether success has been achieved? The means of verification must be valid, reliable and practical in order to generate the necessary data.

Analysis of the situation obtaining in country X through a baseline feasibility study could help clarify a set of objectives for a potential project. In deciding upon these immediate objectives for a project, we would need to consider how they fit in with those of other established projects in that country (see appendix 1.1 for sample project frameworks). This would take us up the left-hand column of the project matrix to consideration of the wider objectives, which are perhaps better seen as *national objectives*. However, it may be difficult for the project manager to be privy to these (see discussion of this in section 1.4.4) and if so the place of the ELT project with respect to these may be difficult to describe with certainty. One could not begin to assess the value of the project in the wider context of, say, manpower planning and human capital theory if this wider perspective were not available.

An added difficulty might arise where the feasibility study suggests a decision against a particular project but because of hidden political agenda it is expedient for a project to start (Iredale 1990). Evaluation of the later success of such projects may be problematic.

Both the wider national objectives and the more immediate objectives will obviously be affected by the prevailing situation in a country. Unpacking this prevailing situation, as far as is possible or permitted, will enable us to more clearly state the assumptions for each of the levels in the left-hand column. These assumptions are perhaps better considered as conditions (or risks) which underlie the successful conversion of inputs into outputs on which the achievement of the immediate objectives will hinge. They may well involve contractual obligations on the part of the host nation.

Let us take a few examples to explore this further. Thought has to be given to the adequacy of resourcing in the light of intended outcomes. If there are local conditions which need to obtain for a project to be successful (e.g. actual jobs for teacher trainees to go to after training), then these should be established and secured prior to the setting up of the project proper. In certain contexts this may not be possible in advance and then the assumptions column would need to clearly state the risks involved so that donors are primed to the exact nature of the funding decision they are taking.

There is a pressing need to establish the viability of these assumptions at the pre-implementation phase and ensure that they are in place before the project starts. For example, if it is vital to project success that the host government will support teachers to attend regional seminars or carry out observations in a province, or provide premises for regional resource centres, there needs to be an agreement on this beforehand. It might be useful to make a division in the project framework submission between donor obligations and recipient obligations with a need for a formalized agreement between donor and host nation to tie these in.

One central requirement is the need to arrive at a sensible estimate of the outputs that must be expected from specified inputs in order to achieve the specified immediate objectives (see appendix 1.1 for examples of project frame-works) – certainly not an easy task for planning educational projects. The emphasis on achievement of objectives in the project framework, and the conversion of inputs to outputs to achieve these, means that there is a heavy onus placed on successful management in ELT aid projects. Smith (1989c) has pointed out the potential for conflict between donor-imposed project requirements and recipient expectations in ELT aid that might threaten the success of projects. Donor re-quirements for specific time-related, quantifiable objectives or for a 'western-style' (Smith 1989a, 1989c) project management approach might be at odds with the organizational culture of the host country. Appropriate resolution of these difficul-ties or at least their identification as risks should be embodied in the assumptions column in project submissions.

The crucial question of the sustainability of projects is related to these issues and also to the less determinate factors of personalities and relations between personnel. It may be difficult to take these into account in advance but employing the wrong type of personality, irrespective of professional aptitude, could be dis-astrous. The possession of suitable and adequate managerial skills on the part of expatriate staff in positions of authority must be ascertained before appointment (Smith 1989b).

Thought also needs to be given to the strategies required to ensure ELT projects are managed jointly by donor and recipients as collaborative cooperative efforts rather than primarily as donor input. The whole area of cross-cultural aspects of management is one which demands more investigation. Various authors in this field (Hofstede 1980, Rodwell 1988, Smith 1989a, 1989b, 1989c, White et al. 1991) have pointed to limitations in project designs which give inadequate attention to the management style of the host organization and the cultural influences on management. In fact this may not be the fault of the designs and subsequent briefings but evidence of the lack of a principled basis for the seeking of answers to the cultural question. Smith (1989c) draws attention to our ignorance in areas such as the management of innovation and the process of change in third world countries and points to potential contaminating variables such as 'informalism' and the environmental uncertainty within which third world educational systems may operate. Crucial too are value differences between expatriate staff and hosts (Phillips and Owens 1986, Rodwell 1988).

As well as this cluster of management issues, there are a number of other areas (categories of information) that it would be useful to consider in the design of project proposals (see table 2.1). We are obviously not suggesting all of these need to be considered (or could be considered) for every project. They are merely an initial list which further use should help refine and reduce. Additionally it should become clearer which data are particularly relevant to which projects. Further, there is a pressing need for establishing priorities in collecting different data for the various types of ELT projects UK agencies might be involved in.

What is crucial is the interface between the goals of the project and the current situation, which will help narrow down the categories of information we need to

Table 2.1 Categories of information

For ELT projects the categories one might wish to collect information on are numerous and a prioritized selection might have to be made from a list which might include the following.

1 *Background demographic information on the education system* Age cohorts, future demographic trends, enrolments, types of school and their status, numbers in classes, size of school, school timetables, time given to English in the curriculum, value it holds, success rates in national examinations

2 *The need for English in that country (target situation analysis)* Key educational policies in the country and their ideological basis, identification of the decision makers, stability of the economic and political systems, official language policy, medium of instruction, role of English in society, language needs, medium, channel, the extent to which ESP is required, who it will be used with, where it will be used, models and standards of English looked to

3 *The current learning situation (learning situation analysis)*

Curriculum issues The form assessment of English takes within the current system, the identity of decision makers, the openness of the system to change in this respect, the system's capacity for innovation (Smith 1989c), history of implementations of the English curriculum, outcomes of previous implementations, attitudes to English in general, to the existing curriculum and its results in particular, motivation of the learners, attendance and drop-out rates (causes of these), preferred learning styles, teachers' qualifications, existing classroom behaviours, attitudes of teachers (e.g. to INSET), socio-economic status of teachers, rate of attrition, nature of existing teacher training, physical and financial resources available (ease with which they could be made available if project funded), availability and nature of teaching materials, premises, current evaluation systems e.g. inspectorate, number of expatriate native speakers already in the system, status of any existing professional ELT organizations (unions/associations) within the power/decision making structure

Management issues Management structure at various levels within the educational system, management style in the host institution, organizational and authority structure within the schools, management and academic direction skills, decision making within the system (and those relating to cultural differences discussed above), capacity to manage change effectively

---

collect data on. The establishment of these data should help refine the specific objectives for a particular project and provide a basis for valid subsequent evaluation, both formative and summative.

The interface among these elements will be crucial for the successful implementation of planned change and empirical research of the type being conducted by Harvey Smith will be essential for identifying those interfaces which are important and which might have the most bearing on project success in the implementation phase (Smith 1989c). No claim is made for the completeness of the list and it is offered only as a basis for discussion. (Harrison 1991, Smith 1989c and White 1988 provide a further discussion of this issue and exemplification of some of the categories.) Debate will refine these categories of information.

The question of best procedures for generating these data must also be addressed, as must the issue of how to constrain the data-gathering process so that the minimum of high quality data necessary for decision making is sought and elicited. There is an obvious danger as those involved in projects move from the 'Garden of Eden' approach to project design (characterized by innocence and an absence of accountability) and attempt to systematize their procedures in working through the current 'Vale of Tears', that collecting such information could easily become unmanageable. *Serious consideration needs to be given to what and how to prioritize in generating these data.* Depending on the nature of the project under review, the needs analysis would focus on categories of background information from the above list which seem most crucial to making decisions about objectives and the assumptions their achievement is premised on.

As part of 'projectization' there has also been much interest recently in exploring the parameters for gathering baseline data at the *start of a project*, before implementation. If evaluators are going to determine what effect a programme has had, they need to establish what conditions were like immediately before it. In other words, they need to gather baseline data which will help to monitor the effects that occur during or after project implementation. If they wish to determine student language improvement they need to test them on entry into courses. The nature of these baseline data (e.g. test data, observations) means that it is likely that the active cooperation of many project members will be necessary especially in the early stages and time and money will need to be allocated for this data collection.

As an example, in a large-scale in-service teacher training programme (INSET courses) it is obviously necessary to provide evidence that such training is having an effect (see section 3.1). It is hard to establish its impact if no baseline data is available for comparison purposes. You cannot say standards have improved if there is no evidence to indicate what they were like before. At the end of the project what has been achieved in comparison with original objectives is assessed. Any changes in objectives are noted and care is taken to establish the most important contributory factors to successes or failures. Consideration is given to whether the results could have been achieved in a more cost-effective manner. Finally, the lessons for this and future projects can be drawn: in this way summative measures can have a formative dimension (Cronbach 1982).

2.3 Collecting baseline data at the implementation stage: The need to measure the effects of a project and its impact

After a project has been approved and started up, the reference point for making judgements on its implementation will obviously relate to baseline data that have already been collected in order to complete the project framework matrix in terms of inputs, outputs and immediate and wider objectives. Progress in terms of these 'vertical' criteria in the matrix will always be relative to this starting point. The indicators and means of verification would show the degree of attainment in respect of each, though obviously monitoring would be more difficult in respect of the less quantitative, less concrete elements. Attention would also need to be paid on a continuing basis to the degree to which initial assumptions were being fulfilled.

It is a common practice in evaluation to compare intended outputs and objectives of educational projects against the actual achievement of these within the given assumptions. Projects will be judged by the extent to which objectives are realized. Smith (1989a) has recently raised some doubts about the very attempt to impose a project culture premised on the achievement of preplanned objectives within a specific time-scale, using preplanned resources to produce outputs that can be assessed in quantified terms (see section 1.4.4 for a discussion of this).

Taking behavioral objectives alone to be an adequate specification of what it is that projects can and should achieve is not without problems, as we discussed in section 1.4.4 (Alderson 1986) and is a controversial issue in education in general. In particular, once a project gets moving, the situation changes and as situational dynamics come into play, even small incidents in a project might have quite unpredictable consequences. The question is whether educational objectives are indeed totally predictable or whether one should expect them to be modified or altered in certain respects as learning proceeds.

Despite the problems in clearly identifying goals, one cannot escape the need for a definition of where a project is going. An attempt to specify objectives at the start of a programme is a valuable and essential exercise. Decisions have to be made on the viability of projects and the likely benefit to recipients assessed. It must be clear to those involved in which direction a project is going and what objectives are sought even if detours might become necessary *en route*. One also needs to be able to assess how far one has progressed along the route. Further, the project approach makes it clear to both donors and recipients what the expected contribution from both sides is to be. As with a syllabus in language teaching, the project approach provides a semblance of order on what otherwise might be a chaotic mess and allows for rational planned action to be taken rather than day-to-day responses to events.

Current ODA approaches to project evaluation do in fact allow for the possibility that projects may change direction or unanticipated outcomes or shortfalls in terms of original objectives may occur. In many project evaluations currently conducted by outsiders, there is a concern to establish systematically what has actually happened in a project, the problems that arose, if the inputs were as planned, if there were any delays and the nature of these, if outputs were achieved, and if not why not, if the management and administration were up to the mark, what the strengths and weakness of the implementation were, what the impact on the host country has been.

Furthermore, in looking at what the project achieved, note would be taken of whether there were any changes of objectives during the life of the project or if any unanticipated results occurred. (It is important that evaluations take account of unpredicted outcomes or effects even if they are hard to define and also for these to be documented thoroughly by insiders.) Care should also be paid to establishing the most important contributory factors to success or failure. Finally, findings would be brought together, key lessons established, consideration given to whether any new light has been thrown on a problem or any additional problems brought to light, the findings compared with similar evaluations, and recommendations made for the project in question and for similar projects.

A project may well be regarded as successful even if there is only a partial achievement of its immediate objectives if it nevertheless has made an acceptable wider contribution to the socio-economic development of the country concerned. However, it may fall to manpower planners and economists (and politicians!) rather than educationists to make judgements of this nature.

2.4 Conclusion

As we noted in chapter 1, the eighties and early nineties have been dominated by 'market economy' thinking in government and commercial circles, which has emphasized the need to identify how resources are being used, whether the purpose of spending has been achieved, and making accountable those who are responsible for the spending (as in state schools in England and Wales, for example). This contrasts markedly with the sometimes rather loose attitude to evaluation that marked ELT programmes and projects in Britain (though not in North America) until the late seventies. Principles of accountability and value for money have led in some cases to the narrow use of attainment tests to measure the gains that pupils in schools make from their point of entry, at key points during schooling, and on leaving it. The intention is to enable authorities to assess the 'cost of input' against the 'value of output'.

Critics of this approach see this as a reduction and simplification of educational processes; almost to that of a chicken farm, in which you would weigh chicks on entry, chickens on exit, and assess the quality of the factory in terms of average weight gained. They would argue that measurement of this type excludes such parameters as social, personal, and motivational aspects of learning and ignores the high degree of variability between learners in what they bring to the educational programme at the outset, both individually and from school to school (see also section 1.4.4).

While we may be witnessing a reaction against extreme applications of free-market thinking, it is probably a fair assessment to conclude that the principle of accountability, and the demand for evidence from a professional audience, are here to stay. However, we would certainly not advocate the universal use of baseline designs (though some might for ideological reasons) nor the exclusive use of 'input-output' measures without reference to other data to explain them. On the basis of our experience (see part II), we would now see the collection of baseline data before and at the start of a project as useful, *but on certain conditions*: that objectives were appropriately and validly measured by the instruments used; that contextual, formative information was obtained in order to explain any baseline results; that there was a constructive place in baseline measures for insider staff; and, finally, that it was *appropriate* and educationally constructive to attempt to measure learner gains between time of entry and time of departure from a course.

In terms of the case studies we present in part II, each situation implies a different degree of relevance for baseline measures. In the case of chapter 4, an evaluation of a relatively short duration English for Academic Purposes programme (100–300 hours), baseline measures could have value as individual learner feedback, and for formative means. However, the short duration of the programme and considerable individual variability in students' acquisition potential means that baseline measures might not in themselves be a fair indicator of programme quality, although they could provide a useful aggregate check on the amounts of progress that is possible in that period. This might eventually prove valuable in briefing funding agencies on the amount of language tuition necessary to bring prospective students up to the requisite proficiency level before entry into their courses of study proper. Chapter 4 is more concerned with improving the service that is provided for reasons of professional rather than contractual accountability. There is also a strong formative, developmental dimension to evaluation of the programme as the institution concerned is committed to improving the quality of its teaching, materials, and resources on a continuing basis.

In the case study presented in chapter 5, a formative evaluation of a teacher training course, many of the objectives do not lend themselves so readily to baseline measurement (e.g. personal development, motivation to continue as teachers, changes in method, etc.). However, English language improvement was a high priority, measurable goal of the two-year full-time course. While baseline measurement of student teacher learning gain was not within the remit of the evaluator, it *would* be appropriate in the context described both for purposes of programme development (to give insiders feedback on the effectiveness of language improvement classes) and for summative evaluation (to assess students' progress and to compare their exit proficiency with 'real world' demands, such as teaching the local English syllabus or being eligible for further training).

However, it is in the case of formal language and training projects (chapter 3) that the case for baseline measurement is most powerful. The systematicity it brings to the management of ELT projects is welcome and timely, but we argue that it needs to be complemented by process data collected by insiders (and perhaps moderated by outsiders) for its full potential to be realized.

The detailed discussion of the baseline approach, above and in the next chapter, reflects the importance the writers attach to it and its pivotal role in developing and crystallizing our thinking in relation to the need for a more *comprehensive* approach to evaluation for both accountability and developmental purposes (see section 1.3). This approach would focus on the use that could be made of evaluation data and the involvement of all concerned parties in a way that is accessible and of value to all involved (Patton 1986: 338). The lessons we learned from the outsider-led, accountability-oriented, baseline approach discussed in chapter 3 suggest the need for some rethinking. We now feel that both insiders and outsiders need to be actively engaged in discussion about what is happening in programmes or projects, where they are going, how they could be improved, and what information is needed to assist in this process. As Patton describes it (1986: 338), 'Ultimately, generating and using information is a personal process. Therein lies the power of evaluation – *in the mobilization of individual energies for action.* As the barrier of uncertainty is attacked and as systematic information emerges to improve program effectiveness, evaluation is used.'

Part II Case Studies

Introduction

In chapters 3–5, we present case studies which are intended to share our personal experiences of evaluation in a number of different settings. Using key terms from chapter 1, we summarize the three case studies in table II.1.

We have given considerable attention to the issue of baseline design in section 1.4.4 and chapter 2 and we include the Nepal baseline evaluation as a case study in chapter 3 below. This emphasis is pragmatic, as the baseline approach reflects a 'cost-benefit' approach to evaluation which is likely to affect many of us in our working lives for the foreseeable future. It certainly contrasts markedly with the far less systematic and mainly developmental approach to evaluation prevalent when we started our careers in the 1970s. We feel that the issue of baseline design and outcome measurement is of central importance to ELT professionals because it demonstrates the increasing need for insiders to concern themselves more fully with evaluation at all stages in the life of a programme or project as economic necessities thrust us all into the arena of accountability in all aspects of our work. In chapter 3, we also focus on *test data and observation* as data sources and try to illustrate some of the problems in their use as well as suggesting that they can be potentially valuable sources of data collection in almost all evaluations.

We feel that the other case studies raise additional important issues for evaluators and subjects of evaluation alike. In chapter 4 we are concerned with the value of insider evaluation for developmental purposes and with the methods that may be used for this. We also explore the dynamics of being subjected to external inspection, and the relationship between this and internal formative programme development. We conclude by discussing the need for a rational synthesis which will lead to a more healthy blend of cooperative evaluation between insiders and outsiders.

In chapter 5, we are concerned with parameters for the evaluation of an initial teacher training project and with the translation of an external intervention into action by insiders – the issue of utilization of evaluations.

In reporting the case studies, our approach is not intended to be prescriptive. There is no one way to conduct evaluation, because purposes and contexts vary. Furthermore, evaluations rarely have the luxury of time afforded to academic research projects, and so typically the evaluator is called upon to strike a difficult balance between meeting professional standards (see section 1.5), developing and maintaining an awareness of the 'hidden' dynamics of evaluations (chapter 8), and also working within the constraints of limited budgets, limited time, and the absolute need to deliver evaluation information in time for it to be used to inform decisions (see section 1.4.7). An excellent report is of no use if the decisions have already had to be made.

We have learned from our own experience and that of others. Indeed, our experiences in the three evaluations led us to reappraise our approach (see sections 1.3 and 1.6 above). Some of the specific lessons we learned are indicated below.

Table II.1.   Summary of case studies

	Chapter 3	Chapter 4	Chapter 5
Context			
Place	In Nepal	In the UK	In Latin America
Course	4-week INSET	12-week EAP pre-sessional	2-year initial teacher training
Funding	ODA project	Fees	ODA project
Number of participants	*c.* 900 teachers *c.* 40,000 students	25 teachers 200 students	7 teachers *c.* 30 students
Evaluation variables			
Why	Contractual accountability	Developmental and professional accountability	Developmental
What	Language-improvement teaching	Language-improvement teaching Materials Client satisfaction	Training syllabus
Initiator	ODA (Evaluation Department)	CALS (BALEAP)	ODA (Education Department)
Who by	Outsider	Outsider and 'insider' teaching staff and administrator	Outsider Insiders
When	Summative	Formative (summative)	Formative
How long	2 years	12 weeks (1 day)	2 weeks
Main methods used	Tests Observation Interview documents Teacher self-report	Tests Observation Interview documents Questionnaire	Tests Observation Interview documents

The experience in the Nepal teacher training project (chapter 3) showed us the need for summative findings (the test data) to be complemented by a formative dimension (the observational data). It also indicated the benefits that could have resulted if we had been able to help structure an insider responsibility for collecting systematic formative data. This would have given us: a wider sample of teacher informants; a clearer picture of conditions across schools; follow-up data on teachers' successes and failures in putting their training into practice and the perceived reasons for this.

In chapter 5 (an initial teacher training project) we report some of the limitations of short-term involvement by an external evaluator and some negative effects of the lack of systematic internal evaluation. However, the experience there suggested the possibility of a common framework for a better integrated evaluation involving formative and summative dimensions. As such, it may offer guidelines for the future development of evaluation activities both in government-funded projects where contractual accountability is involved and in language programmes where accountability to external bodies is valued in the interests of professional identity, status and enhancement.

Our experiences in Nepal and in subsequent ODA projects (see chapters 3 and 5) have demonstrated to us the merit of going beyond a purely summative, 'cost–benefit' model of evaluation to a more cooperative and integrated approach. We now perceive the following broader interpretations of evaluations:

1 the need for funding agencies to accept the value of involving insiders in evaluation for reasons of economy and practicality;
2 the need to encourage the formative improvement of projects;
3 the contribution such involvement would make to post-project sustainability; and
4 the central importance of such formative evaluation data in helping understand the results of summative evaluation.

The lessons from the evaluation of an English for Academic Purposes course described in chapter 4 suggested the value of extending the role of an external inspector to embrace developmental as well as accountability dimensions. We feel a valuable opportunity to obtain another perspective on our programme was missed because of the restricted terms of reference of the evaluator. It also brought home to us as insiders the considerable benefits of responding positively to an accountability-oriented evaluation: in the form of encouraging better documentation (syllabi, aims and objectives, organograms, job descriptions, etc.); and by incorporating new evaluation procedures (e.g. individual tutorials). It reinforced our commitment to systematic formative evaluation for programme and staff development (e.g. materials evaluation by teachers) and added a valuable external perspective on that work.

We hope that by sharing our experiences and the methods we have employed, readers will be able to improve upon what we have done and avoid the mistakes we have made. It is in this spirit that the following chapters are offered.

3 A Baseline Evaluation: Focus on Accountability

3.1 Introductory

The first case study describes the procedures adopted by the writers when contracted to carry out an evaluation for accountability. It took the form of a baseline
evaluation of the effect of a teacher training course on student language performance. It is hoped that the account will lead to constructive discussion of how to
improve the methodology employed. It considers the problems that may be faced
by external evaluators working in difficult circumstances. We are grateful to the
Overseas Development Administration in the United Kingdom for giving us permission to report our methodology. The results of the investigation are at the
moment confidential (see Burton et al. forthcoming for details of these).[1] As a result,
certain issues are not discussed in this chapter: the control of summative information, the form of the report, and the utilization of results. (For a general discussion
of the latter see section 1.4.7.)

If you are running in-service teacher training courses for all the language teachers in a given country over a period of years, it is obviously necessary to provide
evidence that such training is having an effect. It is hard to determine whether it
is having an effect if no baseline data are available for comparison purposes. You
cannot show standards have improved if there is no evidence to suggest what they
were like before the new form of instruction, in terms of either pedagogical input
or student language performance.

As we noted in section 1.4.6, if it were possible to have a control group of classes
taught by teachers who had not received the 'treatment' (the new form of training)
and an equivalent experimental group of the classes of trained teachers, then it
should be possible to administer and re-administer relevant tests to students in
these two groups over a period of time and examine whether significant differences
emerge in their language performance.

If differences do emerge in student test scores then one could argue that it was
worth continuing the training, though one might not be able to fully interpret the
difference between the two. It may be difficult particularly in the cases of general
proficiency, or even reading and listening skills, to express quantitative differences

in qualitative terms. For example, what does a difference between two groups of five marks out of a hundred on a reading test really mean? Such differences may be statistically significant but their meaning in educational terms may be less clear. Therefore in those cases where there are differences, caution is needed in interpreting results. Conversely, if no statistically significant differences appear then funding agencies would question the value of the training and the extension of the funding.

We argued in section 1.4.6 that if no differences emerge in the summative test performances of students in control and experimental groups, we cannot know why this is the case without reference to process data. We would need to know if there were real differences in the classroom behaviour of 'control' and 'experimental' teachers, before one could reasonably criticize the training course. For this reason we felt it important to complement test data with observation and other forms of data. One needs a comprehensive picture of what has happened in a project before one can offer possible explanations. In this sense the role of evaluation is about understanding how a project produces its effects and what parameters influence its effectiveness.

Ideally, the purpose of evaluation should not just be to determine whether a project has been successful or unsuccessful in terms of end products alone but also to provide stakeholders with as detailed a description as possible of all factors contributing to the project's success or lack of it.

3.2 The Nepal baseline study

3.2.1 Background

The SEPELT INSET Project in Nepal was set up to provide 1080 standard grades 8–10 (upper secondary level) English teachers with one month's in-service training, delivered by locally trained Nepali staff, working from a standard course manual and supported by an expatriate training officer. It ran from 1987 to 1989. The long-term goal of the training was to improve students' performance in the School Leaving Certificate English examination. The course provided training in basic ELT procedures designed to enhance the teaching of the national English curriculum.

The Nepal baseline study described in this paper was a small-scale, field-based, non-equivalent group study, contrasting the learning gains of about 750 students in the grade 8 classes of eleven trained teachers and eleven untrained teachers. The study established procedures for measuring the effect of the SEPELT training on students' language performance. It was also concerned with determining the suitability of these procedures for evaluating similar projects elsewhere.

A small-scale non-equivalent control group pre-test/post-test design was employed at the suggestion of the ODA as it offered a tight, practical evaluation design. (Fitz–Gibbon and Morris 1987b provide a detailed account of the range of options open to the evaluator and very useful practical advice on the design, implementation and analysis of evaluations.) In the design selected for the Nepal study, two groups of students which are similar, but which are not formed by random assignment, are measured both before and after one of the groups undergoes the 'experimental' treatment (see appendix 3.1). The students can be assessed at the start of the implementation of the programme to establish their degree of similarity, and statistical modelling (see the section on testing, below) will allow for any necessary adjustments to achieve this. The design is particularly useful in those contexts such as Nepal where random sampling is not a possibility (hence ruling out the true control group, pre-test/post-test design). The use of a control group design as against a single group time series design (Fitz–Gibbon and Morris 1987b) was felt necessary because the funding agency required proof that any impact was due to training and was not just coincidental.

In this case the experimental treatment took the form of instruction by teachers who had attended the SEPELT training course. We were concerned to see if, with faithful implementation of the training, there would be superior learning gains by this group as evidenced by improvement in student language test scores.

As well as testing students we were able to negotiate the inclusion, in the study, of a brief to monitor the performance of trained (experimental) and untrained (control) teachers. In this way we were able to establish whether the treatments received by the pupils were indeed different, i.e. whether or not our control and experimental groups were exposed to different language instruction. This was felt to be particularly necessary as little provision had been made for any formative follow-up of teachers in the main project.

We made short visits to Nepal in November 1988, January 1989 and November 1989. As a result of the first visit, the baseline framework was set up and technical staff were contracted for data collection (The New Era research organization; see section 3.3 for details). These were professional researchers with a good track record in social surveys and fieldwork. A short training course was provided for these technical staff during the second visit. The final visit was made in order to monitor data collection.

3.2.2   The language test instruments

To determine the effects of the training course, baseline tests were administered to the new intakes in grade 8 at a selected group of schools (12 control and 12 experimental in the first instance). This took place at the start of the school year in February 1989. These classes were of both the experimental type, where the teachers had been on a training course, and of the control type, where the teachers had received no prior EFL training. The tests were re-administered at the end of grade 8 in November 1989. Subsequent administrations of the battery are not covered in this account.

Part I of the battery was constructed to sample as widely as possible the structural elements in the English syllabuses for years 7 and 8 in the Nepali upper secondary school system on the basis that such linguistic elements would be accessible to both control and experimental groups (see Beretta 1986b for a discussion of programme fair language teaching evaluation). The two sections of this general proficiency section of the battery were prepared in advance of the November 1988 visit and piloted during that visit.

The general aim of the training was to make teachers more efficient at what they did already and our feeling was that part I of the test adequately catered for this aspect. Our concern in part II of the test was to reflect any differences in kind, in terms of student performances that might be expected to emerge from the new skills practised in training. Details of both parts of the tests are included at appendix 3.2.

3.2.3 The process instruments

The purpose of developing observation instruments in the context of this study was to enable the fair interpretation of test scores through gathering data on the faithfulness of implementation by the trainees. Though these procedures were used primarily for the light they might shed on summative findings, we are aware that they have a clear potential formative value for other training courses. They would enable the fine tuning of training objectives and the validation of training content.

Prior to the November 1988 Nepal visit, an inventory of training characteristics was produced from the project training manual and other available documentation. In discussion with Nepali trainers during that visit, the features that they considered to be both of highest priority and the best discriminators of trained and untrained teachers were selected from the inventory and the resulting short list was then used as the basis for the observation instrument. Additionally, this list helped us identify more clearly those training characteristics potentially capable of effects on measurable pupil performance which would need to be reflected in the tests. This list of *criterial features* proved to be an invaluable document in crystallizing what the project's objectives were.

On return, a draft observation instrument was trialled in a local secondary school's classes of French. The design of the resulting schedule took into account its implementation by technical staff, with an emphasis on simplicity of use and a focus on low-inference observations. The revised form was the basis for observer training in January 1989 (see appendix 3.3 and section 7.3 for details of the instruments and figure 7.7).

It may seem that the data obtained present a somewhat narrow and simplistic account of classroom processes. It should be noted that there is nothing to be gained by making observers' tasks more complex than necessary; that key training and discriminating characteristics can be identified; and that talk in elementary ELT classrooms is intrinsically controlled and restricted in range.

3.2.4 Additional data collection

Two other forms of convergent data were required: that of teachers' self-report lesson descriptions and that of pupils' work.

Self-report On each visit by technical staff, the teachers were given self-report sheets. They were asked to describe three recent, typical lessons they had given. Self-report is often considered unreliable, addressing impression management rather than describing actual practice. However, teachers are unlikely to report doing what they never do, or what is unknown to them. These data were used, with caution, as additional information on the customary practice of teachers in the two groups (see appendix 3.6 for an example of a completed self-report sheet).

Pupils' work As part of the final observation visit, technical staff were asked to obtain samples of work from about five pupils in each class. These data were obtained to help identify discrepancies with observational and self-report data (see section 7.1.6).

3.3 Contracting The New Era for data collection

A decision had been taken in November 1988 that local technical staff should be contracted to collect test and process data on the grounds of economy and their Nepali field experience. The New Era research organization was selected as the best source for such staff. New Era is a highly regarded research organization which had an impressive track record of field-based research studies conducted both for the Nepali government and external donor agencies, including the ODA. As well as providing a very cost-effective service, New Era's management systems indicated efficient monitoring of individual staff performance. The researchers were all social science graduates and well trained in survey methods, particularly questionnaire and interviewing. They offered the possibility, with specific training in observation techniques, of a reliable and systematic data collection service.

3.3.1 Observer training, January 1989

A visit to the Nepal project was made to conduct an observer training session for New Era staff who would be responsible for collecting data on the effects of training on pedagogical practice. A special manual was produced for the observation training seminar. In addition it was necessary to familiarize these staff with the conduct of the language tests. This involved a briefing on the instructions for invigilation and the steps to be taken after testing.

The observer training would seem to have been effective from what emerged in the trialling in Kathmandhu. After joint observations, completed instruments were compared and an acceptable degree of agreement was noted. Where any differences occurred these were the subject of later training sessions.

The best four out of the six New Era staff (i.e. those who had performed best in the training) were selected to carry out the subsequent observations and the testing.

3.3.2 Monitoring visit, November 1989

A final monitoring visit was made in November 1989 with the following objectives:

1 To visit schools jointly with New Era staff
2 To review language test procedures with New Era staff
3 To review collection of observational data, particularly checklists
4 To monitor the selection of sample schools and teachers
5 To make recommendations for future data collection based on points 1–5 above

The following were the outcomes of the visit.

Re point 1: Sixteen schools were visited, and thirteen teachers were jointly observed by New Era staff and the evaluators between 5 and 10 November 1989.

Re point 2: Language test procedures were reviewed in an initial briefing meeting with New Era staff in Pokhara on 4 November 1989; and the administration of tests was subsequently monitored in five schools and found to be satisfactory.

Re point 3: Observation procedures and category interpretations were reviewed and agreed in the meeting and a joint observation held on 4 November 1989; and subsequent joint observations were reviewed and discussed.

On the basis of post-lesson comparisons, there appeared to be a satisfactory level of reliability between observations made by the evaluators.

3.4 Selection of sample

Given the Nepali context and the nature of educational sampling in general, we had no alternative than to base the study on an opportunity sampling. Random sampling was simply not feasible. We would have needed to select about three hundred teachers out of the total for upper secondary if this had been deemed necessary. This would have involved more time and expenditure than incurred in the rest of the project.

Great care was taken in the sampling to ensure equivalence between the experimental and control groups. Details of the conditions for the selection of teachers and schools are included in appendix 3.4.

In summary, the study started with a selection of sixteen control and sixteen experimental schools which were considered likely to meet certain necessary conditions for inclusion. On the basis of screening visits in January 1989, eight of the schools which fell short of these criteria were removed from the study and we began the investigation with an *n* of 12 in each group. In January, one trained and one untrained teacher left their schools and we eliminated their students' scores from the study (see section 3.10.4, point 8 for discussion of sampling problems).

3.4.1   Equivalence of the groups

In the November 1989 visit we attempted to corroborate data on all the schools remaining in the sample. Structured interviews were held with the eighteen teachers who attended a meeting during the third visit. Data were obtained on the following features: years of service in the school; educational background and training; the teacher's place of origin; other occupations; number of pupils in the school; number of pupils in class; student attrition; number of lessons per week; number of lessons in the year; school's School Leaving Certificate (SLC) pass results for last year, both general and in English only; likelihood of teacher continuing with the class in grade 9; an estimate of the teachers' level of oral English, using the British Council ELTS scale.

3.4.2   Language assessment of teachers

During the November visit we were able to interview 18 of the 24 teachers and to assure ourselves that each had a baseline language competence sufficient for them to teach the Nepali English curriculum in grades 8–10. Details of the test administered to teachers are included at appendix 3.5.

3.5   Summary of the data available

By the end of 1989 the following data were available for analysis.

1   Language assessments
    a   Students' language tests: 22 schools (11 trained, 11 untrained); after removing outliers we had 716 students' scripts
    b   Teachers' language tests: 22 completed tests; 18 oral estimates

2   Process descriptions
    a   Observations: 22 teachers, 69 observation forms

b Teacher self-report: 20 teachers (10 + 10), 54 reports
c Sample student work: 20 students (10 + 10)
3 Interviews: 18 interviews (9 trained, 9 untrained)

3.5.1 Product data: Tests

The analysis was carried out using SAS (a software package for statistical analysis) and in particular the General Linear Models Procedure (GLIM; see Hatch and Lazaraton 1991). As a first step, the outliers in the population were removed from the sample by plotting the scores on graphs for each of the three tests: dictation, reading and writing. Their status as outliers was determined by their extreme position on the plotted scattergram. Candidates in the first administration of the tests scoring more than 15/40 on the dictation, or 24/100 on the gap filling, were removed from the sample as it was considered they were too dissimilar from the population we were interested in. This left us with an *n* of 343 students in the experimental group and 373 in the control group.

In all we had data on the performance of these two groups on the two sittings of the gap-filling test, the dictation and the writing. In addition we were able to take into account the effect of a number of other variables on these test scores.

We had collected data on the teachers in the two groups on the same tests and on the grammar test. The size of the classes attending the first test and the estimates of the number of hours of English each class had in the academic year 1989 were also available. The percentage of class time pupils spent talking in English and the number of criterial features of training demonstrated by the teachers were also included in the analysis. Finally, we had more limited data on the general pass rate of the schools in the SLC and the English pass rate at the SLC.

3.5.2 Process data: Observations

The observation instrument produces two quantifiable measures and supporting unquantified descriptions (see section 7.3 for fuller details of these instruments). The quantified data consists of:

1 Pupil English: a raw number of pupil English codings, against codings for all kinds of talk, which can then be expressed as a percentage
2 Criterial features: checklist entries which identify trained teachers' typical classroom activities and untrained teachers' typical activities

Both these measures can be aggregated for the comparison of control and experimental groups. In our study, GLIM analysis included the variables of pupil English and criterial features. The unquantified data in the observation instruments (note form lesson descriptions) were used to conduct internal validity checks, by identifying the consistency between descriptions, checklist entries, and codings.

The fifty-four self-report lesson descriptions were analysed by categorizing reported activities (see Patton 1987b for an account of content analysis procedure), identifying those associated with untrained and trained teachers, and comparing their relative incidence in the two groups.

Samples of student work were not analysed, as an insufficient number matched either the lessons observed or teachers' self-reports.

The two main methods which were employed in the Nepal baseline study, namely testing and observation, will be discussed in some detail below. These are likely to feature in most baseline studies of language projects and consideration of their use in Nepal highlights certain important considerations for this type of study.

3.5.3 Confidentiality

Care was taken to ensure anonymity in all data collection. We guaranteed that no schools, teachers, or pupils would be named in any of the reports. The codings that referred to them in the final report were only known to the evaluators. All data were sent directly from the New Era office in Kathmandhu to the evaluators in Reading.

3.6 Test data as indicators of achievement: The product dimension

Project evaluation has tended to require empirical information rather than qualitative judgement. It has been concerned with collecting hard 'facts', particularly those relating to test scores or gathering biodata about participants. This is largely due to the desire of funding agencies for hard data so that 'single truths' may be identified as a basis for decision making (see section 1.2).

For contractual accountability purposes, using test data is an attractive proposition. Unfortunately, using test data is not as simple, clean, or conclusive as its advocates might wish to believe.

Let us first take the central concern of how to measure student language improvement. This will be an important requirement in any language programme or project and it is in a sense the touchstone of success for teacher training programmes or projects as well. If there is no improvement in student language scores as a result of a massive teacher training project we might reasonably ask if it was worthwhile.

Funding agencies might reasonably ask for test data to be elicited at the beginning and end of a project to show the extent of improvement. Without constructing parallel (equivalent) tests, however, making definite statements as to how much students have improved as a result of following a course of language instruction is problematic. To establish test equivalence is a time-consuming and expensive process. It is necessary to trial both versions of the test on a representative sample of the target population and to analyse the resulting performances. The tests then need to be balanced so that one can confidently administer them either at the beginning or end of treatment and measure improvement in performance as the difference in the results. Unfortunately, on financial grounds alone, the construction of parallel tests is obviously out of the question for most of the language projects we are involved in.

If one does not construct parallel versions and relies instead on administering the same test at the beginning and end of treatment, then one cannot say that improvement is not in part due to a practice effect or to the fact that some of the answers may have been remembered from the first sitting of the test. Given that our purpose is to compare the performance of the two groups, we might reasonably assume that the practice effect benefits both groups equally, especially if there is a sufficient gap between the two administrations and students did not know they would be taking the same test again. If we take scores on the first test into account in the analysis of the second administration, this enables us to contrast gains made by the two groups. If there is a difference between the two groups in performance on the second test administration, it can be reasonably inferred that the training has had some effect.

More difficult to answer are questions relating to the worth of any differences that might emerge, and the issue of whether what has been achieved was in fact worthwhile. In the first instance one has to say what any improvement represents. Whilst this may not be as difficult in the cases of speaking or writing because one has a tangible product to make qualitative judgements about, it does seem to be problematic for assessing incremental gain in listening and reading, where one has to move from a quantitative score on the test to a qualitative description of performance. The judgement to be made on size of gain is in itself problematic when dealing with quantitative scores. If the gain is large the interpretation is better grounded.

In the case where the gain is relatively small, one might wish to consider this from a longer term perspective. One might point to possible exponential as against linear gain in future test scores, given the possibility of initial inertia and old habits. If the teaching of English is to take place over a number of years, any differences between groups might be magnified in future years. This of course argues that in studies of this type monitoring over a period of years would be useful.

It would be imprudent, however, to try to isolate any specific training features as causes for observed changes in test scores. A cluster of associated variables results from training and it is not possible to identify with any certainty the relative contribution of individual variables (e.g. specific elements of training) to outcomes.

As well as concern over interpretation of test scores, there was a prior need to consider carefully the nature of the tests used in experimental designs of this type. In the standard pre-test/post-test, non-equivalent control group design used in Nepal, we had to ensure that some of the tests used in these studies were fair in content to both control and experimental group in order to make valid and fair comparisons. (See Beretta 1986b for an informed discussion on programme-fair language teaching evaluation.) In situations such as Nepal where both groups are using the same course book and working towards the same final school examination, developing tests which were fair to both groups was possible by basing the test items on materials and activities common to both groups. In other contexts where a variety of materials is in use and/or there is not a standard schools examination, this would become more problematic.

In addition, there was a need to try to develop test tasks which were sensitive to novel elements of training. For example, time was devoted in the training to a number of ways of teaching listening comprehension and writing which were not considered 'normal activities' in Nepali secondary school English classes and so test tasks reflecting these were developed to determine whether they had any impact on student language performance. By definition these tests are not fair to both groups.

Devising these tests to reflect differences in pedagogical practice proved to be difficult for two main reasons. First, there is a theoretical difficulty in establishing with any certainty causal relationships between pedagogical treatment and learning outcomes. For example, it is not possible to establish which of the activities and exercises for writing in a training syllabus would have the biggest effect on student performance. As it is not possible to isolate any single activity in this way, a selection of writing and listening tasks for the test had to be made on more subjective grounds. Secondly, there may be problems in predicting which criterial features of training the teachers will make most use of when they return to the classroom. This is especially the case if the training syllabus has been selected without sufficient consideration of major implementation factors. For example, in the Nepali secondary schools the readiness of teachers to use activities from the training programme seemed highly dependent on the composition of the existing SLC test and the single textbook available to teachers. An adequate feasibility stage would have helped prevent this (see chapter 2).

There is a further problem, where a study is designed to measure gain over a period of time, in setting items at a suitable level of difficulty. If the items are too easy then a ceiling effect (i.e. a bunching of the scores at the top of the mark range) would quickly ensue and prevent any long-term comparison. If the items are too difficult, they may be insensitive to gain even over an extended period. There therefore needs to be a balance of items in terms of difficulty. We attempted to do this by basing the tests on book 7, which all students had completed at the start of year 8, and also book 8, which they would have completed by the end of the first year of the baseline study. Given a very low start rate, poor previous learning experiences, and a limited number of hours of English, however, even items based on units covered may be beyond the reach of most of the students. In addition, they may already be severely demotivated and this could interfere with the effects of teaching enhanced by training.

It seemed sensible (in the absence of clear implicational items which had been empirically shown to discriminate between students of different levels of proficiency) to include tests with a large number and range of items in the first administration. In this way any differences would have a better chance of emerging and would enhance the reliability of the results obtained. There is always a danger that long tests might discourage students but observation of test administrations did not suggest such an effect in this situation. Statistical modelling through item response theory might be of some help in long-term studies in the future (Bachman 1990). Such analyses would help identify which items are the most useful indicators of the presence or absence of the performance ability under investigation and enable the tester to discard those which provide less useful information.

It may well be that because gap filling and dictation focus on specific linguistic items, they may be testing constructs which take a long time to develop in learners. There is some suggestion in second language acquisition research that gains in linguistic competence may take a longer time to appear in comparison with skills development and performance. Had we been able to develop practical tests of, say, spoken language ability, gains in test scores might have been clearly marked. This is an area which is in urgent need of research. The practical problems in testing skills such as spoken interaction cannot be ignored, however, and the limitations this imposes on evaluation studies are evident.

A final practical constraint is the length of time that the data even from a small-scale study such as this takes to collect and process. At a conservative estimate it involved around 150 person days. This would be quite a sizeable chunk of a project member's time that would need to be allocated to evaluation.

3.7 Observation: The process dimension

The results of summative test data alone would shed no light on non-significant differences in test performances. They would not tell us whether other variables had affected performance. It could be that the training course was soundly conceived and the training had been effective but this may not be reflected in the test data as a result of the influence of other variables. *Our results may be hard to interpret if there are no data on the process that lies behind the product* (see section 3.10.5, point 12).

In assessing the effects of a teacher training project, observation of trained and untrained teachers might provide valuable data. (One presumes it would be necessary to have done something similar at the pre-project stage in order to determine objectives for the course in the first place.) Observational studies are not without complications, however (Weir and Roberts 1990). In the Nepal baseline evaluation we came across a number of problems.

In the study the number of observations we were able to conduct was not really sufficient to be sure of giving a totally adequate picture of teachers' customary practice. A conventional if subjective view is that about six visits are needed for this. Had we been able to obtain two observations rather than one per visit to each school, the data would have been greatly improved (though the significant differences consistent across the two groups in terms of behaviours observed were quite striking even in our limited number of observations). Practicalities such as cost and logistics militated against more visits and also meant that joint observations were limited except for initial standardization purposes. *The solution to the problem would be to train sufficient reliable local staff in formal and low-inference observation and use outside observers for moderation purposes.*

Quantification of process data is dependent on the identification of adequate units. In this study, coding was based upon the recognition of utterance units rather than, for example, arbitrary time units. As a result, coding boundaries were dependent on interpretation. For example, when teachers or pupils repeat themselves, make false starts, or give one-word responses, or during continuous speech such as in teacher explanation, it is possible that different observers might identify different numbers of utterances. In the case of question and answer exchanges, where counting speech utterance units is considerably easier, greater agreement can be expected. Ideally, it would be worthwhile to train observers in the use of time unit coding, but considerable resources would have to be available (see section 7.2.5).

It is often argued that the performance of observed teachers is influenced by 'impression management'. Teachers may provide 'lessons to order' in which features of training would appear. Triangulation of data is the necessary strategy to validate observations (see section 7.1.6). In this study a number of sources were used, including teacher self-report and feedback forms. Our self-report data suggested that criterial differences continued to be exhibited in unobserved lessons. The returns to an insider post-course evaluation questionnaire in 1988 presented a similar picture. Despite limitations in the generation of observational data, if the differences in criterial indicators between the control and the experimental groups are marked, they are likely to reflect real differences in classroom experiences for students. However, we must bear in mind that *teaching alone may not be exclusively responsible for student performance.* We need to relate student performance to the processes of education and the resources devoted to it. For example, school principals and colleagues may be hostile to the new ideas being espoused by a single, younger member of staff and react negatively; students may be hostile to learning English because they see no need for it; or the hours devoted to English might have been seriously eroded by strikes etc. in the period under study. These suggest the value of a baseline feasibility study of the type discussed in section 2.2.

3.8 Long-distance evaluation

3.8.1 The case for insider involvement

Our experiences in Nepal highlighted the problems of outsider evaluation through long-distance monitoring. As a rule, evaluators working in this way are only able to spend a limited amount of time in the field. By necessity they have to work through others, both in terms of setting up the study and in implementing it. Making practical arrangements such as meetings with teachers, visits to schools, organizing transport and petrol, selecting a sample for the study, are all that much more difficult at a distance, especially when internal communication in the country concerned is problematic.

A feasibility study prior to project implementation (of the type referred to in section 2.2) would have enabled us to scrutinize classroom practice, as would attendance at a wider range of the training sessions early in the implementation period. It would have enabled us, for example, to omit any concern with writing in Nepali classrooms from the study, even though it was an important training objective. Subsequent experience demonstrated that because of the low importance of this in the school leaving examinations and because of time constraints on teachers, this activity was absent from most classroom practice. However, in terms of cost and time required, an extensive initial survey by outsiders may not be funded but could well be feasible and desirable for insiders, assuming availability of local staff and adequate training.

As a result of our involvement, we have come to feel that there is also a strong case for increased systematic internal monitoring by project staff during the implementation phase. This would promote a more accurate definition of the categories of information for use in outsider evaluations, though at crucial points outsider monitoring would be necessary as there is a risk of bias in the data collected by personnel who have an investment in the success of the project.

In general, we feel that observation processes benefit from the need to communicate with an outside audience of some kind. Contracting local but 'outsider' technical staff (see section 3.3) to conduct the observations required explicit analysis of criterial variables and the use of low-inference criteria in observation combined with less structured methods (see chapter 7). It was necessary for the evaluators to develop valid and objective categories in advance as the basis for the observations. This is because the contracted observers could not be relied upon to bring implicit understandings of the project with them to the observation task.

This also suggests that 'insiders' can very usefully and economically collect observational data, but that this would be more productive where there is a need to satisfy an outside audience. This is already recognized as a central characteristic of action research (Ebbutt 1985). In these circumstances the instrumentation of observation should have certain characteristics: either the observation categories should be derived from the same specification of criterial features as any external observation or, better still, a common set of observation instruments should be developed for use by both insiders and outsiders. The initiative in identifying categories of description is best handled through a dialogue between insiders and outsiders (Day et al. 1987). We now feel that where insiders are conducting observations for an audience outside the programme, it is made far more likely that they will produce more objective, explicit, and meaningful observational data. We would see this as an example of the positive effects of a proposed integration of insider and outsider evaluation perspectives.

3.9   Aspects of sampling

The results of our small-scale survey are at best suggestive rather than conclusive, as random sampling was not an option. In the event, we were able to sample 11 out of the 1080 trained teachers.

We attempted as far as we were able to control for a variety of variables which might contaminate the results: class size, school leaving results, language level of teachers, attrition rates, and number of hours of instruction received. By using the GLIM procedure to carry out the statistical analysis, we were able to take account of these variables when determining the effect of treatment on language test scores.

Ethical problems arise in this type of non-equivalent control group design. In particular there must be some concern about the anomalous position of the control group teachers. A small retainer was paid to encourage their participation in the study (preparing self-report forms, attending meetings, etc.). The effect of this was to defer their training. We were also acutely aware that in entering their classes our role was very much that of outsiders looking for evidence of deficit. Careful consideration needs to be given to the interests of teachers in any such control group.

3.10   Lessons to be learned

Through our experience of implementing a baseline evaluation design, and the constructive criticism from within the ODA (see Burton et al. forthcoming), we can draw some tentative conclusions.

3.10.1   The design

1   As a baseline design controls for diverse entry levels, it is the most appropriate means with which to show the effect of different inputs in terms of gains from a baseline point.

2   A baseline design may be most relevant where a project is ongoing: it can then inform subsequent project phases. It may also be justified in pilot projects which are likely to be replicated or expanded in the future. In this way it can perform an educational or formative function. Baseline studies would probably be most effective in long-term and bigger projects.

3   A baseline design may be particularly relevant where information is needed on different 'treatments' (training methods, textbooks, and so on) in the same or comparable contexts.

4   The results of a baseline design are most meaningful if the measured gains made can be assessed against a benchmark set by local needs. In this way a benchmark language proficiency target could be set for each situation – for example, for university entry, employment demands, or eligibility for overseas study, and would enable a pragmatic assessment of the merit of summative scores. Performance of students could be monitored against these benchmarks. An analysis of use of English in the labour market should precede any substantial ELT project and baseline study. Where English has no importance in the labour market, even a highly successful project would have no economic benefit.

In future baseline studies in aid projects, there should be an attempt to define a standard of education required for the labour market and educational systems and monitor student performance against that standard. However, the cost of such an exercise should not be underestimated.

3.10.2   Liaison

5   Key aspects of the evaluation design (such as maintaining experimental and control group distinctions throughout the study) indicate the need for close agreement, cooperation and liaison between host government authorities and the ODA's local representatives, particularly at times when there is a personnel change. This will help avoid contamination of the control group as was subsequently to happen in Nepal in 1990.

3.10.3   Resources

6   Collecting and processing data in a baseline design that is wholly conducted by 'outsiders' requires considerable resources.

An adequate externally conducted baseline study would be most relevant to a large project, where the commitment of resources it demands would not be disproportionate to the total budget. If local players are involved in evaluation there is always a danger of bias and personal interest. The neutrality of an outside moderator would help guard against this. There will perhaps always be a need for some external moderation to lend credence to the results of evaluation. In the case of small projects with limited funding, insider staff could be primarily responsible for collecting baseline data, according to an externally agreed and monitored plan or framework. We would want to argue for the involvement of insider staff in baseline data collection in *all* projects and programmes but would maintain there is a need for some external monitoring.

7   In the case of aid projects, it might be more cost-effective to employ local consultants as external evaluators, but their credibility and training would have to be ensured and their performance supervised.

3.10.4   Technical issues

There are considerable technical requirements for a non-equivalent group baseline design to be adequate.

8   *Sample size*   Given the likelihood of attrition, sample sizes should be large enough at the outset to sustain the study through its length. The longer the period of the study, the larger the number of schools in the sample should be. However, if you have only a small team of evaluators and it takes at least a day to visit a school then the need for a large sample size could be problematic: the longer it takes to complete a series of visits the more likely it is that the pupils in the last school will have had a much greater exposure to English lessons than those in the first school visited. The solution would be a bigger team but this brings with it its own problems. As it stood, the Nepal sample was very small and the problem of generalizability arose.

9   *Composition of sample*   Care in selecting comparable control and experimental groups will reduce the need to adjust for intervening variables to explain differential summative results.

10   *The use of test instruments*   The use of *language test* data to monitor gain in student language achievement is advocated (see section 3.6). Their use can provide clear lines of development for the testing of language at all levels within a school system. More specifically, if properly constructed, tests can help a team monitor closely the effects of certain elements of a training project. The design process underlying the construction of valid, reliable, and practical tests also requires project staff to be very clear about what it is that the project should achieve. In the long term, such tests could have an illuminating influence in those situations where the existing school leaving examinations are at odds with the objectives of the intended training.

Language tests have to be selected with great attention to their appropriacy and their relevance to the objectives of the programme or project.

11   *Monitoring implementation*   The observation instrument, the observer training manual (section 3.3.1), and the use of self-report data offer a proven methodology for monitoring such teacher training projects in the future and also have

a critical importance in clarifying the objectives for such projects in feasibility studies.

It is necessary to obtain data upon the realities of implementation and not to be content purely with test data. This is because an evaluation should be capable of showing a relationship between gain scores and implementation patterns. If there is no difference between the two groups (control and experimental) in terms of the test data, it would have been important to establish why. In such a case the observational data would have been invaluable in establishing whether there was a problem with the training and in what areas this manifested itself; i.e. it would have helped illuminate the effectiveness of the training project. Additionally, there may well have been differences in terms of implementation but no effect on student performance.

Also, implementation data have formative value within the programme/project, for subsequent programmes/projects, and to a wider audience. It is important that teacher training projects should be able to provide a clear picture of what measurable changes in teacher classroom performance the training is intended to achieve. There should be a clear definition of objectives for the training from the outset. This is best served by establishing, with the training and its context in mind, a *trained teacher profile* which would include a criterial list of features to differentiate trained from untrained teachers (section 3.2.3).

Observations of teachers can help to explain the student test results, provide more confidence in the conclusions of an educational baseline study, and provide valuable information on the implementation of training in the classroom (Burton et al. forthcoming). However, *direct observation* is demanding of resources and skilled personnel, and lower cost forms of monitoring might be required (e.g. limited direct observation data cross-referenced to teacher and student self-report data).

We are conscious that further useful data could have been obtained on the teachers' transfer of their training though self-report procedures. Time, financial considerations, and restricted terms of reference precluded these from our external study. However, insiders could have played a valuable role by conducting semi-structured interviews with teachers. The external evaluators could have provided useful input to the design of these procedures and also of questionnaires (see chapter 6).

3.10.5 Ethical issues

12 Where the provision to be evaluated is scarce or in high demand in the local context (such as English language training for secondary school teachers in Nepal), the non-equivalent group experimental design requires provision to be withheld from certain groups while others receive it. This is of ethical concern to outsiders and may lead to dissatisfaction and political pressure targeted upon local bureaucracy.

3.10.6   Sustainability

13   It seems to us that the sustainability of a programme/project is dependent on the ability and readiness of local insider staff to evaluate their own work. This is nearly always the 'missing link' which hinders sustainability. Unless insiders are involved in evaluation, and are trained to carry it out independently, there will always be a debilitating reliance on external inputs into the programme/project. There is thus a possible role for the outside evaluators to help plan evaluations, to train insider staff in appropriate procedures as well as to act as a moderator to control for internal bias. This suggests a new role for external evaluators departing from traditional inspection and summative accountability (see chapter 5 and Weir and Burton forthcoming). Conversely one can expand the conventional role of insider evaluation (for strictly formative purposes) to include data collection contributing to a more broadly based summative evaluation.

3.11   Conclusions

The baseline study described in this chapter has proved feasible even in a country with very limited communications networks such as Nepal. From the results obtained, the procedures employed in the study would for the most part appear to be effective and should be transferable to other similar projects (*mutatis mutandis*).

Baseline studies, designed to generate data for making key decisions, are a necessary part of both project planning and implementation. They are also relevant to programme evaluation in the current climate of accountability. However, baseline studies conducted principally by outsiders make very little contribution to the formative improvement of such projects or programmes. The greater involvement of insiders is a priority in the future. More useful evaluation would result if the evaluation process was defined in such a way as to be meaningful and rewarding for both outsiders and insiders (Patton 1986). Baseline studies would be cheaper if conducted by project staff with limited external supervision. Such insider studies would contribute to effective projectization and sustainability and should be initiated as close to the start date of a project as is feasible. Subsequent experience in baseline evaluation in Guinea Conakry would support this and showed the educational benefit for those insiders involved in carrying out that particular baseline study (Weir and Burton forthcoming).

In the next case study we examine in more detail evaluation conducted for formative developmental purposes in a language programme based in a British university. We report the effect on the programme of the recent need to address public professional accountability considerations with the exposure of the programme to external inspection through membership of a professional body, the British Association of Lecturers in English for Academic Purposes (BALEAP).

Our own experiences of conducting such external inspections for accountability in other institutions are contrasted with the different experience on being on the receiving end of a BALEAP inspection.

NOTE

1   Some of this chapter first appeared in Anivan (1991).

4 The Evaluation of a Language Programme: Development and Accountability

4.1 Introductory

This chapter examines the *procedures* currently employed to evaluate formatively the University of Reading's Pre-sessional English Course provided by the Centre for Applied Language Studies (CALS) in the summer vacations. This course is an annual twelve-week English for Academic Purposes (EAP) programme which has been run since 1974. Between July and August there are three intakes of both privately and publicly funded postgraduates who in many cases will have been recommended to us by the subject departments they hope to enrol in as a requirement for admission. Students with an International English Language Testing System (IELTS) flat profile of 5.5 would normally enrol for the full 300-hour, twelve-week programme starting in early July. In most cases this should enable them to attain the University's language proficiency entrance requirement of IELTS level 7 across the four skills by the end of the course (see Weir 1990: appendix V for full details of the IELTS test). At its largest, the course consists of some two hundred students from over forty countries, with a staff of twenty teachers and three full-time administrators. Most students will go on to join departments in the university. Teaching staff are TESOL qualified, temporarily employed for the three months, and are often former CALS MATEFL students. The course is directed by a permanent member of the CALS staff.

It is not expected that readers involved in similar courses would necessarily use the range of evaluation activities described below, which reflect the distinctive ecology of the programme. Evaluation of the CALS course involves a lot of work and places broad-ranging and intense demands on the staff involved. We are fortunate in that we have been able to appoint an experienced and *professional* group of teachers each year, the majority of whom will return on an annual basis. They represent a capable team who are ready to engage in scrutiny of their work

in an institutional climate which is committed to the improvement of the quality
of the courses it offers as it competes for business in an increasingly competitive
market. Furthermore, CALS is involved in a number of spin-off activities related
to the course, in particular the development of a series of EAP textbooks for a
major publisher, which in itself involves systematic evaluation of pilot materials in
order to develop a quality product.

It is hoped that, through a description of the processes at work in our particular
system, lessons may be learned by other practitioners. Those working in less
developmentally oriented institutions should still be able to identify certain areas
of work where improvements might be made. Even if it was left to the individual
himself/herself to do something about it, the personal value of a commitment to
improvement, in however restricted an area, is incontrovertible. This is after all
what professionalism is about. As Bachman (1987: 39) has noted: 'The most lasting
use of evaluation . . . is . . . the process itself, by which we can foster attitudes and
processes that are at the heart of excellence in teaching'.

Most of this chapter (sections 4.1–3) addresses the formative evaluation issues
already discussed in chapter 1:

• *Why*: the goal of the evaluation and the use of the data it produces (see section
  1.4.1)
• *What*: the appropriate objects of evaluation, e.g. objectives, learning gains,
  materials, teaching, resources etc. (see section 1.4.4)
• *How*: the best means to collect data so that the data obtained are high quality
  and the means of collection are economical in their demands on busy teachers,
  students and administrators (see section 1.4.6)
• *Who*: which stakeholders should be engaged in data collection and interpretation; which stakeholders should have access to information of different kinds;
  who should be involved in decision making, given their prior involvement in
  evaluation processes (see section 1.4.5)

Additionally, in section 4.4 we briefly examine external evaluation of language
programmes. We first present an account of our experience as accountability-
oriented, outside evaluators of language programmes and indicate the difficulties
this may present when faced with insiders' expectations of help in improving their
programmes. Finally, we contrast this with our changed viewpoint when we were
insiders on the receiving end of a similar external evaluation.

This case study highlights a tension between evaluation for improvement which
commonly characterizes insider-driven formative evaluations, and the differing
priorities of evaluation for accountability, most often conducted by outsiders for
reasons of quality control or cost-effectiveness (see also section 1.2, chapters 2 and
3). We conclude by arguing for a synthesis of the two approaches in a comprehensive, utilization-focused evaluation (Patton 1986).

The formative evaluation procedures we describe in sections 4.1–3 have been
carried out internally by ourselves and colleagues in CALS as part of our everyday

work. Evaluations, unlike much funded research, are often constrained by resources that are limited in terms of time, money and personnel. As a result, all evaluators have to make trade-offs in order to provide colleagues/employers/funders with the right information at the right time, and have to accept that evaluations are seldom perfect and need to be planned with the constraint of time uppermost in their minds.

4.2 Why evaluate?

Until 1992 there had been no framework for external accreditation (accountability to an outside body) of university EAP courses, and this is still the case in many countries around the world. The British Association for Lecturers in English for Academic Purposes (BALEAP) only introduced such a scheme in the UK in 1992 (see appendix 4.1 for details of the standards for the scheme and the list of documentation that institutions need to provide).

However, as the provider, CALS has always recognized the need for professional accountability and has been committed to the continuous development of a programme which is its 'flagship' direct language teaching activity. The evaluation carried out by CALS staff on the pre-sessional programme is motivated by a desire for understanding, action and improvement. This chapter is therefore mainly concerned with self-directed, formative developmental evaluation by insiders and in the final section with general professional accountability (the BALEAP inspection).

4.3 What should be evaluated and how?

In this section we examine a number of *focal points* for the evaluation and the *methods* used for each focal point. These are listed in table 4.1.

4.3.1 Focus on objectives

Having determined why we are evaluating, we then need to identify what is to be evaluated, one focal point for which should be the specification of what a programme sets out to achieve. In the case of a course which is already established, there should be *documentation*, course records and descriptions, which would help identify course objectives and other possible focuses for the evaluation.

If you are planning a new course, objectives may be derived from the *secondary literature* – for example, results of previous needs analyses (see Weir 1983 for an example of an extensive analysis of the EAP needs of overseas students in Britain)

Table 4.1 Foci and methods in formative evaluation of the CALS pre-sessional
programme

Focus on objectives

- Examination of documentation
- Examination of secondary literature
- Questionnaires
- Interviews

Focus on student language achievement

- Test data: Proficiency tests, specially designed or existing international tests such as IELTS, course book tests
- Continuous assessment/profiling of achievement
- Questionnaire
- Interviews
- Tracer studies: post-course follow-up

Focus on materials

- Questionnaires
- Record sheets
- Other documentation
- Interview
- Student feedback sessions
- Teachers' working groups
- Teachers' own materials
- End-of-course debriefing

Focus on teaching

- Observations by CALS staff
- Weekly minuted staff meeting
- Monthly pro forma questionnaires
- Group feedback
- Documentation: lesson records, lesson pro forma, student workbooks

Focus on 'customer satisfaction'

- Questionnaire
- Tracer studies
- Interviews
- Correspondence

– or from your own target and learning situation *needs analyses*. Holliday (1983), Holliday and Cooke (1982), Hutchinson and Waters (1987), and Robinson (1991: chapter 2) contain useful discussions of the importance of taking into account both learning and target situation analyses. The rationale for needs analysis is to provide precise and valid objectives at the outset of a programme. Such needs analysis before the course can serve as a feasibility study (see section 2.2) performing a vital appraisal function, for example in determining what the major needs of the incoming students are in terms of required study skills and setting these against the resources available to the course providers. A more comprehensive view of a needs analysis also sees it as ongoing through the life of a programme rather than just as a separate, prior phase of enquiry. (Bramley 1986 and Holliday 1983 develop this view of evaluation as being important before, during, at the end of, and after a course.)

Through documentation or a feasibility study, one should be able to produce a *document model*, an account which outlines the components, outputs, and expected effects of a programme. This can be used subsequently in discussion with stake-holders to check the validity of the initial analysis.

However, a perennial question in programme planning and evaluation arises over the value and status of educational objectives specified in advance. (Alderson 1986, 1992 and Barrow 1984: 134–44 outline the problems in relation to this.) As we pointed out in sections 1.4.4 and 2.3, a sensible view is that these objectives are necessary at the planning stage, but it should be recognized that they may change in the course of implementation. The implications for evaluation design are that an evaluation should be flexible enough to allow a focus on unanticipated outcomes of a project as well as success in attaining pre-specified objectives. By extension, local and contextual factors affecting implementation should also be included in the evaluation (Parlett and Hamilton 1977), which in its turn implies a place for naturalistic study of implementation as well as the quantification of outcomes.

The validation of course objectives by a feasibility study raises further practical questions. While it makes sense to determine if a programme will be feasible before it actually runs, the practical question arises as to who will pay for it. In the case of an institution setting up a new language programme, the problem we discussed above in relation to projects (see section 2.2) presents itself: with finance uncertain or unavailable, how can you fund a study to determine whether the programme will be worth setting up in terms of educational value or marketability? Management would have to resolve the dilemma, that a programme without a feasibility/ needs analysis may fail, but that on the other hand, there might be an outlay with no return if a feasibility study proves negative.

Finally, if an evaluation is *exclusively* focused on programme objectives for its basis, it might be wrongly assumed that this implies priority for external account-ability concerns: showing that you have got results in terms of pre-specified objectives. Of course there may be equally important developmental concerns that merit attention (for example, see sections 4.3.3 on materials and 4.3.4 on teaching). However, we would still wish to argue that an insiders' evaluation should attach some importance to the process of defining objectives, a clarification of where the course is going: for any course to function effectively, it needs a clear statement of objectives even if these may alter slightly during the journey; and, more crucially, the process of clarification can in itself be beneficial for insiders in helping them better understand what it is they are doing, given our lack of a clear picture of the nature of language proficiency or its acquisition.

Methods: Interviews and questionnaires

In our experience these have proved to be useful methods for establishing stakeholders' perceptions of what they think the programme is aiming to achieve (see chapter 6 for a more detailed discussion of the use and construction of these instruments). This initial fieldwork helps establish what the *focuses* for the evaluation are to be and the specific evaluation questions relating to these. (Horgan 1988 provides a description of these methods in use on the CALS pre-sessional course and an account of the processes we went through in determining the focuses for such an evaluation.) The results of such fieldwork might also help in the construction of an evaluation plan which could be used to guide and inform all insiders in a self-directed evaluation (Sanders 1992).

In the case of the CALS language programme it helped us formulate more clearly what our course was trying to achieve and also provided us with clearer and more accessible categories of description for use in subsequent self-report data collection exercises.

4.3.2 Focus on student language achievement

The amount of student language improvement is the 'bottom line' for all stakeholders in a language programme. In the case of the CALS pre-sessional course we are interested in the changes in student performance we can expect after instructional periods of twelve, eight, and five weeks, with some twenty-five hours a week of teaching. To measure these changes one has to assess the nature and extent of gains in language proficiency over these periods (Alderson et al. 1987, Bachman 1989, Green 1983, Hudson 1989, Jafarpur 1987, Marston et al. 1983, Rice and Higgins 1982, Weir 1990, Weir 1993, Wood 1982). Additionally, one must consider measuring possible accompanying attitudinal changes (Henerson et al. 1987).

Methods

Test data   To measure language gains, ideally one should develop parallel tests at the beginning and the end of a course, although we recognize the difficulties here (see section 3.6 for a discussion of the problems). At the very least we need to develop appropriate proficiency tests for use at the end of such courses. There is a very important place for British Council/UCLES IELTS results which are used to determine the EAP proficiency of overseas students (Weir 1990: appendix V). This is because EAP course providers need a valid and reliable indicator of EAP proficiency on entry and exit and, more importantly, a conversion formula to determine the number of weeks of study candidates would need to bring them up to a threshold level of performance in the language (IELTS 7.0 in humanities courses, for example). This is an area in which there is still an urgent need for research. Course providers/evaluators need to develop parallel forms of practical, reliable, and valid EAP proficiency tests to enable the assessment of gain in performance related to hours of tuition.

Continuous assessment/profiling of achievement   Teachers' progress reports are used to enable CALS to provide an early warning to departments about any students who may not make the 'threshold' point in terms of language proficiency. (See Broadfoot 1986 for a useful survey of profiles and records of achievement.) A final end-of-course report, based on course work and a final proficiency examination, is provided to faculties and departments in respect of every student (see figure 4.1). This final report is a composite view based on reports from all his/her teachers and takes account of continuous assessment (tests, quizzes, marked work) and profiles of achievement for oral presentations (see appendices 4.2.1–3) and written work including projects (see figure 4.2 and appendix 4.3). For further details of the development of the assessment criteria applied to students' written work and for details of the Test in English for Educational Purposes (TEEP) developed by CALS and used in a modified form on the pre-sessional course see Weir (1990, 1993). Tonkyn et al. (1993) provide exemplification of one of the few empirical studies of this aspect of pre-sessional evaluation.

Questionnaire   CALS administers end-of-course questionnaires requiring *self-report* estimates of language ability by students (see appendix 4.4). Previously CALS had also administered a questionnaire half-way through the course but difficulties in processing the data and a feeling that this led to a certain amount of 'overkill' (for staff and students) has led us to administer a single questionnaire at the end. The provision of data on the degree of perceived improvement in the various skills areas across the whole population attending our courses is very useful for determining, for example, where the balance of activities in the course might need to be adjusted. In addition, it might bring to light areas where students feel their needs are not totally being met. For example, earlier questionnaire data had indicated that a number of students would have liked more attention to pronunciation and grammar. As a result we have made provision for the former in a self-access mode and the teachers are able to tailor this work to the specific needs of individual students. Students' perceptions of grammar as a priority led us to set up extra weekly optional grammar classes in 1991 and 1992 to focus on grammar, but also to encourage students to consider more carefully whether their perceived need was in fact exaggerated.

Centre for Applied Language Studies   University of Reading

1993 Pre-sessional English Language Course – Final Report

English Ability Rating   Student's name _____

1. *General ability in English*
    (Put X in the appropriate box in the column.)   Approx. IELTS
                                                                     equivalent

☐   Shows native speaker ability   9

☐   Clearly has a very competent command of the language
    and may approach native speaker ability in some areas   8

☐   Clearly not a native speaker because of minor faults
    in English usage, but this does not handicap him/her
    in his/her studies   7

☐   Makes a number of mistakes in English, and this may
    still constitute a handicap for him/her in his/her
    studies   6

☐   Shows many weaknesses in English usage and his/her
    ability is clearly below standard for his/her studies.
    A higher standard is necessary   5

☐   Shows considerable deficiences in English usage, which
    constitute a serious handicap for him/her in his/her
    studies. A much higher standard is necessary   3/4

☐   Shows very little ability in English and is well below
    a satisfactory level   1/2

2. *Individual language skills* (Put X in the appropriate box.)

	Completely adequate	Adequate	Just inadequate	Completely inadequate
Ability to understand spoken English	☐	☐	☐	☐
Ability to speak English	☐	☐	☐	☐
Ability to understand written English	☐	☐	☐	☐
Ability to write English	☐	☐	☐	☐

Comments:

Figure 4.1   Final report

Project Record   Student:_____

	Project 3	Project 4

Content
Development of ideas
Relevance
Adequacy
Clarity

Source materials
Adequacy
Appropriacy
Integration
Acknowledgements

Organization
Introduction/Development/
Conclusion
Organization
Fluency
Logical development
Cohesion

Vocabulary
Range
Word Choice
Form
Register

Language use
Tense
Agreement
Word order
Active/Passive
Article
Preposition

Mechanics
Spelling
Punctuation
Capitalization
Paragraphing

Presentation
Title page
Contents page
Bibliography
A4 paper
Margins
Spacing
Numbers
Clarity

Key: Completely   +   Just   Not   −
      adequate   adequate   adequate

Comment

Figure 4.2   Project record

Interviews A tutorial support system (each student is seen individually at least once every three weeks) provides the opportunity to tailor self-access study to individual needs, wants, and lacks. It also allows for individual, regular, informal feedback on the course.

Tracer studies: Post-course follow-up Staff and CALS MA students (Laaksonen 1987, Langford forthcoming, Tonkyn et al. 1993) have followed up pre-sessional students after they have exited the language programme and they are in their academic subject courses, and through these tracer studies have identified areas of residual linguistic difficulty. (See appendix 4.5 for an example of a questionnaire being used in a current tracer study on reading skills.) Alderson (1985) has also written an informative account of an early tracer study carried out at Lancaster University. Such studies provide informants with the opportunity to reflect back on the value of courses from the enhanced perspective provided by time and experience. There is a danger that feedback provided through questionnaires filled out only at the end of language courses lacks this essential perspective.

4.3.3 Focus on materials

Where published course books are used, the decision to purchase equates with a form of evaluation. If needed, checklists are available to facilitate this (Breen and Candlin 1987, Cunningsworth 1984, Hutchinson and Waters 1987). When new materials are being developed, an important aspect of the Reading University pre-sessional programme, then the process of evaluation and development is more complex and potentially extremely time consuming. The challenge lies in collecting good quality data in the most time-efficient manner, given the time pressure on staff. In this sense, good quality data should be accurate in their account of teachers' and students' reactions and also specific and constructive enough to guide writers in improving their materials. The following summarizes some of the variables to be evaluated, with both published and 'in-house' materials.

* Texts: suitability, length, challenge level
* Tasks: match to texts, challenge level, interest for mature students
* Rubric: lack of ambiguity, brevity
* Unit:

  - length
  - structure
  - completeness
  - teachability within and between units (level, staging, sequencing, accessibility, user-friendliness)
  - usefulness, effectiveness, relevance
  - appropriateness (subject specificity, level)

    – timing
    – interest value etc.

• Teachers' notes: practicality, clarity

Methods

Questionnaires   CALS administers a variety of questionnaires for student and teacher feedback on materials (see appendix 4.4 for an example of one of these prepared by the teachers).

Record sheets   Teachers in the past have been asked to keep running records of materials they were using (see figure 4.3). However, this was not very successful for practical reasons: the teachers felt overwhelmed by the need to fill one out for every lesson. It was felt that these data could be collected as effectively and with less time overload if teachers worked in groups to complete a pro forma about one part of the course only (see figure 4.4).

Centre for Applied Language Studies: University of Reading

Pre-sessional English Language Course: July–September1988

Please fill in after each class.

Group: Spoken . . . . Written . . . . Project . . . .
Tutor . . . . Date . . . . Week . . . .

Important: Please attach one copy of any additional materials used with an indication of how much was actually covered. Where textbook, or supplementary material, please indicate page numbers.

Aim

Activity

Evaluation: (success, difficulties, unintended outcomes–positive and negative–suitability of materials and methodology, suggestions for next time)

Figure 4.3   Student feedback

Other documentation   Coordinators refer to exercises completed by students in their textbooks and to annotated versions of teachers' copies.

Interview   CALS arranges for individual feedback from teachers by making one senior teacher or materials writer responsible for individually interviewing teachers in respect of each of the three skill area classes (spoken, written, and project preparation). An example of an early discussion document on CALS draft materials for written work is provided in figure 4.5.

Student feedback sessions   Each month, staff hold a feedback session with students which is followed immediately by a staff meeting in which both teachers' and students' views on materials are minuted (see figure 4.6). It provides a useful, immediate feel for how the clients are reacting to materials, teaching, and the course in general.

Teachers' working groups   Small informal groups of teachers are formed, each focusing on a particular aspect of materials (e.g. the accessibility of tasks in a skills booklet). They are left free to arrange meeting times but have a brief to minute their discussions and provide this as data to a coordinator. In the view of the materials writers, this has proved to be the *most effective and useful* way of obtaining high quality feedback for improving the materials. This is probably due to the combination of focus and self-direction given to the teachers.

Teachers' materials   Where teachers developed their own supplementary materials these are collected and used to identify possible shortcomings in the existing materials.

End-of-course debriefing   In advance of the meeting, staff are asked to identify specific areas of the materials that need change or improvement and record them for the attention of the CALS coordinator. This gives the staff as a body the opportunity, in a final whole-day discussion, to reflect at length on specified aspects of the course away from the pressures and demands of daily classroom life. The coordinator is then responsible for developing a plan of action for improving the course the next time around in the light of these data and those collected through other methods.

4.3.4   Focus on teaching

The classroom performance of teachers is a vital factor in the climate of the whole programme. Therefore, a number of means are used to learn what goes on in the classrooms. This is now partly because CALS is the teachers' employer and is responsible to outside interests (the British Council, University departments and now BALEAP; see section 4.5 for a discussion of recent developments in this area).

Centre for Applied Language Studies
Pre-sessional Writing Course 1992

Evaluation

WRITING Unit no._____

1) Which activities/steps worked well in your group? Please give details.

2) What difficulties did you experience? Did you adapt/alter any material in response to these? Would you change anything in this unit if you taught it again to a similar group?

3) Did you feel a need for or use supplementary exercises or 'input' of your own? Please give details.

4) Please comment on how effectively this unit has been integrated with the corresponding READING I unit in terms of a) topics b) rhetorical functions c) other features. Is there enough cross-referencing?

Evaluation of a Language Programme 95

---

5) Please comment on one or more of the following:

- aims & achievement of aims
- language focus & development
- clarity of rubrics
- time taken
- choice of topic
- range/variety/sequencing of activities
- development of writing skills shown in essays
- development of skills in critical evaluation of writing
- overall user-friendliness, etc

Course: July/Aug/Sept

Proficiency level: Group _____ out of _____ groups

Figure 4.4   Evaluation: writing unit

Centre for Applied Language Studies
Pre-sessional: Integrated Reading and Writing Course

Evaluation Conferences with Teachers

Questions for individual discussion

1 Level of group; numbers in class

2 Nationalities

3 Any 'blocks' of nationality of subject area in group?

4 How good are the group dynamics generally in your class? How willing are they to discuss various issues?

5 Did you have to 'sell' the process approach heavily in the beginning? Was there resistance? What forms did this take?
   a Have you done or felt the need for supplementary sessions on 'grammar'? Why?

6 Describe how you conduct the writing process.
   a Do you ask them to evaluate each other's plans?
   b When and how much do you intervene?
   c How helpful do they find the checklists? How do you guide the use of them?
   d Has their awareness of audience translated effectively into structure, style, etc.?

7 What differences are there between how well this process of peer evaluation and rewriting works now and when they did the first unit?

8 Have there been major problems in the dynamics or results of peer evaluation at any point?

9 Have students now accepted the process approach? Do they themselves perceive any benefit from it?

10 In your own view, has this approach yielded concrete results/improvement in their writing? Details?

11 READING I:
   a Major problems?
   b Major successes?
   c Comments on individual units/tasks?
   d Did you do the optional timed essays? Conditions? Results?

12 WRITING
   a Major problems?
   b Major successes?
   c Comments on individual units/tasks?

13 In your view, how effective is the integration of these two?

14 How much use, if any, did you make of the READING II units? Details?

Figure 4.5 Evaluation conferences with teachers

Week ....

We would welcome your comments on the classes you have had this week.
(For example: what you did not like, what you would like more of, what you would like
less of . . .)

First class 9.15–10.45   Teacher ....

Second class 11.15–12.45   Teacher ....

Project class 2.15–4.15   Teacher ....

Figure 4.6   Student feedback

We are also responsible to the students themselves to ensure that they are receiving competent instruction. Apart from this 'quality control' aspect, CALS is often asked to provide work references and needs to see the teachers at work to do so. Additionally, it is clearly necessary for the CALS coordinator to visit classes to evaluate how the course is going, how students are responding, and how materials are being used.

Methods

Observations by CALS staff   From the outset, temporary teaching staff know that a number of visits will be made to their classes, and the reasons for them that were given above. They are given a choice in the focus of the observations (either negotiated in advance to look at certain agreed features, or a more broad spectrum observation using the standard RSA/UCLES Dip TEFLA performance criteria in appendix 7.3) and they are also consulted in advance on the timing of visits. The quality control aspect is largely a safeguard against the unlikely case of an incompetent teacher being engaged, so certain basic efficiencies are looked for rather than an approved pedagogic approach, and the diversity of teachers' personal styles and strengths is fully recognized. The goal is to make the observation as constructive as possible, and contributive to teachers' participation in the overall development of the programme. Thus observations have a developmental as well as an accountability focus, and approaches the comprehensive view of evaluation we advocated in chapter 1.

The biggest problem is that time and effort are required to timetable these observations in an already packed summer schedule. CALS is fortunate in having five qualified RSA/UCLES assessors on its permanent staff to share the responsibility. Their experience and expertise are valuable here as questions might otherwise rightly be raised as to the credibility of the observer(s) to pass judgement on the teaching of others. The fairness and the credibility of an assessment system has a direct relationship to the working climate of the institution (see chapter 8).

Weekly minuted staff meeting   Teachers discuss their own teaching in staff meetings, which are minuted, and so help all concerned build up a picture of teaching across the whole programme.

Monthly pro forma questionnaires   Students are asked to complete a pro forma questionnaire to record their reactions to instruction (see figure 4.6). The questionnaire is not highly structured and is designed to encourage them to record any matters of concern to them or indicate what they feel particularly happy about. The completed questionnaires are returned to the Director of Studies and these are discussed in staff meetings to determine any general trends in responses, whether they are positive, negative, or throw light on specific teaching issues. The questionnaires are then returned to the teachers concerned. Caution must be exercised in considering the use of individual student feedback as it may well be idiosyncratic. In isolated cases of hostile, negative comment, close support of the colleague involved may be necessary to ensure a balanced response to the feedback.

Group feedback As in the evaluation of materials, feedback on teaching may be obtained in the informal class discussion on the last Friday of the month prior to the staff meeting, and in the summative questionnaire to students (see appendix 4.4).

4.3.5 Focus on 'customer satisfaction'

Clients' sense of current satisfaction with the course is always of importance to providers. Apart from measurable gains in learning, the quality of the pre-sessional programme is continuously monitored by recording the perceptions of students in the ways discussed above and by using the professional judgements of staff. However, it is important to note that the value of some aspects of the programme will only be confirmed to the student once real study conditions have been experienced. Similarly, some deficits in the programme may not be realized until some time after the course itself. The departments within the university are crucial stakeholders, both as 'customers' of the course and as colleagues of permanent staff, and there is a strong sense of accountability to them. Similarly, the requirements of bodies funding our students are of central concern.

Methods

As previously mentioned, students' satisfaction levels can be assessed through end-of-course questionnaire returns (see appendix 4.4), tracer studies (Alderson 1985) and interviews.

Contact with departments is maintained throughout the programme. Particularly in the case of 'borderline' candidates, individual contact with their future supervisors is seen as extremely helpful both by CALS and the departments. Reports are sent on students half-way through their course and at the end (see figure 4.1). In the case of those students who appear unlikely to achieve the necessary level of language proficiency in the time they have available for language instruction, departments are given an early warning and close contact is maintained with them.

After each language programme, evidence on the subsequent performance of the pre-sessional students is of great value to course development. We need to take into account that departments can vary considerably in their expectations of students' language performance. Tracer studies, interviews, and correspondence are all used to assess the linguistic performance and needs of our students once they are engaged in academic study. Tonkyn et al. (1993) provide a detailed and informative account of one of the few empirical studies conducted in this area. Also, from time to time extensive post-course evaluations are carried out by our MA students for their dissertations (Langford forthcoming, Laaksonen 1987, Horgan 1988).

External bodies also have a stake in the programme: many students are sponsored by outside agencies, such as their ministries or the ODA. It is perhaps surprising that until recently there were no external accountability structures. External inspections are now carried out every three years by the BALEAP organization (see appendix 4.1), which evaluates the course in action.

4.4 Who conducts the evaluation?

In an *internal* evaluation, it is of great importance that the 'insiders' (students, teachers, director of studies) feel able to participate freely, confident that their views will be attended to, and used for the purposes initially agreed. For this to occur there is a need for a climate of trust and commitment. Without this climate, the real experiences and perceptions of teachers and learners may never be voiced to improve the programme. It is generally agreed that a positive school climate is central to effective staff and curriculum development (Fullan 1982, Wideen and Andrews 1987). The manner in which evaluation is conducted will affect this climate (see chapter 8). Stakeholders need to be consulted at both the planning stage and at the implementation stage, otherwise they may well feel excluded and react negatively to involvement. Exclusion from such studies can affect participants' self-concept and produce a sense of threat because evaluation raises the sensitive issue of change in collective and personal practices and questions the worth of existing modes of operation (Rudduck 1988). Great care must therefore be taken to ensure such evaluations are both ethically and technically correct. All stakeholders need to be clear and in agreement about why such evaluations are taking place and who will do what, to whom, where, when, and how.

4.4.1 Factors linking evaluation to effective change

In the CALS programme the teachers are briefed about their involvement in an introductory three-day workshop at the start of each summer course and have the opportunity to identify the issues for review and the methodological procedures for investigating these. In this way we hope to empower the staff and encourage full participation in programme development. (See section 1.4.7 for discussion of ways to improve the link between data collection and action for improvement.) The evaluations in CALS aim as far as possible to be *problem oriented* and are motivated by a desire for improvement in the EAP service we provide.

From day 1 the teachers are regularly involved in the formative evaluation of the course. Their experiences and views are shared in a number of ways: weekly staff meetings; individual/group discussions with materials writers and with periodic observers of their classes; daily informal contact with the Director of Studies; completing pro forma or annotating materials; and debriefing sessions at the end of the course. As we mentioned earlier, we are fortunate in that the staff we employ are familiar with the institutional culture of evaluation for improvement. If we were dealing with staff with little or no previous experience in evaluation and/or who were not predisposed to scrutiny of their practice by others, a more gradual step-by-step approach would be necessary. For example, materials review sessions might be started which would have a general focus and not be specifically related to the classroom practices of particular teachers.

Students' views are regularly elicited through filling out the pro forma feedback sheet on the course, the review sessions in class on a Friday, and in completing the feedback questionnaires at the end of the course. Individual tutorials allow them to put forward their own personal response to the course and the academic and social problems they have can be dealt with.

The Director of Studies and the two senior teachers have the responsibility for facilitating the formative evaluation of the course and servicing the process administratively. All teachers are also asked to contribute to the revision of a summative questionnaire given to the students at the end of the course. This questionnaire has a formative dimension when the data are used for planning subsequent courses in those cases where it is possible to clearly identify areas in which the course might be improved (see appendix 4.4). The administration of the questionnaire, the collation and analysis of responses, and the final interpretation of the data are carried out as far as possible with the full participation of all staff. All staff are given open access to the data, and decisions affecting the future of the course are discussed with the teachers involved. The final decisions on changes to be made to the course rest with the course director but these are based on views elicited from both staff and students and will have been discussed thoroughly with staff beforehand. Every effort is made to act on findings and to try to ensure fairness, favouring no particular stakeholders over others. An annual report is written for the CALS steering committee and is available to all staff connected with the programme. The course administrator is responsible for the collation and filing of evaluation data.

4.5 Reflections on external evaluation of language programmes

4.5.1 An inspector's view: Outside looking in

So far in this chapter we have considered the evaluation of a language programme from the viewpoint of the insider committed to professional accountability, for *formative purposes* (see also section 1.2). Increasingly, however, such language programmes are also externally accountable. The British Council and ARELS-FELCO (1991) run an English Language Schools Recognition Scheme which is intended to guarantee minimum standards of efficiency in these institutions.

Given the increasing exposure of language programmes to such external inspection, we feel readers might benefit from our experience both in conducting such evaluations and being on the receiving end. We now turn to the topic of the external evaluation of language programmes. We first describe our experience as accountability-oriented, outside evaluators of language programmes and indicate the difficulties this may present when faced with insiders' expectations of help in developing their programmes. We then contrast this with our very different viewpoint when we were insiders on the receiving end of a similar external evaluation. For us this brought out a tension between evaluation for improvement which commonly characterizes insider-driven formative evaluations, and the differing priorities of evaluation for accountability, most often conducted by outsiders for reasons of quality control. It further clarified for us the need for a synthesis of the two approaches in a comprehensive, utilization-focused evaluation (see also chapters 3 and 5 and section 1.3).

The ARELS-FELCO inspection is normally carried out by two inspectors who have been appointed on the basis of suitable qualifications and their wide experience in the field of ELT. They have to be demonstrably impartial and be able to make evaluations with full professional independence. They must not have had any previous connection with the institution being evaluated and the institution has the right to veto the choice of up to two inspectors without explanation. The panel of inspectors is chosen so that individuals can be selected from it whose experience is relevant to the activities of the organization they are to assess. There are regular briefing and standardization sessions for inspectors and newly appointed inspectors have to undergo a period of induction alongside experienced inspectors.

The criteria on which schools are evaluated (management and administration, premises, resources, professional qualifications, academic management, teaching, and welfare) are described in the *English Language Schools Recognition Scheme Handbook* (obtainable from the British Council's Accreditation Department, Manchester office). These represent a thorough and praiseworthy attempt to guarantee customers and donor agencies value for money. A number of issues have arisen as a result of our own involvement as inspectors in these accountability-oriented evaluations and these are discussed briefly below. They represent our *personal* response to the inspections we have carried out and should in no way be taken as representing the views of the British Council or ARELS-FELCO.

Role conflict

An issue which has begun to trouble us in conducting external inspections is whether the role of the inspector is to be limited to quality control or will also include a developmental function: whether only to assess the providing institution against agreed standards or also to introduce this formative dimension so that the inspector can offer suggestions on the way improvements might be brought about (see chapter 1 for discussion of the differing pulls of the accountability and developmental paradigms).

In carrying out these external inspections ourselves, we considered our terms of reference as restricting our role to an accountability function, to determine whether the school provides a reasonable service for clients. From this perspective the aim of inspection schemes is to eliminate the 'cowboy' operators and to protect standards in a field of free market competition. In this case, there is a need for inspectors to be seen as neutral, impartial outsiders with no personal axes to grind. The inspectors need to closely identify areas of deficit or excellence but it would not be their job (in this view) to offer advice on how any problems might be remedied. Indeed, this might compromise their attempts at an objective stance, applying standardized criteria.

However, we often found that external inspection was viewed by the school as a way of receiving advice on how to improve – an expectation leading to disappointment when the inspector does not provide advice at all. Differences may exist within the inspectorate, even among those who view it within their brief to offer suggestions, as to how much advice and what type of advice to offer. In either case, there can be the problem of unfulfilled expectations ('. . . last time, So-and-so gave us a lot of help . . .').

In the interests of reliability and standardization of treatment, we had felt that the external inspectors' primary purpose was to make an impartial decision on whether certain standards were being met, and to describe accurately what is seen, read, or heard. Once they step over this line, this central purpose may be compromised.

Against this can be set the view that the external evaluator could be used in a critical role to help insiders establish for themselves the criteria and procedures for conducting evaluation. The external evaluations we discuss below as yet do not have this function as part of their terms of reference. We will return to this issue at the end of the chapter.

Sufficient sampling?

Most external evaluations are marred by the problem of adequate sampling (see discussion of this in relation to the Nepal study in chapter 3). In our role within the recognition scheme, we came to question whether a one- or two-day external evaluation once every three years, when conducted solely by outsiders, is sufficient to evaluate all the significant features of an institution (i.e. the issue of validity). Additionally, there must be some concern whether sufficient sampling of implementation (for example, the number and frequency of classes observed) and consistency in judgement are achievable, to a degree which will ensure fairness and accuracy in judgement (i.e. the issue of reliability). As an inspector, one obviously has some reservations about the possibility of making valid and accurate judgements in terms of all proposed criteria in a visit of only one or two days. After all, there is the probability of impression management (the desire to look good) which might suggest that spot checks would give a more truthful picture than the institution knowing three months in advance the precise dates and times of the visit. However, some might claim that such surprise visits produce their own form of distortion; in particular, some teachers might under stress fail to do themselves justice. More seriously, such sudden visits would not have the positive formative effect that planned inspections can generate, as we discuss below.

An alternative might be to encourage more internal school self-evaluation structured to take account of likely summative demands. This might, for example, involve providing assistance in the setting up of an internal system(s) of observation, with an increased role for the Director of Studies in monitoring teaching. In this broader revised scheme the external evaluator would play a moderating role when an inspection visit takes place. It would also mean that we need to explore what other documentation institutions could be asked to make available to ensure that reliable judgements can be made.

The criteria themselves

In any evaluation, high-inference areas (for example, teaching quality, the comparability of professional qualifications, and the standard of academic management) will not necessarily be as easy to judge objectively as compared with criteria which demand less inferencing (such as the description of premises and resources). It is easier to make criterion-referenced judgements with low-inference criteria, as the evidence is concrete or quantifiable. The inspector can tell if a chair is broken; whether there are reports on teachers observed or evidence of student feedback on courses or accommodation; whether any student work is displayed; the number of OHPs and tape recorders there are; whether there is a social programme, a staff room, sets of books, and so on. (See section 7.1.4 for further discussion of low- and high-inference observations.)

However, high-inference categories are subject to different personal expectations and theories, and may be difficult to apply equitably to the contexts and purposes of differing institutions. Unfortunately, these are important dimensions of a programme and present an unavoidable dilemma for educational evaluation.

The evaluation of *teaching* is regarded as centrally important in the recognition scheme and schools would not receive recognition if they do not pass on this. This is an extremely effective ground rule as it ensures that institutions do not employ inexpensive unqualified staff to boost their profit margins (as is unfortunately the case in some EFL settings).

However, the evaluation of teaching is highly contentious: 'Good teaching is a direct function of the judge's value systems. And judges do not always agree' (Brown 1975: 10). There is general agreement that prescriptive, behavioral criteria alone are not appropriate, that judgements on teaching reflect wider value judgements, and that context and teacher personality and intention should all be taken into account (Brown 1975, Kyriacou 1985, Kyriacou and Newson 1982, Mackay

1989, Poster and Poster 1991, Rosenshine 1971, Sanderson 1982, Stones 1975, Turney et al. 1982a: 26–37, 1982b).

There is, therefore, a real problem for the inspector in assessing teaching on limited evidence and on too subjective a basis. Observation of teaching, particularly in large schools, takes up the biggest proportion of inspection time. However, what you can learn by sitting in on a teacher for one or two classes is very limited. There is no guarantee that this is a representative sampling of that teacher's pedagogical ability. Additionally, the reliability of the judgement of a single observer may be questioned. Additional data are necessary for fairness. Paired observation might provide a more reliable judgement. Also, much more pedagogic information could be provided, such as lesson plans, schemes of work, student workbooks, records of observations conducted internally (Turney et al. 1982b: chapter 7). If these extra data were made available in an accessible form, one might have more faith in the 'snapshots' the external inspector can get. Again there would seem to be a case here for a more systematic formative contribution from insiders, which could provide the external inspector with a wider database for making judgements, as is the case in both the UCLES/RSA Certificate and the Dip TEFLA moderation schemes. In these successful schemes, prevalent at the time of writing, the judgement of a visiting inspector on a teacher is compared with and negotiated against the fuller record kept by training staff. (See appendix 7.3 for the Dip TEFLA criteria.) A further solution might be to integrate high- and low-inference categories in one observation instrument.

4.5.2 Subject to inspection: Inside looking out

Having described a number of issues arising from our experience of carrying out inspections, we thought it might be useful to note our perceptions when we at CALS were evaluated by outsiders for accountability purposes, under the new BALEAP scheme (see appendix 4.1 for details of their criteria). Such reactions are inevitably personal and other colleagues in CALS (teaching staff and co–directors) might have responded differently to the experience. What was interesting for us was the different way we viewed such evaluations when we were on the receiving end as subjects! The value of such reflection for us is that it should make us more understanding of what people are going through when we visit them as external evaluators. Additionally, it does point to *the need to try to develop an eclectic approach to evaluation which might build on the strengths of both insider and outsider contributions* (see chapter 1 for fuller discussion).

Workload The first thing we noted was the sheer amount of time it took to get documentation together, organized and copied, in preparation for the external inspection. There was a tremendous effort and strain in getting it ready on top of all the other demands on our time in an extremely hectic summer programme. However, though it was so time consuming to do from scratch, feelings of annoyance were tempered by the realization that this was very useful internally in systematiz-ing our documentation and procedures, secure in the knowledge that it would be easier to do the next time. We were also aware that we might never have forced ourselves to do this without the need to satisfy the external criteria.

Workload on inspectors   A potential problem in providing such full documentation is that some of the materials might not be read by the inspectors before arrival – a danger of information overload. What remains to be established is what *criterial documentation* inspectors should see beforehand. The paradox is that the less they see beforehand will reduce what they can actually achieve on the day. A possibly unfair and unreasonable immediate reaction to the prospect of the visit on our part was: '*Given the documentation, how necessary is the visit?*' On reflection, we had to admit the need to verify that the written information was true, hence direct observation and contact are necessary.

Internal systems   We also felt that collecting documentation was valuable in that it can provide evidence of internal monitoring systems (for example, of the observed effectiveness of teaching on a number of occasions) so that the restricted coverage and depth of the external evaluation may not be as serious an issue (see 'Sufficient sampling' above). The external inspection might in time more usefully be seen as a moderation of internal monitoring. The value of neutral outsiders would then complement the wider sampling insiders can do.

Reflection and overview

The external evaluation certainly had important effects on us *in preparing for the inspection*: it made us think very hard as an institution about what we were doing; we prepared more thorough teaching syllabuses for spoken language (which had not received the research and development focus and massive inputs that our reading and writing courses had); we clarified in written documents our manage-ment structure, responsibilities, lines of authority and duties (useful in what had hitherto been a fairly informal system); we gathered all documentation relating to the course in one master file (see documentation list in appendix 4.1), and, most important of all, it made us step back and take a long hard look at the *overall* programme. Internal, developmental evaluation described earlier in the chapter had been comparatively 'bitty', tending to focus on specific problem areas such as reading and writing materials. The need to satisfy an external evaluation forced us to look at the programme as a whole and was extremely valuable as a result. We were thus encouraged to examine critically our overall management, our academic management, our resources, our premises, and our social and welfare programme as well as the more immediate teaching concerns which tend to be the usual focus of attention in internal evaluations.

The positive impact of getting ready for such an external inspection can be greater than the evaluator's report. This in itself may be an argument against spot checks and in favour of giving prior warning of a visit in order for the benefit from preparation to accrue. In general, the imminence of such evaluations motivates course providers to find the time to carry out activities and build in monitoring systems, such as teacher observation. It led us to consider and implement pro-active innovations such as a regular tutorial system covering all the course and not just the supervision of projects, which previously had been only reactive and informal.

So even the very occurrence of an external evaluation, whatever its quality, can be a cause of positive change in that it encourages institutions to make necessary improvements and put their own houses fully in order. In some ways it is compar-able with the MOT (the former Ministry of Transport) certificate for road vehi-cles. 'Tinkering with the machine' may keep a poor vehicle on the road but it is the threat posed by an outsider inspection (as in the annual MOT inspection with the dire consequences of failure) that is usually the spur to any serious repair work. In institutions such as CALS, which already provide a reasonable service and we hope a quality product, the glare of outside public attention is a further stimulus to our commitment to self-evaluation.

The need for criticism

There can, however, be a downside to such evaluations in the affective responses of those on the receiving end. Colleagues and ourselves felt a range of emotions, from relief and delight that it was over, to a certain amount of frustration and disappointment that we did not appear to get a hard enough time during the evaluation! Behind our disappointment there was a feeling that 'if they haven't asked about something or seen something, how can a rounded view be made?': the practical constraints of time and cost and availability intruding on fairness. It certainly raised for us the issue of sampling and the time-span of such evaluations and highlighted the dilemma of the external evaluator 'jetting in and out' (Alderson 1992). A period dedicated to discussion between the insiders and outsiders might well help alleviate some of these tensions and prove a very useful cooperative feature. The case for a more judicious mixture of both internal and external evaluation certainly surfaced once again. In a way this is a further argument in favour of the type of internal documentation of systems and procedures that the BALEAP inspection demands. If these are in place then maybe all the inspectors need to do is check certain of the elements in the record and moderate internal judgements, say, on the teaching.

Perhaps the reaction to inspection in our own particular institution arose from the fact that where there is a genuine commitment to improvement, lack of nega-tive feedback is paradoxically disappointing. If the external inspectors had identi-fied serious problem areas or blind spots in our programme, it might well have been a stepping stone to real development. If the organization is basically healthy, insiders should be able to get over and respond constructively to negative feedback.

This is of course as true for an organization as it is for an individual in receipt of negative feedback (chapter 8, Fuller and Manning 1973).

So, in contrast to our experience as external evaluators, as recipients of such evaluations we were very keen to hear from the inspectors where they thought we could improve and how they thought we might achieve this. The absence of such advice (not as yet within the evaluators' brief) left us in a similar position to the heads of those schools we had inspected and disappointed by not helping them to solve their own problems.

A parallel can be drawn with the reaction of some of the teachers in the external evaluations we carried out in Nepal (described more fully in chapter 3). Their interest was in finding out how they might improve their performance in the classroom, our purpose as external evaluators was to establish whether their teaching exhibited certain criterial features or not.

4.6   Conclusions

In external evaluations which are conducted purely for accountability purposes, there would seem to be an inevitable tension between the interests of the external evaluator and the desire for improvement on the part of those being evaluated. This tension is not likely to be resolved until one can achieve a more productive, fairer integration of development and accountability purposes (see chapters 1, 3 and 5; also Alderson and Scott 1992).

A more comprehensive approach to the evaluation of ELT programmes would imply a judicious blend of insider and outsider evaluation, involving a commitment on both sides to formative and summative dimensions (see chapter 1). Such an approach (along the lines suggested by Patton 1986) should generate appropriate, credible data for the intended users through a balanced, practical, situationally responsive design planned and carried out through collaboration and consultation between insiders and outsiders. These data would address the issues of utility: 'What needs to be known to get the program from where it is to where it wants to be?' (Patton 1986: 216–17).

Patton offers a picture of such a synthesis (1986: 215):

> The utilization focused evaluator works with stakeholders to design an evaluation that includes any and all data that will help shed light on evaluation questions, given constraints of resources and time. Such an evaluator is committed to research designs that are relevant, rigorous, understandable, and able to produce results that are valid, reliable and believable. On many occasions – indeed, for most evaluation problems – a variety of data collection techniques and design approaches will be used.

The work described in chapter 5 suggests how an external evaluator could be used in a critical role to help insiders establish for themselves the criteria and procedures for conducting evaluation. The external evaluations we have discussed above did not have this function as part of their terms of reference. In the coming decade it would strengthen such external evaluations if they were to seriously consider widening their brief to include helping institutions with the development of their own internal formative evaluation procedures.

5 Evaluating for Development: An Initial Teacher Training Course

This chapter is an account of an *external, development-oriented* evaluation of an initial training course for non–native speaker teachers in Paraguay. We do not attempt to provide a complete portrayal of the project but to give a context for comments and guidelines which may be of use to others for an evaluation of this type. Therefore, this chapter attempts to:

1 introduce some of the issues in doing an external formative evaluation,
2 present a framework for the review of an initial training course for teachers of English (section 5.3.3),
3 summarize sources and methods that were used (section 5.4),
4 indicate some of the development proposals that arose (section 5.5.1),
5 outline the characteristics of an appropriate summative evaluation, should it be required (section 5.5.2),
6 comment briefly on some lessons learned by the evaluator (section 5.6).

Since this was intended to be a supportive and formative evaluation, and insiders would be responsible for course development, their sense of ownership of the process, or lack of it, was a central concern throughout.

5.1 Terms of reference

In 1990 the writer was engaged by the Overseas Development Administration (ODA) for a two-week external evaluation visit to a project at a tertiary institution in Latin America (henceforth the College). His role was to advise and support the English Language Teaching Officer (ELTO) and local staff.

5.2 The project

In the early eighties the host government came to recognize that the poor standard of English among school leavers was obstructing the acquisition of technical knowledge and expertise from abroad, badly needed for the development of the country's economy. The ODA had already had a number of successful agricultural projects in the country and in 1986–7 they and the host government negotiated a jointly funded education project whose goal was to upgrade English teaching in secondary schools through a two-year 'Certificado' (Certificate) training programme at the College and a related secondary school textbook project. Local staff were to take over the programme from mid-1991.

ODA input took the form of a three-year ELTO post (1988–91) to support both the textbook and Certificado projects; books and equipment; external evaluation visits; and UK postgraduate training for counterparts, the local staff who will replace expatriate staff on the completion of their project involvement (on MA course and three one-term Certificate courses). The implementation of the project was controlled by the College administration, and monitored by the British Embassy. The objective of the new Certificado course was to produce some twenty well-trained English teachers for the state secondary school system each year, and to become established and self-sustaining within the College.

A Certificado is not equivalent to a degree: the course was designed for an intake who would not be able to enter the elite degree courses at the national university. As most of the intake had to be self-supporting, the programme was concentrated into two years (four fifteen-week semesters) with four intensive inter-semestral blocks so as to reach the legally required total of taught hours. Classes ran from 5 p.m. to 8.30 p.m. to allow students to work or care for families in the daytime. The twenty-five classes each week were split between some ten on general subjects, such as educational administration, psychology and didactics, and some fifteen for the specialist English programme.

The specialist teaching load of thirty classes a week was split between the ELTO, two full-time counterparts and three part-timers. Course assessment was based on semester and mid-semester tests, marked on a 1–5 scale with 2 as a passing grade.

The external evaluation visit was made in September 1990, the final year of the ELTO's contract and the first intake's fourth and final semester. Of this intake, thirteen were still on roll, of whom six were teaching both in state secondary schools and privately, three were teaching privately and four were either not working or were doing non-teaching jobs. Of the next intake, in their second semester, thirteen of fifteen students were still on roll. Dropouts were usually not for academic reasons.

Progress on some aspects of the project had been disappointing, largely due to difficulties with support from the College administration and poor liaison with outside bodies such as teachers' organizations. Many key aspects of the Certificado programme had not been under the ELTO's control (for example, enrolment and teaching practice), and so the ELTO had to take responsibility for programme development without full control over it. However, a new College Director had been appointed a few weeks before the visit, which led to an improvement in support from the administration and in staff morale.

5.3   Principles in the approach to the formative evaluation

5.3.1   Starting with staff concerns

The evaluator assumed that the concerns of insider staff would be the starting point of this formative evaluation, since they would have long-term responsibility for programme development. This was reinforced by the short, 'one-off' nature of the visit. Therefore, the evaluator's approach was to identify problems and tentatively propose solutions based on staff perceptions of needs, issues, and problems. These were elicited in a series of individual and group discussions which were then summarized in a discussion paper presented to full-time staff in the second week of the visit. Such an approach may not meet staff expectations of a visiting 'expert' and the external evaluator should expect to meet some resistance or role confusion when probing insiders' accounts of internal issues and problems rather than providing instant nostrums.

5.3.2   Sustainability, self-evaluation, and climate

The evaluator's view was that effective action by counterparts could only arise from their independent ability to frame problems and to evaluate their actions without outsider direction. Therefore, he hoped to guide staff towards setting up feedback and evaluation structures within their programme which would allow informed self-evaluation and would additionally facilitate summative evaluation if it were required at a later date.

As is argued more fully in chapter 8, internal programme development depends on staff collaboration and acceptance of responsibility, which in turn depends on a supportive climate in interpersonal and role relations in the institution. Therefore the agenda of the development-oriented evaluator should include monitoring this climate and trying to influence it for the better. The evaluator felt that the quality of collaboration between programme staff was crucial to their ability to self-evaluate and sustain the project (Fullan 1982: chapter 5, Rudduck 1988) and this in fact emerged as a serious obstacle to sustainable development.

5.3.3   A framework for formative evaluation

The evaluator felt the need for a framework to guide the 'what' of the evaluation (see section 1.4.4) – that is, what aspects of the course might need to be reviewed. This was to ensure that he attended to significant aspects of the programme and also so as to relate the programme to the larger systems within which it functioned – the College and the secondary school systems. Before the visit, the checklist of parameters below was prepared to guide the investigation of an initial training course of this type. While it aimed to be comprehensive, it was also provisional, as some important variables might only be identified 'on the ground'. It proved to be a helpful framework, though its comprehensiveness contained some hidden drawbacks (see section 5.6.3) in that it produced a wide range of information that proved hard to prioritize. Readers will have to develop their own checklists relevant to their circumstances, but even if they are not able to apply the full range of categories below, they should find it a helpful starting point.

Checklist of parameters in an initial training programme

Mission, programme aims, course objectives

- The history and institutional setting of the programme
- The mission and explicit aims of the programme, and the objectives of courses
- Appropriacy, relevance, and worthwhileness of objectives
- The model of teaching represented by programme aims and objectives
- Evidence on achievement of objectives

Intake and entry levels

- Entry requirements
- Entry profile of students/nature of intake (levels of English; experience of being taught; prior teaching)
- The match of the entry profile to first-year courses
- Numbers applying; numbers admitted; transfer and dropouts (numbers and reasons)

Graduates

- The knowledge, experience and skills of students on graduation (measured either as gain against entry levels or against prospective employment requirements)

Programme structure

- The organizing principle of the programme syllabus
- The progression of courses; the entry and exit levels at different stages over time
- The relative balance between courses in terms of teaching time, study load on students, and assessment weightings
- Coherence of courses, in terms of content linkage, overlaps, or omissions
- Contact hours
- Structures for student choice (e.g. modules/option courses)
- Effect of institutional norms and constraints on programme structure

Programme content

- The relevance of course syllabuses to the mission, and aims of the programme, and to the objectives of the particular course
- The relevance of the programme to mastery of the school curriculum
- Course texts
- The scope and 'up to dateness' of course content
- The adequacy of descriptive language study
- The adequacy of language skill development
- The adequacy of pedagogic training
- The adequacy of teaching practice arrangements (in terms of supervision time, practice time, and a teaching practice syllabus)
- The relevance of professional content (e.g. on the national education system)

Teaching

- The quality of teaching (accepting different approaches)
- The effectiveness of teaching methods
- The consistency of teaching methods with the programme's goals and content

Assessment

- The match between assessment, course content, and objectives
- The ability of assessment to discriminate student performance
- controls over fairness of assessment

Staff characteristics

- Number, grades, qualifications, training, and experience
- English language competence
- Staff stability
- The cohesion and interaction between staff
- Availability of staff development

Staff roles

- Individual staff responsibilities
- The quality and balance of research and other activities of staff
- Basis of employment (tenured; occasional; full- or part-time)
- Teaching loads and presence on site

Accountability

- Authority and accountability within the programme; within the institution; between the institution and outside agencies

Internal administration

- The efficiency and scale of record keeping of individual students; courses; evaluation findings; staff meetings; policy
- Support of staff and students

Monitoring and evaluation systems

- Methods for the monitoring and evaluation of the programme
- Evidence that the views of stakeholders (staff, students, administrators) are known
- The presence of systems by which monitoring and evaluation findings contribute to programme decisions

Funding and staff levels

- The source and allocation of funds
- Current staffing level; staff–student ratio; teaching loads; contractual demands on staff
- Use of funds

Resources

- Provision of resources, and their actual use
- The adequacy of teaching facilities

Liaison

- The forms of liaison with other departments, with the institution, and with outside bodies

Stakeholder concerns

- The strengths and weaknesses of the programme as seen by staff, students, and administrators
- Issues of major current concern to staff, students, and administrators

This framework was developed through reference to the literature (e.g. McDonald and Roe 1984, Wallace 1991) and personal experience. It should serve others as a useful starting point for the planning of an initial training programme; for the structuring of an internal development oriented review; or for an external evaluation, either for development or contractual accountability purposes. However, in evaluation for development it is essential to prioritize concerns in order to decide what action to take (see sections 5.3.5 and 5.6).

5.3.4   An exploratory approach

Following Parlett and Hamilton's (1977) 'illuminative' model, the strategy of moving from 'open' to 'closed' data collection was attempted (see also section 6.3.4):

1   an 'open' phase in which the evaluator is familiarized with programme; followed by
2   consolidation and focusing, in which themes, issues and factors are identified collaboratively by evaluator and insiders; leading to
3   a 'closed' phase, in which more focused information getting takes place, and in which provisional analyses are presented to insiders for discussion.

This strategy does require explanation and careful 'timetabling' since it entails a series of contacts with insider staff which change in their purpose as time goes by.

5.3.5   Priorities for action

When combined, a comprehensive framework and an 'open' approach to identifying staff concerns are very likely to produce a lengthy and diverse initial list of issues and problems. To move forward to planning and taking action requires collaborative reduction of this 'master list' to a limited set of agreed priorities. As is discussed in section 5.6, this process could not be completed by the evaluator and was left in the hands of insiders.

Prioritizing requires a structured approach, which can be led by an insider or by a neutral outsider. Some well-tried procedures used to agree priorities are summarized in appendix 8.1.1–3. It should be noted that their use is not merely a technical means to elicit staff needs, but a social means to bring staff together to collaborate on the development of a programme, using methods that explicitly defend their individuals rights (see in particular the Nominal Groups procedure). They are therefore a means to develop staff ownership of programme development.

5.3.6   Work within an institution's systems

Those with the power to carry through changes resulting from formative evaluation have to be at the centre of a consultation process, which should be done bearing in mind that it is the counterparts who have the long-term power base, and not the ELTO.

In this case the ELTO and the Director of the College were the key figures, with the ELTO as the planner, course leader, and 'on the job' trainer of counterparts; and the Director offering strategic direction and administrative/political support.

Therefore the evaluator met with the ELTO almost daily, and also had formal and social meetings with the Director.

5.4 The conduct of the formative evaluation

5.4.1 Time planning

The evaluator used the first week as an 'open' phase: getting to know staff, trying to form good relationships with them, and learning about the programme and its context. This involved observations and interviews (see section 5.4.1 and appendix 5.1). A more focused stage began early in the second week when staff met to discuss the evaluator's draft discussion paper based on individually elicited accounts of staff needs and possible solutions (see section 5.5.1 below for an extract). The purpose of the paper was to bring into the open issues which might be worked on by the ELTO and local staff after the evaluator's departure.

The need for several meetings with the same people meant checking personal timetables on the first day, and arranging a series of meetings with staff, singly and in groups. This was not always easy, owing to their other work commitments. Also, not all meetings could be coordinated: a diagnostic meeting with the part-time staff could only take place on the *same day* as the draft paper was discussed with the ELTO and full-time staff. This was unfortunate and tended to reinforce an existing divide in the staff. In time planning, the evaluator also had to allow some 'slack' for short notice contacts, e.g. to meet senior administrators and to talk to students at times convenient for them.

A helpful outcome of the Certificado timetable was that it allowed the evaluator to meet the ELTO in the early afternoon; to meet students and staff and attend classes in the evenings; and to use the mornings for record keeping and reflection.

5.4.2 Institutional climate

Along with interviews, classroom observation and the study of records and materials, the evaluator informally observed the behaviour of staff and students out of the classroom. He was also given 'messages' by different parties: being used as a means to pass on points of view which could not be put directly. From these informal sources, it seemed that the frustrations and false starts in the early phase of the project had left a legacy of poor relations among staff. There seemed to be no real interaction between some staff and very little systematic collaboration over all. This was, for example, reflected in the layout of the staff room, which did not contain a table around which staff could sit for discussions. This pattern was greatly reinforced by the staff's personal timetables which overlapped infrequently due to external commitments full-time staff had taken on, and to the large proportion of part-timers on the staff. This climate seemed not to provide good conditions for a handover of responsibility from the ELTO to the local staff, since course-related decisions were not being shared, and very little informal 'side-by-side' training was going on. However, this perception could not be presented to staff overtly: it would appear too negative and could lead to personalizing. Therefore, the evaluator tried to use the joint discussion of problems to bring staff together, and also tried to present the behaviour of their colleagues to certain individuals in such a way that they might reframe their negative perceptions of them. He was aware of the limited time for such an approach to take effect, however.

The evaluator's activities are summarized in appendix 5.1 (a day-by-day resume) and in table 5.1. This is followed by examples of the formative evaluation itself (section 5.5.1).

5.5   Outcomes

5.5.1   Course development proposals

The discussion paper prepared for the second week summarized areas of need and suggested steps to tackle them. After discussion and revision, the proposals were copied to the ELTO and Director and also included in the evaluation report. The issues arising were: counterpart needs on withdrawal of ELTO in 1991; specification of Certificado objectives; student language performance; programme structure; course contents; entry levels and admissions; monitoring and evaluation. A few extracts are given here for illustration.

Counterpart needs on withdrawal of ELTO

A particularly important and unpredicted concern voiced by counterparts was their desire to prepare themselves for the ELTO's departure. We feel that the points they raised are of interest for others concerned with project sustainability.

1   *Need*: Familiarity with courses taught by ELTO
Counterparts will need to understand not only the content of ELTO's courses, but also their rationale, objectives, and appropriate classroom management. They will also need session-by-session materials on which to base their teaching.
Proposal: Team teaching with ELTO
Staff who will take on the ELTO's courses should observe and team teach these classes with him/her in the first semester of 1991. This requires the counterpart staff to be available for pre-class planning and discussion, team

teaching, and post-class discussion. Therefore the 1991 timetable needs to be structured to allow the availability of counterpart staff for these activities.

2 *Need*: Counterpart teamwork and development of courses

Counterparts recognize that as yet they have not been working as team. They put this down to the constraints of their timetable. They recognize the need to work together on course development and teaching.

Proposal: Overlapping timetables

The 1991 timetable should be planned so that there are periods when all counterparts are at College but not teaching. This could be for a period of two to three hours weekly. As a first step, the issue should be raised with the Director and a draft timetable submitted to the College coordinator no later than December 1990.

Proposal: Staff meetings

Staff meetings (with agenda and minuted) should be held at regular intervals, but not so frequently as to interfere with other activities.

Proposal: Joint responsibility

Some courses should be jointly prepared, or at least discussed, by paired staff. This would improve the exchange of ideas, and improve the consistency between individual courses. This should apply to courses for 1991, first semester.

3 *Need*: Native speaker input to the course

An English native-speaking teacher or colleague helps set a standard for student and staff levels of aural comprehension and oral accuracy/fluency. Interaction with the native speaker tends to counteract the effect of pupils' limited English on that of student teachers, and that of student teachers on staff.

Proposal: Recorded materials

Increase the stock of audio and video recorded materials (particularly those with transcripts) for use by staff and students.

Proposal: English Club

Start up a Certificado English Club, based at College. Native speaker guests (e.g. from the business community) would be invited to meet students in appropriately informal settings. Video recorded films or other programmes could be watched and discussed. The timing of the meetings (perhaps within the normal timetable), and their location (perhaps the cafeteria) have yet to be decided.

Proposal: General subjects

Encourage the appointment of teachers of general subjects who can teach in English or bilingually.

Programme structure

Weighting This section reviewed the coherence and weighting of courses within the whole Certificado syllabus. A general problem referred to by all staff and many

Table 5.1 Methods, sources, and topics

Method	Source	Focus
Interviews	Embassy staff	Policy
		Project history
		'Messages'
	Administration	Policy
		Priorities
		'Messages'
	ELTO	Project history
		Priorities
		Perceived goals and needs
		Information on course, staff, and resources
		Perceptions of staff
		Attitudes on emerging issues
		Future actions
		'Messages'
	Counterparts	Project history
		Priorities
		Perceived goals and needs
		Attitudes on emerging issues
		Future actions
		'Messages'
	Students	Feedback
		Motives for study, aspirations, work lives
		Language assessment
Documents	Correspondence	
	Course descriptions	Objectives; 'Perfil profesional'[1]
	Course records	Reports; admissions data; student records (entry tests, grades, attendance)
		Teaching files
	School syllabus	Demands on teachers' English; teaching activities
Observation	School	School and class conditions and 'climate'
		Teacher and pupil behaviour; classroom norms
	Certificado classes	Student behaviour
		Teacher behaviour *vis-à-vis* objectives: discrepancies and awareness
	College	Material indicators (tidiness etc.)
		Patterns of interaction and relations between staff, and between students and staff

Table 5.1 (cont.)

Method	Source	Focus
Language tests	Students	Compare with entry levels Compare with exit needs (eligibility for scholarships, teaching secondary syllabus) Diagnosis for language improvement

1 A descriptive profile of a 'typical' graduating student, as a means to reflect course objectives

students is lack of time for coverage of content. The ELTO also noted the inefficient use of contact time during the inter-semestral 'blocks'.

1 *Need*: English language classes are now in blocks (six periods split into three blocks of two, three, one class periods) whereas the classes should ideally be daily. The 'blocking' seems to be due to the demands of teaching staff.
   Proposal: A draft timetable should be drawn up no later than December with daily English language classes, and presented to the College coordinator.

Omissions This section dealt with perceived gaps in the existing curriculum.

2 *Need*. Insufficient coverage of syllabus and materials design
   Students should be able to differentiate syllabus types and materials, and be able to abstract key content and exercise types from textbooks.
   Proposal: Incorporate practical textbook analysis and syllabus study into methodology in semesters 3 or 4.
3 *Need*: Insufficient coverage of practical achievement testing.
   Proposal: Introduce an achievement testing block in the fourth semester after the skills blocks, requiring students to prepare and pilot tests for their own materials.

Monitoring and evaluation

This was an area the evaluator had to draw to the insiders' attention.

1 *Need*: No systematic means for obtaining student feedback, though the evaluator found students to be well in touch with their needs.
   Proposal: Find means for informal discussions about the course; administer anonymous, short form questionnaires; institute staff–student meetings; use the intensive blocks for more formal evaluations.

The whole paper contained a considerable number of proposed areas for change. It was left with staff for subsequent work *but without external support* (see point 4 of section 5.6.4).

5.5.2   Guidelines for a summative evaluation

A further outcome of the formative evaluation was to suggest the nature of an appropriate *summative* evaluation, should it ever be required. The draft guidelines below result from an approach to summative project evaluation which emphasizes a positive role for insider staff (Simons 1982c; also sections 1.3, 1.6, 3.8, 3.10, 4.5 and Introduction to part II). However, as discussed in chapter 2, conventional summative evaluations for accountability serve the needs of funding agencies, and in many cases 'insiders' can attempt to negotiate conditions but not demand them, though we would wish to extend the role of insider contributions. The evaluation questions (the 'What' of the outline) derive from the original framework the evaluator worked from (section 5.3.3) and through discussion with insiders (section 5.5.1). If used openly and collaboratively with insiders, such guidelines could empower them by: (a) opening up the structure of an accountability-oriented evaluation to criticism and (b) enabling record keeping and programme development in advance of the evaluation (see also chapters 1 and 4).

Summative evaluation guidelines

1   The evaluation should be conducted on terms agreed by the Director of the College and staff.
2   It would be essential to confirm with insiders that the criteria and procedures planned for the evaluation were fair to the programme and fair to them (Beretta 1986b and chapters 1, 3, 7, 8). There should be an opportunity for insiders to comment on proposed criteria, and suggest indicators they see as appropriate. (See also references to criterial features in chapters 2, 3, and 7.)
3   All data collection plans should take into account the positive role of insiders as data collectors (see chapters 1, 3, and 4).
4   Evaluation methods should anticipate problems of access to Certificado graduates, especially in the context of a short visit by an outside evaluator.
5   One essential measure would be of Certificado student language performance, obtained from written work and independently conducted language tests (see discussion in section 3.6).
6   Levels of expectation regarding the stated objectives of the project would have to recognize structural social factors (such as the pay differential between private and state teachers which exerts a very strong pull toward private teaching).
7   Because much of the data collection could be done by insiders, certain external evaluator functions (such as review of assessed work) could be done at a

distance, while evaluation activities during a visit could focus on key independent data collection along with validation of insiders' data.

8 Evidence relevant to project sustainability would need to be obtained: the extent to which counterparts have been prepared to take over from the expatriate staff.

Appropriate indicators

Relevant indicators could be classified as follows.

Programme outcomes

1 Current teaching activities of graduates (hours per week; nature of employers)
2 Current teaching activities of undergraduates (hours per week; nature of employers)
3 English language performance of graduates (as against baseline measures, demands of secondary school syllabus, and demands of further professional development)

Programme delivery

1 Application, enrolment, and attendance figures
2 Calculation of students' class contact time
3 Calculation of students' teaching practice contact time (observing and teaching)
4 Appraisal of students' assessed work against stated objectives, and demands of secondary level syllabus
5 Appraisal of staff performance in relation to negotiated indicators (which could include English testing)
6 Description of staff roles, and timetables

Programme resources

1 Presence of adequate documentation (e.g. teaching files)
2 Fabric and upkeep of resources

Programme sustainability

1 Evidence of shared preparation and teaching of courses
2 Evidence of training in formative evaluation methods
3 Evidence of existing formative evaluation frameworks

Further qualitative indicators

1 Appraisal of the relevance of programme objectives to requirements of secondary level teaching (in terms of language, syllabus, testing, etc.)

2   Course appraisal by staff
3   Course appraisal by students
4   Course appraisal by graduates
5   Course appraisal by employers (school directors)
6   Evidence of proposed changes in courses being introduced and evaluated by staff
7   Evidence of support from Director
8   Evidence of support from Ministry of Education
9   Evidence of support and interest from teachers' organizations
10 Evidence of readiness and competence of counterparts to replace ELTO functions and maintain evaluation frameworks

5.6   Commentary on the evaluation

5.6.1   Evaluating teacher training

There is relatively little published work available on ELT initial teacher training evaluation – though in the private sector, UCLES (The University of Cambridge Local Examinations Syndicate) is currently conducting an important review of its Cert. TEFLA and Dip TEFLA programmes. This is in marked contrast to the literature dealing with other aspects of training which has developed considerably in recent years (e.g. Bickley 1987, Bowers 1987, Brittan 1985, Freeman and Richards 1993, Flowerdew et al. 1992, Jarvis 1992, Richards and Nunan 1990, Thornbury 1991, Wallace 1991) aided by the publication of *The Teacher Trainer* journal. Also, while not directly concerned with ELT, Dove (1986) addressed issues relevant to ELT teacher training for non-native speakers in less developed countries.

Where evaluation is formative in purpose, both the procedures used here and the issues of ownership and change are probably relevant in institutional contexts comparable to that in this account. Distinctive issues do arise, however, as regards the assumptions of trainees, trainers, and evaluators as to what the *process* of learning to teach actually is and in what ways trainees might be expected to change through their training experiences. A great difficulty here is that knowledge about learning to teach in ELT is very limited (see, however, Woods 1991 and Gebhard 1990). In the case of summative evaluations, these challenging theoretical questions have to be addressed and firm positions taken, since they determine the way in which training objectives are framed, which in turn determine the focus of formative and summative evaluations. These questions turn upon the extent to which trainees' behaviour and their subjective theories about teaching are seen as an object of change, and also upon the question of what can and should be expected as an outcome of any initial training programme as against subsequent experience in schools (Calderhead 1988, 1990). The timing of an evaluation is an issue consequent upon these theoretical questions: whether the proper focus of measurement should be at the point that trainees leave their training course; or whether a valid evaluation should assess the subsequent career of trainees in schools. The dilemma here is that while the latter option seems sensible, the performance of new teachers in schools is subject to many more variables than merely their training (Calderhead 1990).

5.6.2 Baseline design

An objectives-led evaluation of the Certificado course would be appropriate, assuming that the objectives and attainment targets were framed in terms of the demands upon students of future employment. Therefore, it would be appropriate to obtain measures of student teacher *language performance* on entering and leaving training, since this is so central an objective in the preparation of non-native speaker teachers of English, and findings could have both formative and summative value, depending upon the tests used.

5.6.3 Design and pupil learning outcomes

It would not be recommended to attempt to assess the effectiveness of the newly qualified teachers in this situation in terms of the learning gains of their pupils as compared with those of an appropriate control group of untrained teachers. This was possible in the Nepal study where all the teachers in the study (trained and untrained) were experienced (chapter 3). However, in Paraguay the only control group available would have been teachers with considerable experience in the classroom but with no adequate practical training. (See Weir and Burton forthcoming for a discussion of similar problems in the Guinea baseline study where the experience of the control group cancelled out any training effects in the experimental group.) As regards the variable of the teacher's English, one can see that the graduates from the training programme *should* have superior English to that of the average secondary school teacher, due to the hours of English instruction recently received and the poor level of language proficiency prevailing among the teaching population. A comparative study of the attainments of pupils of graduates and of 'control' teachers would have to be in terms of samples comparable in language performance. As a result, any comparison between the two groups would have been confounded. In addition, research (e.g. Calderhead 1990, Kagan 1992, and Zeichner et al. 1987) suggests that in subsequent teacher performance, initial training is only one variable among many, and is arguably less powerful than the immediate influences of the school, the pupils, available teaching materials, and the curriculum itself. It would therefore be extremely difficult to isolate the variable of Certificado training processes from these other variables. Finally, a comparative summative study would emphasize any differences in pupils' test scores, whereas the most valuable information for the development of this or any other initial training course would lie in the experiences of graduates once working in the school system. Thus a strict experimental/control group pre-test/post-test design would not be useful.

If there were an interest in this context to relate training to subsequent pupil learning effects, this could be more appropriately done as part of a multiple-site case study design (Yin 1989) which would be oriented to improvement in the initial training. These case studies could apply both qualitative and quantitative measures (Lynch 1992). Through qualitative information (interviews and questionnaires), confirmed by direct data as access and resources allow, it should be possible to identify aspects of teachers' school work for which the Certificado prepared effectively, needs in school not met by the training, and perhaps aspects of the training that are perceived as irrelevant or unhelpful. This information would be used to develop and validate programme objectives, the achievement of which could then be the focus of a summative evaluation.

5.6.4   An evaluation of the evaluation

The merit of an intervention such as the one reported here is best assessed by the nature of subsequent changes and improvements – in other words, according to levels 6 and 7 of Patton's (1986: 173) hierarchy of criteria (see appendix 1.3). Unfortunately, the 'one-off' nature of the visit limits the assessment to the evaluator's own reflections.

1   *Needs*   The evaluation made public a detailed listing of needs and issues with proposed responses (section 5.5.1) which enabled insiders to set priorities and plan how to develop the programme. It could also facilitate subsequent internal evaluations. How far staff would work on these proposals depended on their readiness to subject themselves to a process of change. As Rudduck (1988: 208) points out: 'If we accept that practitioners' own sense of self is deeply embedded in their teaching it should not be surprising to us that they find real change difficult to contemplate and accomplish.'

2   *Checklists*   Detailed frameworks for review and for summative evaluation were produced (sections 5.3.3 and 5.5.2). These could be of use both internally and to a wider professional audience, but only as 'maps' for a programme review. The change process is dynamic and personal in nature and depends upon conditions of ownership, trust and control, rather than technically proficient forms of analysis (Rudduck 1988, Simons 1984a, and chapter 8).

3   *Priorities*   The development process was incomplete. The Certificado staff were left with a long agenda of areas for development, *without having been helped to prioritize and work out their best 'next steps'* in the immediate future. This is probably the most serious criticism to level at the conduct of this evaluation.

4   *Support*   To translate a searching formative evaluation into action usually

requires further support. That this was not provided was due to time pressure and the enforced ending of contact between the evaluator and staff on completion of the visit, which in turn was due to: ODA ownership of the final report; distance and communication barriers; and the evaluator's other work commitments. It is interesting that more recent project policy (e.g. Rodwell 1988) emphasizes a longer term relationship between local project staff and visiting external evaluators. The ODA's policy has shifted towards more in-country training inputs, with longer term bilateral links with UK institutions, a model which would probably have benefited the project more than the long-term UK-based training and short-term outside inputs it received.

5   *Intervention*   Structural internal problems cannot readily be resolved by an outsider intervention if that intervention is short term. The evaluation process may have been effective in presenting an agenda to which staff had contributed, but it could not address some covert structural problems. The evaluator's view was that the Director was aware of these structural problems and had the skills to tackle them. However, one should not underrate the positive effects on insiders of even a short visit (see chapter 4) in terms of stimulating critical thinking about the programme and a greater awareness of the accountability dimension. It is also quite likely that some further external intervention would have stimulated more effective internal evaluation and required better collaboration by the insider staff (see also the last section of chapter 4).

6   *Design*   The Certificado course would have been appropriate for the adoption of a baseline evaluation design to assess student improvement over the two-year programme for both professional and contractual accountability purposes. Entry and exit language testing was already taking place, and the language improvement of the students was recognized by all to be of prime importance. However, the design of baseline entry measures is dependent upon an adequate definition of objectives and exit targets, which was still in progress when the visit was made (the first group of students had still not completed their training). It may be that a 'shaking down' period is needed in the life of a new programme before valid and realistic objectives can be specified in the detail that baseline testing requires.

7   *Skills for responsibility*   'Power sharing' in evaluation can have beneficial effects, as is argued elsewhere in this book. However, in the case of the Certificado, to achieve it would have required changes to project structure, including a revised job description for an already hard-pressed ELTO, specific training of insider staff, and a long-term synthesis between outside interventions and internal data collection and interpretation.

In part II of this book we have presented three accounts of our work as evaluators:

*   as summative external evaluators for contractual accountability, where we came to feel that a formative dimension was needed in the study, involving our own design and the greater inclusion of insiders (chapter 3);

• as insider formative evaluators in our own language programme, subject to external evaluation, where we came to see the dynamic benefit of external intervention upon internal processes, and the formative potential of such evaluation (chapter 4); and
• as outsider formative evaluators, where we came to see the need for counterpart involvement in formative processes, and the potential for its integration with possible summative external evaluation (chapter 5).

We now turn in part III to more general issues of methodology, focusing on self-report and observational data collection.

Part III Methodology of Evaluation

Introduction

Part III consists of chapters on two major methods of collecting information: self-report (interviews and questionnaires) and classroom observation. We assess these methods as means to achieve differing evaluation purposes, examine their particular strengths and weaknesses, and summarize good practice in their use. In this general introduction, we consider the links between the choice of method, the purpose of evaluations, and practical constraints.

Purpose and evaluation method

A data collection method should be chosen because it is the best means to tell you what you want to know. Therefore the first step is to determine *exactly what it is* that you want to know: what the objectives of the evaluation are and what information will help achieve these objectives. For example, in an evaluation with a narrow summative focus for accountability purposes, methods generating quantitative evaluation data would be required in order to match formal plans against measurable low-inference outcomes (see description of the use of test data in chapter 3); or in a more comprehensive summative evaluation, additional methods would be used to obtain process and implementation data – for example, on the transfer of training, as in the Nepal study (see section 3.2.3). However, in the broader approach to evaluation argued for in previous chapters, we would expect far more involvement of insiders in data collection, the broader focus of which would lead to a more varied and eclectic use of methods (for example, the range of indicators suggested as appropriate for the summative evaluation proposed in section 5.5.2 would involve a wide range of methods for collecting both qualitative and quantitative data; see also section 1.4.6 for an outline of the range of methods available).

Where the purpose is largely developmental, as in the study of the CALS pre-sessional course (see chapter 4), data collection can fulfil more diverse functions: to document its actual development; to provide course records; to record unintended outcomes; to map the evolution of objectives; to identify the contextual factors affecting implementation; to record the perceptions and reactions of teachers and students to the programme; to monitor progress in language learning; to support and inform materials development; to monitor classroom processes; and to show how far criteria of quality and worthwhileness relevant to the programme are being met.

In the past, there has been a tendency among some evaluators to adopt one paradigm of enquiry to the exclusion of any other: some adopting naturalistic and qualitative design and others relying wholly on experimental and quantitative models. However, it is now a more widespread, and in our view far more sensible, view that the purpose of the evaluation should override such quasi-ideological preferences in favour of principles of utility and relevance (Patton 1986). Our position is greatly reinforced by a preference for a broad, inclusive approach to evaluation (see section 1.6). Patton (1986: chapter 8) provides a full and stimulating discussion of these issues (see also Cronbach (1982) whose support for methodological eclecticism, and for the value of qualitative studies, was extremely influential in developing a wider approach to evaluation). Patton concludes (1986: 213): 'All in all, these trends and factors suggest that the paradigms debate has significantly withered. The focus is now on methodological appropriateness rather than orthodoxy, methodological creativity rather than rigid adherence to a paradigm, and methodological flexibility rather than following a narrow set of rules.' Patton's helpful summary of the emphases of different approaches to method can be found reprinted in appendix III.1 (Patton 1986: 216–17).

Methods should therefore be chosen according to the information required by different evaluation purposes, *and also* according to the realities of logistics (access and resources) and the characteristics of informants. It should be stressed that while evaluators must attempt to obtain information of the best possible integrity (see chapter 1 on standards and chapters 6–8 on good practice) and have to anticipate challenges to their methods and findings, evaluations are *rarely perfect*. Funded research allows time to meet the strictest criteria for data collection and analysis, but in comparison most evaluations are constrained by time, money, and personnel, so that evaluators often have to make 'trade-offs' in order to provide the most useful information possible at the right time for it to inform decision making. Furthermore, evaluations take place 'in the field' and rely upon the cooperation and actions of others subject to the demands of day-to-day living. We now turn to the constraints that affect data collection before returning to the issue of matching method to purpose.

Method and logistics

Quite as important as the purposes of data collection are the logistical and other practical factors which determine how data are collected, and who is involved. In terms of *logistics*, methods are determined by such issues as the following.

Access Who can you actually reach for data collection? How long can you expect informants to be involved in giving information (e.g. being interviewed, being observed, filling in questionnaires)? Potential informants will all have their own commitments and demands on their time, which evaluators will often have to work with rather than against. For example, to see a busy teacher might require quite careful advance arrangement.

Communications How reliable and quick are communications? For example, is there a functioning telephone system by which to reach schools? How far off the road are schools located? Is there a functioning public transport system?

Resources What time is there to get, analyse and present information? What are the cost limits on data collection? For example, can staff be employed in data collection or analysis, such as observers or clerks?

Access consequences Who is affected by the data collection methods you use, and your sampling decisions? The choice of informants and the route by which data is obtained will be affected by possible interpersonal consequences of data collection. For example, there could be individuals who will object if they are excluded. (Jansen-Strasser 1989 reports an interesting account of colleagues who were upset because their classes were not observed.)

Could your actions be perceived as going behind anybody's back? Are there local 'hidden agendas'? For example, in a centralized system those in authority may resist consultation with teachers because of the implications this might have for the power structure, while the teachers may resist involvement in evaluation because they perceive data collection as a form of inspection and control.

When considering access consequences, the advice of Sanders (1992: 1), though somewhat idealistic, should be well taken: 'One must always consider three aspects of good program evaluation – communication, communication and communication. As long as you listen and respond, share information, discuss your intentions and obtain feedback, clarify expectations, provide clear and useful reports in a timely manner, and maintain an open evaluation process, the evaluation seas will be smooth.'

In the real world of evaluation the seas tend to be a trifle choppy, in that logistic considerations require most evaluators to make difficult trade-offs in order to provide the best data they can at the time they are needed.

Method and focus of data collection

In evaluating the implementation of a programme, one may attend to a wide range of classroom features relevant to learning, as follows:

1 Milieu (including cultural norms)
2 Teaching activities
3 Mode of approach
4 Subject matter
5 Materials and equipment
6 Student involvement and attitudes to study
7 Interactions (verbal and non-verbal)
8 Aspects of authority and models of knowledge
9 Curriculum balance
10 Curriculum adaptation
11 Levels of expectation
12 Staff patterns (individual, group, etc.)
(after Goodlad and Klein 1974)

In very general terms, these features can be described through asking, reading, and watching: self-report (chapter 6), analysis of documentary records, and observation (chapter 7). (The feature of learning outcomes, not specifically mentioned by Goodlad and Klein, would of course be measured by achievement tests. See Weir 1993 for a detailed account of how to construct these and also some reservations we have in section 1.4.6.)

Examples of the method–purpose–focus match

In the Nepal evaluation (chapter 3) a variety of data was collected to meet its purposes and the terms of reference of the evaluators. To measure student learning gains (the key summative indicator required by the funding agency) language test scores were obtained and compared. In order to get some direct evidence on the implementation of training in the classroom, observational data were needed. To complement these direct data, teachers' unstructured self-report accounts of their lessons were also needed because resources did not allow a large enough number of observations. Focused interviews were carried out too because biographical data about the teachers in the study were needed. Thus a variety of methods was used to describe different facets of the programme, each method chosen as it gave the particular type of information required.

Similarly, the choice of self-report method can be determined by a combination of resource constraints (sample size and access) and the nature of the information sought. For example, in a case where large samples are necessary, or personal access is a problem because of travel or time constraints, then postal questionnaires would be an appropriate means of data collection. However, postal questionnaires (completed by informants on their own) are most suited to low-inference, *factual* questions – for example, information on conditions of service, or target situation needs. On the other hand, high-inference information (such as teachers' levels of expectation, reactions to a new course book, or students' perceptions of what they have been taught) is more suitably gathered by interviewing because it affords greater scope for questions of complexity and depth (chapter 6 and Patton 1987b: 108–43). Interviews are particularly useful where explanations of behaviour or affective responses are needed and as a means to pursue pedagogic issues in depth (see Millar et al. 1992 for a full and informative discussion of this method).

Table III.1 (from Siedow et al. 1985: 138), in which teacher and learner characteristics are related to a range of data collection methods, further illustrates how methods vary according to the focus of evaluation.

Features of self-report, documentary, and observational data: A summary

At the risk of some repetition of chapters 6 and 7, we summarize here some of the key features of the three major data collection methods.

Table *III.1* Methods for evaluating various objective types

Objective Types	Evaluation Methods
Teacher Beliefs	Pre/Post: questionnaires interviews observations review of lesson plans
Teacher Abilities	Observations/videotapes Self-assessment quizzes Pre/Post: questionnaires interviews observations review of lesson plans
Teacher Practices	Record of activities Lesson plan reviews Observations/videotapes Interviews Questionnaires
Student Behaviors	Student interviews Student questionnaires Teacher logs Observation Teacher interviews
Student Learnings	Chapter/unit tests Standardized test Teacher logs Student assignments Comparison of present term grades to previous grades (or grades of another group of students) Student interviews Teacher questionnaires Student questionnaires Teacher interviews

Source: Siedow et al. 1985

Self-report

Self-report accounts (for example, questionnaire or interview data obtained from classroom teachers) provide only second-hand, indirect information about classroom events and as such are filtered by the perceptions of informants, who are likely to have an interest in the descriptions they provide. Their accounts may reflect what they espouse, aspire to, or what they think the questioner wants to hear, rather than what has actually taken place. Furthermore, given the complexity of the teacher's task and the number of cues competing for his/her attention, it is to be expected that teachers' recall of lessons will be selective and often far from complete: it tends to be in terms of their pedagogic intentions and the cues in learner behaviour relevant to carrying them through (Bromme 1987, Doyle 1977).

Therefore, self-report data on classroom events are not entirely reliable and where possible should be verified by other sources of information (see the process of 'triangulation', below). However, self-report data are an essential means for understanding teachers' perceptions and beliefs concerning classroom variables. Without this understanding it is doubtful that one can make a valid interpretation of many evaluation findings.

Documentary information

Programmes produce their own records: examination papers, administrative files, teaching materials, attendance records, teachers' lesson notes, students' work, and so on. (See Sanders 1992: 31–2 for a discussion of the use that can be made of these and methods of analysis.) If these are 'banked' in an orderly way by staff (see discussion in chapter 4) they can provide evaluators with valuable direct information on many of Goodlad and Klein's categories listed above. However, documents have limitations. Classroom processes can only be inferred from them; collection and analysis can be time consuming; and free access may have to be negotiated. Also, documentation may not be complete, and there may be resistance if the evaluator wants to burden staff with additional record keeping in areas of interest only to him/her.

Observation

Observation is the only way to get *direct* information on the classroom behaviour of teachers and learners. It is hard to justify an evaluation of the implementation of curriculum materials or of a training programme, without observational data. By focusing upon relatively low inference features (of activities or talk), the evaluator can identify objective patterns in classroom events which can test the achievement of objectives and also can underpin interpretations of participants' perceptions and beliefs. Additionally, evaluators will learn about the real life of a programme by visiting schools and watching the interactions between participants in and out of classrooms (see chapters 3, 4 and 5). Both developmental and external accountability-oriented evaluators have to understand the milieu in which informants work, the complex interaction of factors and the diversity of sites and participants. Only in this way can they truly understand their own data. It is worth noting that self-directed observation also can have a crucial role in internal development-oriented evaluation (see appendix 7.1) since it requires insiders to clarify their pedagogic intentions, and to identify the classroom features which can give feedback on their achievement (Roberts 1993 and chapter 7), though we argue for the desirability of an outsider audience of some kind to maximize the value of this.

Though essential as a means to describe implementation, systematic observation is demanding and in some ways problematic. It requires considerable resources; it demands special skills; and it intervenes in the school and the classroom. Furthermore, there can be real difficulties in meeting validity and reliability criteria, in the choice of observational categories, in controlling for the 'observer effect' (see section 7.1.7) and logistical problems in attaining an adequate sample.

Some general considerations

There are a number of considerations that all evaluators need to address whatever methods they employ. We briefly summarize them below and then return to them in more detail in our discussion of interview and questionnaire methods in chapter 6, and of observation in chapter 7.

Planning

In each of the methods discussed in this part of the book considerable space is devoted to the planning stage. Evaluators need to be aware of the advantages and disadvantages of the various methods available to them and be familiar with what constitutes good practice in the use of these methods. In many ways, planning is the most crucial stage, as once the evaluation is implemented it is difficult to make radical changes to the instruments being used or the procedures being followed. Any changes made will cause problems of comparison with data collected earlier. The comment on piloting below is obviously relevant here.

Validity

In all of the methods we discuss in this book (and in the less formal methods suggested elsewhere, e.g. Rea-Dickins and Germaine 1992) the cardinal principle is to establish clearly what you want to find out. Validity is concerned with *measuring what you want to measure*. It is crucial to be explicit about what is to be measured and to take steps to ensure that your data collection procedures provide you with the data for this purpose. Methods should be selected which best allow you to do this in your particular context.

Triangulation

A combination of data sources is likely to be necessary in most evaluations because often no one source can describe adequately such a diversity of features as is found in educational settings, and because of the need for corroboration of findings by using data from these different sources, collected by different methods and by different people (i.e. 'triangulation'). It is now widely held that multiple methods should be used in all investigations (Patton 1987b: 61). However, it is important to note that of the three methods we discuss in detail in part III, observation is the only one that can provide *direct* information on what is taking place in classrooms.

Reliability

It is imperative for all evaluators, whatever methods they employ, to try and ensure that the data they collect are as reliable as they can make them, i.e. *to what extent can we depend on the results obtained from these enquiries?* Obviously triangulation from different data sources will help here. In addition, evaluators need to take steps to ensure consistency in the use of different methods and to provide evidence of such in their reports (see section 7.3).

Practicality

Particularly in the case of hard-pressed, 'part-time' formative evaluators, it is imperative to choose the most efficient methods for generating the required information (section 1.4.6). They are often denied the time and the resources that are available to the outside summative evaluator. However, even outsiders may suffer from serious time constraints, as we saw in section 4.5. Data should only be collected if they are going to be used, and only in a form which will enable *best use* to be made of them (see section 1.4.7). It is far better to collect a limited quantity of high quality (informative and reliable) data rather than a larger amount of low quality information that is possibly unusable. This is best ensured by *continual reference back to the decisions which these evaluation data are designed to inform*. In many situations, logistics, and time pressure may force compromises, in which priorities for collecting information would have to be decided.

Sampling

As we noted in the Nepal study reported in chapter 3, for results to be credible we need to take a reasonable sample of data relating to the evaluation focus under review (see Patton 1987b: 51–60 for discussion of the logic of purposeful sampling). The more restricted the sampling – for example, making judgements of teacher effectiveness on the basis of a single thirty-minute visit (see section 4.5 for a discussion of this) – the more the data is open to question in terms of both its validity and reliability. It is important that stakeholders consider carefully what would be an adequate sample size for them to have faith in the results that emerge. Increasing the sample size has obvious knock-on effects in terms of practicality. However, if compromises are to be made, practical expediency should not ever threaten the validity and reliability of the study. The results of an evaluation must be valid (this obviously implies that they are also reliable), otherwise there is no point in collecting the data.

Piloting

In all methods, the value of piloting instruments before actually employing them in final data collection is paramount. The biggest single threat to the reliability and validity of a study occurs when insufficient attention is paid to the design and piloting of evaluation instruments. All too often, attention is concentrated on the actual collection of data and their analysis (Davies 1992: 208). Sufficient time and attention must be allocated to the refining of evaluation instruments. They at least need to be tried out first on colleagues and then preferably on a small sample from the intended target group of informants (see also sections 6.2.2, 6.3.3, and 7.2.6 for discussion of piloting interviews, questionnaires, and observations). This will help identify ambiguities, other problems in wording, and inappropriate items, and provide sample data to clarify any problems in the proposed methods of analysis prior to the collection of data in the study proper.

Reporting

Davies (1992: 208) makes the important point that 'An evaluation is not a history but an abstraction . . . An evaluation must be an interpretation.' Care must be taken to ensure that the audience for any reports have sufficient information to judge the reliability and validity of the procedures followed, but they need to be able to separate the wood from the trees. A surfeit of information should be avoided. Volume 9 of the Sage Program Evaluation Kit, *How to Communicate Evaluation Findings* (Morris, Fitz-Gibbon and Freeman 1987), is an essential reference in this respect as it provides useful information on the structuring and presentation of evaluation reports. The 'transmissibility' of data is an important consideration (see section 1.4.7). The value of an evaluation is a function of its usefulness and accessibility to immediate stakeholders and perhaps eventually to a wider audience. An avoidance of jargon and overloading with detail, a coherent argument written in simple English, and clearly drawn lessons are counsels of perfection for us all.

Having considered some of the 'strategic' questions in choice of method, we now go into greater detail on tactical aspects of 'asking and watching' in chapters 6 and 7. In general, our approach to the discussion of evaluation design and data collection methods in this book has been to try to raise our readers' awareness of these strategic and tactical issues, according to broad headings of 'Wh' questions (see 'Why, What, Who, When, and How long' in chapter 1) and key considerations and standards rather than to offer a 'blueprint' in the form of a step-by-step planning guide (see section 1.4.6 for further discussion of this). Readers who feel the need for more detailed guidance can do no better than to refer to the Program Evaluation Kit – in particular, *How to Design a Program Evaluation* by Fitz-Gibbon and Morris (1987b), *Evaluator's Handbook* by Herman et al. (1987), and *How to Assess Program Implementation* by King et al. (1987) – and, for using qualitative methods, Patton (1987b, 1990). In these, both formative and summative evaluation planning is dealt with in well-exemplified, lucid and economical terms.

6 Self-report Methods: Interviews and Questionnaires

6.1 Introductory

The authors acknowledge the debt they owe to the work of Judith Bell (Bell 1987, Bell et al. 1984), of Cohen and Manion (1980) and of the contributors to the Program Evaluation Kit published by Sage (particularly King et al. 1987 and Patton 1987b) in developing the ideas on collecting data reported below. These works influenced us greatly in the early evaluations we conducted and our comments below owe much to the ideas they contain. We recommend them strongly to all would-be evaluators.

Our aim in this chapter is to provide insights and awareness of two important self-report methods and to make readers aware of the criteria by which to judge these means for data collection. It is not intended to provide a detailed step-by-step guide for users (see section 1.4.6). However, the reader is referred to sources on evaluation methods listed at the end of this chapter for further information.[1]

6.1.1 Definition and purpose

Interviews and questionnaires are commonly referred to as *self-report* methods because information is obtained at second hand through informants' accounts, rather than by direct 'first-hand' description such as test scores, documentary evidence, or classroom observation.

Self-report data can be seen as:

the personal responses of program faculty, staff, administration, and participants . . . Self reports typically take one of two forms: questionnaires and interviews. Questionnaires asking about different individuals' experiences with a program enable one evaluator to collect information efficiently from a large number of people. Individual or group interviews are more time consuming, but provide face to face descriptions and discussion of program experiences. (King et al. 1987: 72)

Evaluators cannot provide a comprehensive account of a project or programme on their own. They need the accounts of insiders (learners, teachers, administrators, parents, education authority officers, and others) because they need to elicit insiders' experience of events to verify their descriptions. Also, insiders' reported experiences and perceptions of the programme help outsiders understand their actions and the personal impacts of the programme.

Different stakeholders are not at all likely to provide perfectly matching accounts: their interests, responsibilities, and contact with the programme or project diverge and so a single agreed truth is unlikely to emerge. There should, however, be discernible trends or patterns in these accounts which the external evaluator can identify. Additionally, discrepancies between participants may have an explanatory value regarding the implementation of the programme or project.

6.1.2   Limitations of self-report data

Self-report data, by definition, are 'indirect' in nature, as they either consist of a description of events through the eyes of an intermediary, or represent the views and perceptions of an individual, which cannot be directly accessed. In general, the less direct data are, then the harder it is to defend their credibility. On the other hand, in educational settings direct evaluation data (documents, observations, test scores) may be desirable, but they may be unobtainable; furthermore, the perceptions of participants, however subjective, are a crucial means to understand programme implementation and effects and are only obtainable by self-report methods (e.g. see appendix 4.4 for student feedback and self-assessment questionnaires).

Self-report data are unreliable if unsupported by other data because of 'post-event reconstruction' by the informant, and the tendency for interviewers or question wording to affect responses. Post-event reconstruction is the tendency to create an account of reality which is favourable to ourselves: we have a vested interest in 'sounding good' when we report what we have done. The interviewer effect refers to the tendency of an interaction between informants and interviewers to bias responses: there is a known tendency among respondents to wish to provide what they think is wanted of them; indeed in some cultures it is impolite not to do so (Coleman 1992: 233, Phillips and Owens 1986). Interviewers can sometimes reinforce this by 'cueing' respondents when this is taking place. Low (1991), drawing upon the conversational analysis literature, suggests that there might be a reluctance to disagree in spoken interactions. Finally, there is a tendency for the nature of question wording to influence answers, a fact fully recognized in market research. This is not so much the case where questions are objective (such as years worked in an institution, age, etc.) but it may occur in the case of 'opinion' questions. For instance, the opinion poll questions:

'Do you believe that it is time for a change?'
'Do you intend to vote for the Opposition?'

might be answered 'yes' and then 'no' by the same person. These are contradictory but result from the nature of the questions asked. The evaluator needs to try as hard as he/she can to ensure that questions are not loaded. Structured questionnaires (e.g. multiple-choice types) should be less susceptible to bias as a result of the 'sound good' problem or the wish to provide what is thought to be wanted.

The issue of question formulation requires a detailed treatment beyond the scope of this book. The reader is referred to Labaw (1980), Low (1988, 1991), and Slembrouck (1987) for informed discussion of the nature of the communication between respondent and researcher, the semantic aspects of rating scales and the need for clear hypotheses as the basis for research design.

In many cases data can be elicited through self-report which is objective and/ or quantifiable (e.g. appendix 6.3, questions 1–6). However, in those cases where self-report data are supplied in response to open-ended questions, where they are not elicited in a structured fashion, or responses are subjective and not open to quantification, there may be some inherent limitations, particularly as regards reliability and generalizability. Some evaluators might wish to restrict the role of such data to the verification of more quantifiable data, and only to prefer it if logistics demand. Some evaluators would go further than this (e.g. Cronbach 1982, Cronbach et al. 1980, Parlett and Hamilton 1972, Patton 1987b: 30 and Stake, R. E. 1986) and would argue that qualitative data is essential so as to understand participants, the learning milieux and programme outcomes. The largely ideological controversy between those favouring 'hard' and 'soft' data is now, thankfully, at an end since after Cronbach (1982) it is generally recognized that both quantitative and qualitative dimensions are relevant to the description and evaluation of programmes (e.g. Lynch 1992; see Chapter 1 and Introduction to part III for a discussion of this). This is because of the need to 'triangulate' data – that is, to confirm data from one source by cross-referring it to data from another (Cohen and Manion 1980). It is also because the forms of data can be complementary: quantitative findings (classroom interaction patterns, test scores, attendance figures, etc.) can identify objective trends and patterns; qualitative, self-report data can help us to understand them (Delamont 1976, Lynch 1992).

6.2   Interviewing

6.2.1   Advantages and disadvantages

Advantages

Depth   Whereas questionnaire responses have to be taken at face value, an interview response can be clarified and developed through follow-up questioning. If the respondent is unclear on the interpretation of a question, this can be resolved. The interviewer can probe, follow up on clues and comments, and can develop unanticipated lines of enquiry. Interviewing is therefore suited to the early, exploratory stages of an enquiry when variables are being identified, and also to the later explanatory stages which put 'flesh on the bones' of a questionnaire or other quantified data. It also allows the investigator to check on the accessibility and clarity of questions he/she might wish to include in a questionnaire.

Personal contact Additionally, apart from verbal information, the personal contact between the evaluator and programme insiders allows responses to be illuminated by the manner in which the response is made, which can be as informative as their content. Furthermore, the evaluator needs personal contact to develop his/her own proper understanding of the programme as a whole, of the relationships between the people involved (for an example, refer to the experience of this in the Paraguay study in chapter 5). There is usually a high response rate because of this personal contact and it offers less chance for collusion by informants.

Language When respondents have language difficulties (e.g. they are non-native speakers or there are literacy problems), questionnaires might confront them with problems of understanding or self-expression, whereas in an interview these difficulties can be more readily overcome.

Disadvantages

The interviewer effect In an interview there can be very powerful interactions between interviewee and interviewer which bias responses, so making the data inaccurate. Interview data are not objective facts: an interview is a discourse constructed by two individuals contributing their own assumptions, interests, and concerns. It is self-evident that great care must be taken over the wording of questions (see 'Planning the interview' below). However, bias can also arise from the interviewer's responses to answers: for example, by giving selective attention to things he/she wants to hear which cue the interviewee to elaborate on them. As we noted above, this effect is strengthened by the tendency of interviewees to wish to satisfy the interviewer. Bias can also arise from personal or role interactions that stem from race, gender, class, or status, or just personality (Millar et al. 1992: 69–76, Powney and Watts 1987: 35). These may lead to an interviewee's 'closing up' or taking a line hostile to the interviewer or simply 'yea saying' in order to get rid of him. Alternatively, the interviewee may be too ready to defer to the interviewer's interests.

To combat bias, interviewing demands personal skills deriving from the training, attitudes, and experience of the interviewer (Fowler and Mangione 1990). It is essential to be able to attend to what is said, not to talk too much, nor to misdirect the discourse. Also, the creation of trust and rapport (where this can be achieved in the face of language problems or power differences, for example) will help to elicit rich information which otherwise might not be volunteered (Millar et al. 1992: chapter 3, Pring 1984).

Sampling   The time-consuming nature of interviews will affect the composition of the sample interviewed as well as its size. In many evaluations, limited resources and problems of access tend to restrict the numbers who can be seen, because of the time it takes to set up and conduct interviews, and to analyse and reflect on the data. The result may be that random sampling is hard to achieve so that opportunity samples often have to be used, which could bias the data.

In an educational setting, hierarchies will indicate who should also be sought out as informants: one would normally include decision makers and other key personnel, partly for reasons of diplomacy and partly because of their influence in the system. (See Fullan 1982, 1986 and Harrison 1987 for good advice on how to set about identifying the 'key players'.) There may, however, be cases where the concern is *only* with what the pupils and teachers think.

6.2.2   Types of interview

The formal interview

Description   A formal interview is highly structured, with no variation in the form of questions, with a standardized question sequence and with answers recorded from a set of limited response options (e.g. Mitchell 1992: appendix 1). This structuring enhances the comparability of the data collected, in that one can be confident that each set of individual interview data was elicited in the same way. Also, its standardized form improves the reliability of the data collected and makes it easier to collate and analyse. In terms of coverage, detailed and personal information can be collected which might not be volunteered in an informal interview. In response options, a questionnaire or a checklist may be used, especially by an inexperienced interviewer, so that informants are asked to select one of a set of categories presented to them, choose from a range of responses, or give some other limited response.

Limits   This type of interviewing is *not* appropriate for exploratory phases in an enquiry (see section 6.3.4), as it lacks the potential richness of the informal interview: the pre-determined and unvarying specification of question wording and sequence naturally limits the interaction that can take place and leaves little room for the idiosyncratic or unexpected. The nature of the enquiry is constrained by the questions on the page. Furthermore, the formal interview depends on the assumption that the questions are valid: that they are relevant, real, and significant. Without proper piloting, however, questions decided on may not be the right ones, and the data obtained could therefore be of very limited value.

The informal interview

Description An informal interview is discovery oriented, appropriate to the early stages of an enquiry when relevant issues are still being uncovered. It would have been extremely useful to have conducted follow-up interviews with trained teachers in Nepal at the start of the baseline study described in chapter 3. This might have helped avoid some of the mistakes we were to make.

An informal interview makes no prior limiting assumptions on the topics or content that the interviewee will provide. Therefore, the interviewer's aim is to stimulate the subject to talk freely about the area under study so that interview discourse follows the course set by interviewees. (This procedure is advocated for teacher student tutorials in the language programme discussed in chapter 4.) Very general cues and questions should be used at first, though narrower, more focused questions may follow up on responses from the interviewee. (King et al. 1987: 76 ff. provide a useful discussion on types of question.) The most appropriate means to record the interview data is by verbatim notes or recording. Obviously, limited response options would not be appropriate.

Quite often, a *group* discussion will be very useful to elicit a wide range of concerns, views, and priorities at the very start of an enquiry. Also, an informal approach could be used as a 'warm up' before moving on to a formally structured interview. This again illustrates the need to match the method with contextual features to ensure maximum utility (Patton 1986).

Limits Informal interviews require rapport between interviewer and interviewee, skilled and trained interviewers, and reflective, forthcoming, and articulate interviewees. They can provide deep, illuminating information that cannot be obtained in any other way. However, the lack of structure leaves the data open to challenge: that certain key questions may have not been addressed, or that the interviewer effect has not been controlled.

In terms of analysis, recordings or verbatim notes are time consuming to transcribe or summarize (see also section below on Planning: Recording responses). Perhaps more seriously, there can be great difficulty in finding a common framework by which to categorize the data since the order, form, and very occurrence of questions will vary from interview to interview, with obvious implications for the reliability of the data. In this case, a form of content analysis (systematic classification according to repeated terms, concepts or issues occurring in the data) is the appropriate form of analysis (King et al. 1987: 122, Miles and Huberman 1984, Patton 1987b: 149). However, its appeal to the non-statistically minded should be tempered by the very time-consuming and skilled nature of good qualitative analysis.

The focused interview

Description The focused interview (Bell 1987: 71–3) is a compromise between fully structured and unstructured approaches, so that pre-determined topics can be covered but there is enough flexibility for interviewees to develop areas of concern or volunteer unpredicted content. (See chapter 4 for a description of the focused materials feedback sessions conducted with teachers.) The interviewer is free to modify the sequence or wording of questions as he/she sees fit, and can also explain questions or add to initial probes. It is a less artificial personal encounter than the formal interview and can encourage more openness from the interviewee.

In contrast with informal interviews, a degree of focusing provides comparability and structure for analysis, which is particularly important in a study where time and resources might be restricted.

Limits   As open elicitation is used, there can still be problems of comparability and interviewer bias.

6.2.3   Planning the interview

General preparation

Objectives   As we discussed in the Introduction to part III, it is essential for the evaluator to be clear about his/her general aims and purposes and the specific function of interviewing. In strategic terms, he/she should be true to his/her terms of reference (summative or formative) and should determine the level of description thereby required: for example, whether portraying implementation, isolating key features, describing variation between sites, or seeking causes for observed effects. Such decisions should facilitate both focusing the evaluation and exclusion of less useful items and issues from interview schedules.

Schedules   Once the detailed objectives of the interview are clearly in mind it will allow the preparation of an *interview schedule* in which questions (form and sequence) and response modes are prepared. The questions must be very carefully devised: see the detailed section below on questionnaire design criteria and common pitfalls. While these criteria are very important they are slightly less critical in interviews because there is always the possibility of repair should a question 'go wrong'.

Apart from their form, one must decide if questions can be omitted, or others added, and if the order is appropriate. For this purpose, it is useful to write questions on cards at the pilot stage so that the question sequence can be readily adapted. Piloting is *essential* in preparing questions, as relevant responses cannot otherwise be guaranteed (see 'Piloting', section 6.3.3).

Sampling   Along with the interview schedule itself, the evaluator has to prepare a sampling plan in which he/she has decided the number and characteristics of informants to be seen. He/she also must decide when and how often to see them in the light of logistical constraints balanced against validity criteria: for example, periodic contacts may be demanding of resources but can build rapport and can also allow fresh and therefore credible accounts of current activity. They would therefore be very suitable when closely monitoring implementation. If a single retrospective interview is to be held, perhaps for logistical reasons or as a validity check, then it is most important for the credibility of the data that the time gap between the interviewee's relevant experiences and the interview is as short as possible. These considerations apply to both insider and outsider evaluations but this is an area in which compromises may be forced upon them.

Question types   Questions are likely to be of five general types (Bell 1987: 58–60, Patton 1987b: 118–20):

1   Opinion/belief

    Examples: What do you think is the best textbook available to you?
                What is your opinion on the present school leaving examination?
                In your view, why did so few teachers use group work?

Their aim is to elicit people's goals, intentions, desires, and values. They require considerable self-disclosure which informants may not be prepared to undergo, and may also change over time.

2   Feeling

    Example: How do you feel about using drills?

Their aim is to uncover the emotional responses of people to their experiences, and the perceived behaviour of others. The interviewer is looking for 'adjectival responses' – sad, happy, pleased, etc. They require rapport with the interviewer, can be quite unstable in nature according to contemporary events, and in some cultures may be subject to strong taboos.

3   Knowledge

    Examples: What is covered in your official syllabus?
                What age range are your children?

Their aim is to obtain facts, or to assess the informant's knowledge of relevant topics.

4   Experience/behaviour

    Examples: What techniques do you use to teach speaking skills?
                How do you usually introduce a new grammar point?

Their aim is to elicit experiences, behaviours, actions, and activities. In the case of teachers, they can on occasions report what they think they do or what they think they should do rather than what they actually do. In other words, they describe their 'espoused theory' rather than their real practice. Triangulation is therefore required to confirm this information.

5   Context

Examples: How many years have you been at this school?
Where were you trained?
What year groups do you teach?

Their aim is to build a factual profile of informants. Relevance must be balanced against respecting the informant's privacy.

Question sequencing   On the whole it is best to start an interview with questions that are least demanding to recall and require least interpretation. For example, questions about the present tend to be more readily answered than those about past or future. Similarly, context or experience questions would be preferable to opinion questions. This is so as to put the interviewee at his/her ease and not to challenge him/her to self-disclose or express an opinion at the outset. It is also to provide a shared factual basis for the subsequent elicitation of interpretations, opinions, and feelings about these facts.

Probes and reacting   Probing is a means to elaborate on an initial response. King et al. (1987) illustrate how this can be done by picking up a point or verbatim phrase from the interviewee and asking him/her to elaborate on it, either through open questioning or a general request to elaborate on a point. They suggest frequently used probes such as: 'Can you tell me a bit more about that?', 'Why do you think that happened?', and 'Thank you. Is there anything else?' If you are in doubt about a reply you can simply repeat it to the interviewee to see if they confirm it or change it. Skilful probing requires very careful listening and a sense of when to stop trying to elicit more, when the interviewee either cannot or does not want to go further. Similarly, one must prepare strategies in the event of aggressive or defensive responses from the interviewee.

Response modes   According to the type of interview, different means will be used to record responses. In an informal interview, this may be entirely unstructured: a blank piece of paper for verbatim notes, or a tape recording. In a more formal interview, where greater reliability and comparability of the data are required, then structured response categories are appropriate, and the respondent can be asked to provide short answers to specific questions, to complete sentences, or to select from certain fixed alternatives presented to him. These could include:

- Completing a rating scale of agreement or frequency
- Ticking items in a checklist
- Rank ordering
- True/false choices

Recording responses The general principle in recording what is said is to ensure that you can understand what you have written when the interview is over, that the format used is suitable to the question item, and that you know before you record anything how you will analyse it. Recording interviewees' responses presents greater problems in the less structured, informal interview. Either tape recording or detailed verbatim notes are suitable. Tape recording provides an objective and complete record but it can make some interviewees uncomfortable, and taping without the interviewee's permission is not ethically acceptable. Furthermore, taping commits you to at least three hours' transcription to each hour of interview and far more if you do not have a transcriber, or if there are audibility problems. An effective alternative, if the interviewee is happy with it, is to employ a 'scribe', seated out of the interviewee's line of vision, who provides a full record, releases the interviewer to concentrate on the interview itself, and allows the possibility of checking the data afterwards. If the interviewer depends on his/her own notes taken during the interview then they must be written up as soon after the interview as possible to minimize inaccuracies. The writing-up process is also time consuming, and there is the risk that the data will be 'skewed' if the interviewer summarizes or rephrases the actual record. The account eventually produced should be verified by the interviewee, especially if it is to be quoted in a report.

Informal interviews generate unstructured, 'narrative' data, and an explicit method *must* be used to organize, reduce and, if appropriate, quantify the occurrence of certain categories or items in the data. The alternative, an unprincipled selection from the content, would risk generating a version of the interview which merely confirms the analyst's assumptions and expectations. (See King et al. 1987: 120–3 for helpful advice on this; see also references in section 6.4.)

Pitfalls There are well-known, common pitfalls in interviewing (see also the following section on questionnaires and Bell 1987, on which this section is closely based):

1 Unclear questions: Questions should be clear and unambiguous. If the respondent finds difficulty with questions, repeat or rephrase them.
2 Leading questions: Avoid leading questions such as 'How happy are you about the course?' This focuses the respondent on satisfaction when you want to know their opinion along a scale (satisfaction – dissatisfaction). Open questions are preferable when seeking this type of information, e.g. 'How do you feel about . . . ?', 'Would you like to comment on . . . ?', 'What do you think is the reason for . . . ?' Leading closed option questions should similarly be avoided, e.g. 'Did you enjoy the course?'
3 'Portmanteau' questions: Ask one question at a time and avoid complex 'multi-part' questions. The interviewee will be confused by several questions in one and later interpretation of answers will be difficult.
4 Inattention: *Attend* to the interviewee: this means listening *and* looking, as well

as showing interest and attention to the interviewee. You should give support and reinforcement to encourage the volunteering of ideas and information.

5 Talking too much: Do not talk too much yourself. An interview is *not* a discussion. The interviewee does not necessarily want to hear your views and you are not there to give them.

6 Interruptions: Do not close a response too soon by summarizing or asking another question: allow the interviewee time. You may need to change topic if the interviewee is particularly long-winded or if the conversation is completely 'off the track'. This should be done politely and if you intervene, do so at a 'natural' point, such as a pause. Do not interrupt or redirect to confirm your own views or some point you particularly hoped the interview would bring up.

Interviewers Where a sample size is representative but large, additional interviewers may need to be engaged. However, principled decisions should be made as to who is to be selected, and how, and the skills that they are expected to have. Furthermore, additional staff should be in sympathy with the method being used by the evaluator. It is for this reason that formal interviews are often the safest type to use when additional staff have been engaged.

Piloting As in all forms of data collection, it is *essential* to pilot the interview, in order to discover unanticipated difficulties in the questions, in recording, or in analysing data. It will also develop fluency and skill if the interviewer is inexperienced. Interviewees at a pilot stage should be a small, randomly selected sample of the real population, with colleagues simulating in a 'pre-pilot' trial. (See section 6.3.3 on piloting of questionnaires and discussion on general considerations in the Introduction to part III.)

6.2.4 Conduct of the interview

Before the interview

1 Arrange to meet the interviewee (or interviewees if it is a group interview), securing all necessary permissions and warning respondents when you will be coming, and explain how confidentiality will be kept.

2 Arrange for a location in which you will not be overheard or interrupted.

3 Ensure that you have covered all the points under 'Planning' above.

On the day of the interview

4 Arrive on time with the interview instrument (which should contain a statement of purpose, a reminder of the confidentiality ground rules, and a principled order for the interview).

5 Try to arrange for seating which promotes relaxed conversation. For example,

do not have a big table between you; sit at a comfortable distance apart; lighting should not be too strong or on the interviewee(s). You should also guard against distractions and interruptions.

6 If necessary, you should introduce yourself and explain why you are visiting: interviewees have the right to know why they are being questioned. It is *essential* to be honest about what you are doing, the way you are doing it and the way you will report it. You must explain how the confidentiality of the interview will be respected. Describe the report you will make and how the information the respondent gives you might affect the programme. Explain what will be expected of the respondent(s) during the interview and say how much time you will be taking up.

7 In general, you should begin by trying to put the interviewee(s) at ease. A successful interview depends on the trust the interviewer inspires. Positive attending signals and a friendly but neutral manner promote full and candid responses: the interviewee(s) should not feel subject to judgement. It is essential to exhibit *genuine respect* for the interviewee, much of which is communicated through your body language and kinesics such as voice pitch and intonation.

8 Pauses and silences can be very important to allow thinking time: you should not always fill them too quickly. If there is a long pause or a non-reaction to a question, then do not overreact but reformulate your question or move to a different topic.

9 If you want to change topics, indicate this clearly to the interviewee(s).

10 Keep to the agreed time: it is an aspect of respect for the interviewee(s), and it also avoids inconveniencing the interviewee(s) or others who may need the room you are using.

11 Thank the interviewee(s) for their time.

After the interview

12 Send follow-up letters of thanks and, where relevant, also thank those who arranged access.

13 Regarding the dissemination of the evaluation results, you should only promise what you can deliver (e.g. a digest of results or a record of the interview rather than a full copy of the report).

In all matters, the guiding values are respect for the informants and the concern to obtain truthful accounts.

6.3 Questionnaire

Many of the points made regarding interviews hold true for the use of questionnaires, especially as regards the nature and framing of questions. Some repetition in this section is therefore unavoidable. The dissimilarities between the two methods largely derive from their medium: oral and interactive as compared with written and 'one-way'.

Questionnaires often have the following advantages:

- They are a cheaper and more cost-efficient form of enquiry than interviewing.
- They allow wider sampling.
- They ask everybody the same questions.
- They provide anonymity.
- They give more time to think about answers.
- They may prove easier to analyse.

However, they can also have some drawbacks:

- They may be affected by low response rates.
- They require respondents to write at length if open questions are included.
- They are often completed in a rush.
- They present difficulties in making questions clear and unambiguous.
- They lack flexibility.
- They may allow the possibility of collusion between respondents.

6.3.1   Questionnaire items

The development of good items in a questionnaire is a mixture of art, science, common sense, and practice (Bell 1987: 58–69) and is usually dependent on adequate piloting (see below). Your questionnaire should meet the following criteria (see Introduction to part III for additional discussion on these and other general considerations in design and implementation).

Validity   Establish first exactly what it is that you need to find out and whether a questionnaire is the most suitable method for doing so. Questions must relate directly to the purpose of the enquiry. For example, if your purpose is to determine the target situation language needs to cope with academic study in the United Kingdom, it could be that frequency information ('How often do you do X?') is less useful than importance information, e.g. in establishing students' language needs ('How important is it to be able to do X?'). Students may not perform an activity very often, such as an oral presentation, but this may be very important. They may only write exams at the end of their course but this may be the sole form of assessment. The questionnaire contained in appendix 6.2.1 could be improved in this respect.

Reliability   Ensure the questions are answerable (for example, by ensuring that rubrics are clear, unambiguous, and accessible, and by piloting the questions). Your aim is to minimize the potential for erroneous responses in your final version

Figure 6.1 A flow chart technique for question planning. *Source:* Cohen and Manion 1980: 104

of the questionnaire. To do this, you need to engage informants' interest and cooperation, and to elicit answers as close to the truth as possible.

Practicality Ask for the minimum information required. Make it as simple as possible for respondents to complete and return the questionnaire; for example, by providing a stamped, addressed envelope.

Types of question

Having first identified the topics and specific information required, questions may be generated during an exploratory phase (see 'Model stages' in section 6.3.4) or from the literature, or from the investigators themselves. To plan the sequencing of questions, use the use flow chart technique (see figure 6.1).

Open responses It is useful in first drafts with a limited sample to start with more open-ended questions because they can obtain richer, more divergent information that is not limited to the areas pre-determined by the evaluator. These data should provide the researcher with the descriptive categories for more structured responses in the questionnaire proper. Open items may still be combined with closed items in the final questionnaire where explanatory or illustrative data is required (e.g. 'If no, please give your reasons').

Closed responses These can be answered by yes/no choices, or ticking off from categories (e.g. rating scales, lists, categories, quantities, a grid). Closed responses generate discrete and convergent data which is usually easier to compare and analyse than that from open-ended, unstructured questions (Bell 1987: 59–60 provides a full description of these; also helpful are Oppenheim 1992 and Youngman 1986.). Their validity of course depends upon an adequate prior open stage in developing the questions. Closed questions in themselves provide less information in depth. Low (1988) provides an insightful discussion on the semantics of the rating scales often employed in closed responses and provides thoughtful advice on the labelling of midpoints, the differential gradability of adjectives, and some limitations of Likert-type questions.

Types of question to avoid

The following badly written questions are imaginary and may seem self-evident or even silly but errors of this type are almost always made in first attempts at questionnaires. Clearly, questions of this kind would contaminate your findings.

1 Leading

   Examples: Have you stopped boring your students?
             Do you favour the use of games?

   Here, the form of the question suggests the response to the informant.
2 Difficult to answer

   Examples: How many students pass the English paper in the School Leaving
             Certificate?
             What grades did students get at FCE in your school?
             How proficient is a student with Cambridge Proficiency?

   Respondents may not be able to answer challenging or specialized factual questions.
3 Ambiguous

   Example: To what extent are you involved with the institute's curriculum?

In this case, the meaning of 'involved' is open to different interpretations: in general, avoid words that can be interpreted differently by different people.

4 Over-general

Example: What difficulties do intermediate students have?

Questions may need to be more concrete, and more clearly related to the experience of the informant.

5 Double questions

Example: Do you teach English in grades 8 and 9?

In this case, the meaning of a 'yes' or 'no' answer is ambiguous.

6 Double negatives

Example: I would not do X if:
   a) Y was the case
   b) Y was not the case

These are likely to confuse the informant!

7 Offensive

Examples: Do you feel you are too old to be a teacher?
   Do you think your government is doing an adequate job in education?

No wording should be objectionable in any way to the respondent. Also, a stereotyped or defensive response may result from an emotional reaction to the question.

8 Presumptuous

Example: What communicative exercises do you use with your students?

In this case, there is an unwarranted assumption about the informant, which may be resented or may act as a leading question.

9 Hypothetical

Example: If you had all the resources you wanted, what improvements would you make in your language classes?

Such questions invite speculation and unless this is appropriate to the enquiry they should be excluded.

10   Jargon

    Examples: How often do you finish your turn with a sympathetic circularity
              sequence?
            Do you use pyramid discussions in group work?

    Vocabulary should not be hard to understand or demand specialist knowl-
edge.

6.3.2   Design criteria

Layout and elegance

In general, when writing a questionnaire one is seeking simplicity of design and
clarity of wording (Bell 1987: 64). The questionnaire should be neat, and well
presented (see figure 6.2). It makes a much better impression on informants and
improves response rates when it is well typed, clear, and well laid out. The use of
different coloured paper can clarify the overall structure of the questionnaire.

    The theme of a questionnaire should be clear, with unambiguous instructions so
that respondents understand exactly what is being asked of them. Also, there
should be a clear differentiation between instructions and questions. In layout, the
answer to a question should not be influenced by its position in relation to other
questions, nor by the content of preceding questions.

    You need to keep the questionnaire as short as possible, consistent with the need
to obtain target data. Long questionnaires are likely to have a poor return rate.

    Completion should be made as easy as possible by a means familiar to respondents,
such as ticking in boxes or circling pre-coded numbers in a margin. Responses
should be positioned in the same place to the right of the page, with response
boxes aligned, and free space left for analysis and coding by the evaluation staff.
To criticize your own design you should try to view it as an informant, and also
think ahead to the analysis and use of the responses.

    Questions should be within the frame of reference of the respondents. When
possible, ask specific questions to encourage respondents to think concretely. Also,
you should allow people to admit to being unable to answer the question, by
providing some form of 'don't know' or 'unsure' category.

    Questions should be arranged so as to maximize cooperation on the part of the
respondent: try to put interesting and readily answered questions first, with open
questions at the end if needed. Similarly, the order of questions should be logical.

    At the end of the questionnaire, solicit prompt return and give a target date.
You should provide a stamped, addressed envelope or make it as easy as possible for
questionnaires to be returned. Personal contact may improve the chances of return.

    Ensure that your accompanying letter thanks the informants, guarantees ano-
nymity, and is written in an appropriate style. If return rates are disappointing,
follow-up reminders may encourage non-responders.

Business English Course Questionnaire

Here is a list of activities where you may use English. The numbers on the left are for you to show how important the activity is for your job and the numbers on the right are to show how difficult it is for you.

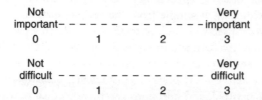

Please circle the number to show your answer.

Example

Important		Difficult
0 1 ②3	Writing telexes	0 1 2③

Please answer all the questions

Important		Difficult
0 1 2 3	Conversation with one person	0 1 2 3
0 1 2 3	Informal meetings	0 1 2 3
0 1 2 3	Giving formal presentations	0 1 2 3
0 1 2 3	Chairing meetings, conferences	0 1 2 3
0 1 2 3	Giving instructions and training	0 1 2 3
0 1 2 3	Reading reports and correspondence	0 1 2 3
* 0 1 2 3	Writing letters	0 1 2 3
0 1 2 3	Writing reports, minutes, instructions	0 1 2 3
0 1 2 3	Telephoning	0 1 2 3
0 1 2 3	Participating in formal meetings	0 1 2 3
0 1 2 3	Following a training course	0 1 2 3
0 1 2 3	Being entertained abroad	0 1 2 3
0 1 2 3	Entertaining foreign visitors	0 1 2 3
0 1 2 3	Reading technical journals, manuals, etc.	0 1 2 3

If there are any activities that have not been mentioned, please add them in the boxes below.

0 1 2 3		0 1 2 3
0 1 2 3		0 1 2 3

Figure 6.2 Business English course questionnaire. *Source:* MATEFL students, CALS, University of Reading

6.3.3   Piloting

Piloting is a crucial stage to iron out faults in your data collection instrument: it is not possible to recover from errors in a full-scale postal questionnaire survey, since it is typically an unrepeatable opportunity. Piloting should be done first on colleagues and then with a small sample from the real population.

Piloting allows you to see whether the method of collecting data is suitable and whether the questions are adequate in terms of clarity, and so on. The efficiency of the instructions, the adequacy of the response categories, and the analysis of the data can all be evaluated. On the basis of pilot results, items that do not provide useable data can be omitted, and questions can be refined so they come closer to producing the information you require. On reviewing the data produced by the pilot questionnaire, ensure you have got all the information you need and that you have done a dummy run analysis on the data.

6.3.4   'Model' stages in data collection: An example from questionnaire survey

The purpose and method of data collection is also affected by its function at various stages of a study. For example, in a large-scale study in which questionnaires are a central element, if logistics allow data collection over a period of time, then there is a certain 'classic' sequence which is commonly followed to obtain the best possible information. This sequence characteristically moves from an exploratory phase (stages 1–3) to focused data collection (4–9) and then ends with an explanatory stage (10) where findings can be validated or explored further prior to the production of the final report. The stages would be as follows.

1   Examine all existing documentation (reports, records of attendance, teaching records, etc.).
2   Do exploratory observation.
3   Do exploratory, unstructured or semi-structured interviews or group discussions.
4   Identify themes, issues, and topics emerging from stages 1–3 and use them as headings for the preliminary organization of the data you have.
5   Write draft question items for structured interviews or questionnaires.
6   Pilot and trial a questionnaire.
7   Conduct interviews as a validity check.
8   Administer the final questionnaire.
9   Analyse data.
10 Conduct follow-up interviews to illuminate or explain questionnaire response patterns.
11 Produce report.

Following these steps would help optimize the data you can obtain. Steps 1–3 help meet challenges to the validity of your data; steps 4–7, to its validity and reliability; further validation and explanation of initial findings can be obtained through step 10.

For further discussion of questionnaires, the reader is referred back to the use made of these in evaluating a language programme, the CALS EAP course, described in chapter 4. We discussed there the value of questionnaire data in giving us a wider perspective on participants' reactions to the course than is available from other means such as interview, tutorials, or group discussion. We also noted that questionnaires cannot be used too frequently or an adverse reaction may set in on the part of respondents. Copies of some of the questionnaires used in evaluating that programme are located in the appendices to that chapter (see appendix 4.4). Some additional useful examples of questionnaires are provided in appendix 6.2.

6.4 Qualitative and quantitative data analysis

As we have argued above (see Introduction to part III), there are no rigid rules to help readers make data collection decisions beyond ensuring that the methods chosen are appropriate to the situation and for the purposes for which information is sought. The qualitative and quantitative dimensions of data need not be isolated from each other, and can be complementary. For example, in section 7.1.3 we suggest the possibility of quantitative observation data acting as a starting point for a qualitative comparison of teaching styles (Delamont 1976). Similarly, we suggested in section 3.7 that summative quantitative data were necessary but not sufficient as evaluation findings, and required qualitative data (e.g. field notes on page 3 of the observation instrument; see figure 7.7) in order to be able to interpret them. As Cronbach (1982) has observed, it is not adequate or desirable to try to compress educational outcomes into a single dimension of measurement (see also section 1.4.6, where limitations of test data for the evaluation of a teacher training project are discussed). Conversely, it is good practice in questionnaire or interview design to start from open-ended elicitation to more focused, quantifiable response categories (see section 6.2.2 for a discussion of this in relation to interview types, and 6.3.1 on types of question; also 6.3.4).

Qualitative methods are often closely associated with naturalistic inductive designs and are guided by a search for patterns rather than by hypotheses (Patton 1987b: 15). They are normally exploratory, descriptive, and discovery oriented in purpose. They try to describe complex events, attitudes, and sets of behaviour in depth and detail. They can take account of unforeseen or diverse reactions and perspectives of stakeholders. They can provide information on how teaching and learning processes actually take place and what they mean to participants. The data may take the form of verbatim descriptions, interviews, written responses, or unstructured observations. Qualitative methods allow depth and flexibility, as in the unstructured interview (see discussion of the method in 6.2.2 above).

Quantitative methods normally rely on constraining people to respond in terms of fixed response categories, as in the example of the summative questionnaire for students used on the CALS EAP programme in appendix 4.4 or the target situation analysis questionnaire for Business English students in figure 6.2. Quantified data tell us the frequency with which certain responses are ascribed to the sample under review and allow us to determine whether these frequencies are reflected in subsamples within the data set – i.e. the extent to which people differ in respect of specific pre-determined critical variables. Patton (1987b: 9–10) observes that:

> The advantage of the quantitative approach is that it measures the reactions of a great many people to a limited set of questions, thus facilitating comparison and statistical aggregation of the data. This gives a broad generalizable set of findings. By contrast, qualitative methods typically produce a wealth of detailed data about a much smaller number of people and cases. Qualitative data provide depth and detail through direct quotation and careful description of program situations, events, people, interactions and observed behaviours. The detailed descriptions, direct quotations and case documentation of qualitative methods are collected as open-ended narrative without attempting to fit program activities or people's experiences into predetermined, standardized categories such as the response choices that constitute typical questionnaires or tests.

6.4.1   Analysis of qualitative data

Qualitative data collected in response to open-ended questions may well be invaluable in the interpretation of events but they are obviously more difficult to code and analyse than the quantifiable data which result from structured questions. The categories of description are inducted from raw data rather than imposed from 'outside' these data on the basis of a pre-determined and circumscribed set of categories. Thus no *a priori* decision is taken as to what is important. A recognized method for analysing data obtained by open-ended questions is to develop, with reference to the data, a number of categories by which they might be coded. (Patton 1987b: 144–64 provides a very useful summary of basic directions for qualitative data analysis.) Other helpful guides to qualitative data collection and content analysis include: Budd et al. (1967), Cook and Campbell (1979), Cook and Reichardt (1979), Fetterman (1988), Guba (1978), Guba and Lincoln (1983), Hatch (1983), Holsti (1969), King et al. (1987: 120–3, Miles and Huberman (1984), and Welch (1983). The extent to which one might generalize from such data is, however, open to debate. Concern about the neutrality or balance of such investigations should also encourage us to triangulate through the use of different methodological procedures in studying the same programme (Cohen and Manion 1980: 254–70 and Patton 1987b: 161–2).

6.4.2 Analysis of quantitative data

The analysis of quantitative data is in some ways easier in that there are clearer procedures laid down for us to follow and the researcher can more readily use standard statistical techniques to search for relationships in the data as well as employing descriptive statistical procedures to summarize patterns in the data (e.g. Bell 1987: chapter 11, Brown 1988, Fitz-Gibbon and Morris 1987a, Hatch and Lazaraton 1991: chapters 5 6, Woods et al. 1986: 8–47).

Display Having obtained the raw quantitative data, it is desirable to summarize the data in tables which can then be represented in a variety of graphic forms (see examples in section 7.3). In this way, any patterns or trends will be made that much more apparent. Often simply 'eyeballing' the data presented in this fashion can give you a reasonable idea of what the data set suggests. See appendix 6.1 for examples of the ways data were summarized in the authors' investigation of the language problems of overseas students studying in Britain. A full discussion of these data appears in Weir (1983, 1988).

The most obvious way of condensing data is to convert numerical data to percentages as in appendices 6.1.3 and 6.1.6, to graphs as in 6.1.4, or to use symbols as in 6.1.6. Appendices 6.1.5–9 illustrate the use made of the raw numerical data from over 1500 students collected in response to question A6.1 in appendix 6.1.5. As a first stage the raw data were mapped onto summary sheets (Bell 1987: 104–17) and then converted to percentages (see appendix 6.1.6). The data relating to this particular difficulty were then displayed as part of an overall picture of the listening comprehension problems encountered by overseas students through condensing the data by using symbols as illustrated in appendix 6.1.8. Further use was made of these data, as illustrated in appendices 6.1.9–10 to indicate the primacy for overseas students of the particular difficulty of understanding when people talk quickly.

There are other ways of representing data and examples of some of these are given in section 7.3. The reader is also referred to Bell (1987: 111–17), Brown (1988: 20–8 and 63–94), Fitz-gibbon and Morris (1987a: 13–30) and Hook (1981: chapter 13) for detailed practical guidance.

6.4.3 Statistical analysis

In some situations you might want to take the analysis further and examine the differences between groups of cases (comparing their means). t-tests and analysis of variance (ANOVA) are the more commonly employed measures for establishing the statistical significance of any differences and the magnitude of those differences (Brown 1988: 154–81, Fitz-Gibbon and Morris 1987a: 38–73 and Woods et al. 1986: 176–93 for t-tests and 194–223 for ANOVA).

In other cases you might want to examine the nature and strength of functional relationships between variables; for this you might wish to establish the correlation coefficient: the degree to which two sets of data vary together (Brown 1988: 126–53, Cohen and Manion 1980: 149–69, Fitz-Gibbon and Morris 1987a: 78–94, Hatch and Lazaraton 1991: chapter 15, Woods et al. 1986: 154–75).

Finally, you might wish to compare frequencies of the number of people who fall into particular categories. Chi-square is a commonly used procedure for this (Brown 1988: 182–97, Fitz-Gibbon and Morris 1987a: 98–104, Woods et al. 1986: 132–53).

6.4.4   Endnote

Controversy has existed about whether to use qualitative or quantitative data. However, the general 'issue' of qualitative versus quantitative methodologies now seems less than contentious, at least in the professional literature. (A further sensible discussion of these issues is provided by Beretta 1986a, 1986b, 1986c, Cook and Reichardt 1979, Cronbach 1982, Hutchinson et al. 1988 and Lynch 1992). Pockets of resistance may still remain, however, especially at the bureaucratic level, with a preference there for 'hard' quantifiable data. Patton (1987b: 169) summarizes the current and widely shared state of opinion:

> A consensus has gradually emerged that the important challenge is to match appropriate methods to evaluation questions and issues, not to advocate universally any single methodological approach for all evaluation situations . . . evaluation has moved into a period of methodological diversity with a focus on methodological appropriateness . . . Today's evaluators must be sophisticated about matching research methods to the nuances of particular evaluation questions, the idiosyncrasies of specific program situations, and the information needs of identifiable stakeholders.

Having examined self-report data in some detail, we now turn in chapter 7 to the use of observational data, certainly a more 'direct' method of collecting information.

NOTE

1   A number of helpful examples of questionnaire and interview instruments and data can be found in Alderson and Beretta (1992: (appendix: 'Evaluation Materials', 305–66) and Gibbs and Haigh (1984). Borg and Gall (1989), Fink and Kosecoff (1985), Labaw (1980), Molenaar (1982), Oppenheim (1992), and Slembrouck (1987) are good sources for detail about developing questionnaires. Useful advice and guidelines on interviewing can be found in Briggs (1986), Fowler and Mangione (1990), Millar et al. (1992), Moser

and Kalton (1971), Patton (1987b: 108–43), Powney and Watts (1987), Simons (1982a), Walker (1985) and Wragg (1980). Bradburn and Sudman (1983), Fink and Kosecoff (1985), Fowler (1989) and Youngman (1986) provide useful advice on the design and use of self-report instruments and the analysis of data resulting from these methods of enquiry. For useful discussion of all aspects of planning and implementation of surveys we have found Cohen and Manion (1980) to be an excellent reference work on interviewing and questionnaires, and we would recommend it to anyone collecting information by these means.

7 Classroom Observation

7.1 First principles

7.1.1 Introductory

This chapter concerns the use of classroom observation procedures to evaluate programme implementation, illustrated in sections 7.2 and 7.3 by its use in an evaluation for accountability (see chapter 3). As it is based on our experience in external summative evaluations, the procedures we have described below reflect the level of rigour required in these types of evaluation design. These systematic procedures can also have their place for insider, formative evaluation purposes: instruments developed by external evaluators could also be exploited by insider staff for their own purposes. For example, the observation procedures we developed for the Nepal study could be adapted for other comparable teacher training programmes (obviously modified to take account of different criterial features of training obtaining in that context). Indeed, this has already occurred in projects in Guinea (see Weir and Burton forthcoming) and Bangladesh. The reader should note that the more time efficient and less formal procedures that can be adopted for formative evaluation by insiders working under pressure of time are given less attention here. Field notes, checklists, annotated classroom plans all belong in this category. This is not to imply that such methods are unimportant or not of practical value. Indeed, some reference is made elsewhere to the use of these methods for developmental purposes (see section 1.4.6, appendix 1.2, and appendix 7.1). Rea-Dickens and Germaine (1992) provide much helpful guidance for teachers on these less structured, practical methods suited to formative evaluation. Hook (1981) also gives thorough and practical guidance to teachers on the flexible uses of checklists and other observation methods for developmental purposes. Other useful background ELT publications in this area are referred to at the end of this chapter.[1]

As already discussed in the Introduction to part III, observation is the only way to get *direct* information on classroom events, on the reality of programme implementation. This can be used to assess the achievement of programme objectives and to illuminate participants' expressed perceptions and beliefs. By getting into classrooms, external evaluators learn about the real life of a programme and how participants interact and relate to each other. From the formative standpoint, self- and peer observation is also a valuable tool in internal development oriented evaluation (see appendix 7.1). However, systematic observation is demanding and presents difficult theoretical and practical problems, discussed below. It also re- quires considerable resources and skills.

The first section of this chapter presents some key concepts and issues in doing classroom observation. The second section presents the steps needed to plan observations, while the third gives a detailed 'worked example' of quantitative data analysis and presentation. Observational data collection is also referred to in chapters 3, 4 and 5.

7.1.2 Selective description and explicit systems

Twenty five years ago I tried to bring home the same point to a group of physics students in Vienna by beginning a lecture with the following in- structions: 'Take pencil and paper, carefully observe, and write down what you have observed'. They asked, of course, what I wanted them to observe. Clearly the instruction, 'Observe' is absurd. . . .

. . . Observation is always selective. It needs a chosen object, a definite task, an interest, a point of view, a problem. And its description presupposes a descriptive language, with property words; it presupposes similarity and classification, which in turn presupposes interests, points of view, and prob- lems. (Open University 1979: 21)

We cannot report everything we observe. We have to select, and selection is directed by prior decisions as to what is relevant and significant. These decisions must derive from prior theoretical or value assumptions. This is as true of un- structured observations (see 7.1.5) as it is of structured category-based systems, such as interaction analysis (see 7.2.4), of which Long (1980: 12) comments: 'observational instruments are, in fact, no more (or less) than theoretical claims about second language learning and teaching'.

It must be noted that the selectiveness of the observer will tend to pre-determine the nature of the data that he/she presents, which may then reinforce the observer's prior theoretical assumptions through the exclusion of alternative data. However, some stakeholders may not share the assumptions which determine the observer's selection and so they could contest the selection as biased. For this reason, obser- vational data should be obtained by a system capable of description to others. Otherwise, these data may be seen as no more than a reflection of the observer's personal expectations. In the case of evaluation for accountability, there is an *absolute* need for an evaluator to be recognized as independent and unbiased. For these reasons, the basis for selection in observations must be made explicit when reporting results (see section 7.1.6). Furthermore, given that stakeholders' interests may be affected by his/her findings, the evaluator must anticipate criticisms of the validity and reliability of the data he/she presents (see section 7.1.7), plan how to meet these criteria, and account for them in the report (see also chapters 1 and 8).

7.1.3 Quantitative and qualitative categories of description

Quantitative observational data can be expressed numerically. They are obtained by coding talk and behaviour according to a limited set of pre-determined categories (see chapter 3). Where low-inference categories are used (see section 7.1.4), relatively objective and reliable data can be obtained. Quantification allows comparison between groups and individuals according to a standard measure, and where sample sizes are large enough, it enables statistical inferencing to identify objective patterns and trends (e.g. Ross 1992, Spada 1990). The pie charts in figure 7.1, for example, represent two lessons contrasted by Bowers's system coding: 'The first is of a lesson comprising presentation of a new structure to the class, followed by some controlled drills. . . . The second is of a lesson based on a translation exercise from a course book. Note the differences between the two lesson patterns' (Malamah-Thomas 1987: 55).

However, there are also considerable limitations to observational data based on the frequency of pre-determined categories (fully discussed in Delamont and Hamilton 1976). While quantification can reveal objective patterns and contrasts in the frequency of discourse and activity features, it does not follow that what is *infrequent* is necessarily insignificant. Also, quantification cannot explain what these discourse and behavioral patterns mean to teachers and learners. This requires consultation and interpretation, a value-loaded process. Also, the construction of observational categories is not objective, as discussed in section 7.1.2. Finally, not all categories used in coding processes are themselves entirely objective: where they refer to intention, then their interpretation rests upon the observer. Therefore, while the analysis of quantified data may be objective, the interpretation of categories may not be, and the initial selection of categories is not. (See section 7.2 on the development of observation categories.)

In comparison, qualitative data categories are descriptive and narrative in nature, referring to motives, intentions and the meaning of utterances and actions to participants. Naturalistic method,[2] associated with qualitative data categories, is one in which the observer begins from a set of general evaluation issues or questions, but does *not* attempt to work from pre-determined categories of description. The aim is to produce a valid, 'programme fair' description (Beretta 1986b) of indigenous and relevant issues, variables, and categories. In this approach, the first phase would be open, to describe the programme as it really is by diverse and responsive methods (Parlett and Hamilton 1977, Patton 1980, 1987b) which could

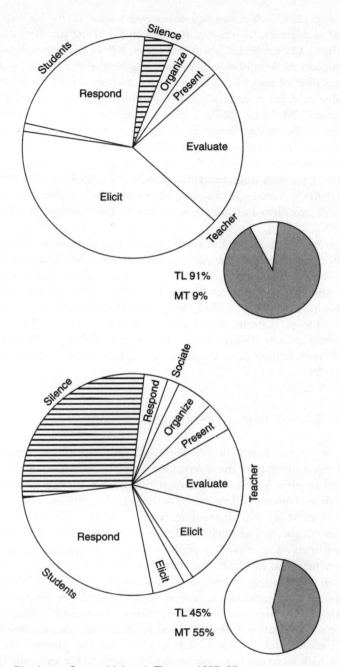

Figure 7.1 Pie charts. *Source:* Malamah-Thomas 1987: 55

combine observation, self-report and documentary analysis. At this stage, a combination of unstructured description (see section 7.1.5) and provisional checklists
could be used. Once relevant issues and patterns have been discovered, further
analysis can take the form of more systematic and focused description, which could
include quantitative measures. Categories for analysis should be inferred from
unstructured description, and rigorously tested for their contextual validity (Miles
and Huberman 1984, Patton 1987b), a process demanding validation by stakeholders.

However, qualitative data categories contain their own limitations. The observer/
analyst's own 'world view' is certain to affect both the data and the classification
terms used in description, so that the description still should be recognized as an
interpretive rather than sbsolute account. Rigour in the analysis of qualitative data
therefore requires system and criticism, otherwise there is a great danger that the
observer will only discover whatever it was he/she hoped to find in the first place
(Patton 1987b).

There is no necessary conflict between these two dimensions of description.
Quantifiable, low-inference data such as category frequencies have to be understood in terms of the reality of classroom life and the meanings they have for
insiders. Similarly, narrative description is usually capable of representation by
quantifiable indicators of some kind, though the relevance of these indicators must
be confirmed by participants themselves. Lynch (1992) gives us a helpful account
of using combined data of different sources and types. Delamont (1976) also shows
the use of quantification prior to qualitative explanation in studying contrasting
teaching styles.

7.1.4   Low- and high-inference observations

'Pupil comes to the board' or 'Teacher says: "It's a pen" six times' are low-
inference observations, since the observer has described behaviours. A low-inference
observation requires little or no interpretation by the observer and so there is
relatively little room for differences of description by different observers. High-
inference observations are, for example: 'Pupils did not understand'; 'The lesson
was too slow in pace'; 'The pupils used their mother tongue because they did not
know what to do'. Typically, they apply to motives, mental states, and the interpretation of particular incidents. Such categories of description have been inferred
through the selection and interpretation of a complex of observed behaviours. As
inferencing entails interpretation, it must be influenced by an observer's expectations, which derive from his/her past experience of comparable events, and his/
her theoretical orientation. Categories used in structured, category-based observation (see sections 7.1.3, 7.1.5 and 7.2.4) may be either low inference (e.g. 'teacher
smiles') or high inference (e.g. 'teacher is enthusiastic'). For example, its authors
have divided the TALOS instrument (Ullman and Geva 1984), into separate high-
and low-inference sections (see figure 7.4 for an extract of the high-inference
section where the majority of the categories are high inference in nature and the

ratings require subjective estimation). High-inference categories allow more diver-gent interpretation by observers than low-inference because they will tend to carry different meanings for different individuals (e.g. 'pace', 'communicative', 'interest-ing'). They can readily be challenged as unreliable or open to bias as a result. It is evident that low-inference observations will be relatively less open to challenge on the grounds of observer bias. However, their initial selection and their validity are equally open to challenge on the grounds of relevance and fairness to the context and to teachers' values and objectives. It is for this reason that low-inference observation categories were central to our approach to observation in the Nepal study (see section 3.2.3 and appendix 3.3) and care was taken to base the categories on criterial features of the training programme. We also complemented the use of low-inference categories with methods based on higher inference categories, namely field notes, and a short checklist of criterial features.

7.1.5 Structured and unstructured observation

A structured observation method, such as a coding system or checklist, will use pre-determined categories of description, and other data selection criteria such as time samples, nature of subjects, and so on. Unstructured methods put no prior restrictions on an observer as to the categories of description employed, who is observed, with what duration, and so on. The instrument for wholly unstructured observation is a blank piece of paper!

Selection in unstructured observation is led by the observer's theory as to what is significant and this theory may have to be inferred by the reader, rather than be explicitly stated by the observer. Where a structured method is used, the structure itself indicates the theory upon which a description is based, though too often this theory is otherwise left inexplicit.

Unstructured observation is appropriate at an exploratory stage of investigation, when the observer is trying to become familiar with a context, and trying to discover variables that are relevant in it. As such, it is a tool in a naturalistic approach to description. Unstructured description need not necessarily be im-pressionistic and informal. It can be systematic and rigorous if disciplined procedures of analysis and validation are employed. (Miles and Huberman 1984 provide a detailed account of strategies to achieve this.) It should not be confused with informal or *ad hoc* observations, in which there is no real control on observer bias.

Structured observation is appropriate once a valid focus for observation has been identified. It lends itself to quantification and comparison between individuals and groups. Its main danger is lack of validity: that the prior choice of categories might exclude critical features from the data. This is a particular risk to an evaluation if an existing instrument has been 'borrowed' rather than designed especially for an evaluation. Borrowing an instrument may be a good time-saver, but it is also risky: it is unlikely that an existing instrument was designed for exactly the same purposes as your own evaluation unless you are engaged in some kind of replication exercise. Therefore it may not provide relevant data.

7.1.6   The principle of triangulation

When data are obtained by a human rather than a machine, we cannot rely on their accuracy as we would on a thermometer or a seismograph. We need to corroborate its accuracy by checking it against other sources. This is the process of *triangulation*, in which independent measures are made of the same subject, and their degree of consistency assessed (Cohen and Manion 1980: chapter 11). Consistency may be possible at a level of direct corroboration. For example, a teacher may report students producing written work of a certain kind, and this work may be available for inspection. Where direct confirmation is not available, then the evaluator may have to rely upon findings which are indirectly related but mutually consistent. For example, a teacher may refer to using group work in written self-report as in the Nepal study (see section 3.2.3) and also be able to give evidence of this in interviews (for example, by showing experience of practical problems of implementation). This would be a case where 'the results from any one of your instruments coincide logically with results from other implementation measures' (King et al. 1987: 55).

Equally important as this search for confirmation is the search for negative cases when data presented by one measure (for example, coding of talk) may be contradicted by another (such as self-report). Where inconsistencies are found, the evaluator is faced with the problem of assessing which data may be right, and how to resolve contradictions. This could entail checking back for sources of bias, or noting previously unrecognized variables. The discrepancy may uncover a mismatch between what teachers claim to be doing and what they actually are doing (Argyris and Schon 1976). The use of such data must be highly circumspect, since the confrontation of a teacher with such discrepancies represents a major intervention: the teacher may find this confrontation threatening and disorientating, and would need support and discussion to be able to come to terms with it.

For reasons of limited time, it is possible that triangulation will be done on a 'spot check' or sample basis rather than of all the data, a fact which should be acknowledged in the evaluation report.

Observational data can be triangulated by obtaining data on the same questions by alternative means. Individual observations can be triangulated by joint observations, transcription, and comparison of items.

Joint observation   If resources allow, independent observations may be done in pairs, a practice which enhances their reliability, assuming adequate observer training has ensured that both are equally consistent in their judgements.

Transcription   The analysis of transcribed classroom talk may be an option as a data source but while it is very 'fine grained' and objective in nature, it is laborious, time consuming and expensive to do. If it can be done, perhaps on a smaller sample of the whole data, then it provides a record against which rival accounts and interpretations may be compared and their accuracy assessed. Conflicting interpretations may not always be resolved by reference to a transcript, however, as some observed behaviour may be interpretable in differing ways.

Item consistency Observation instruments can contain their own internal checks. The basis for this should be low-inference items (e.g. codings, behavioral checklists) capable of contrast with more global or high-inference measures (e.g. global checklists or field notes – see section 7.3).

Observational information can also be cross-referenced against other types of information, such as self-report or documents.

Self-report Teachers' and students' accounts of lessons (by interview, questionnaire, or unstructured written description) can be matched with other measures, either for direct corroboration or for logical consistency. The tendency of respondents to contrive accounts in the direction of an ideal or model must be recognized. In interviews, interviewees typically look for cues from the interviewer so as to provide the 'right' answers. In questionnaires, there is a tendency to 'yea saying'. However, a number of independent informants are unlikely to consistently report what they do not do or do not know about, as we felt was shown in our teacher self-report data in the Nepal study (section 3.7).

Documents Records can be reliable sources for direct corroboration or logical consistency – for example, by comparing teachers' notes and student work against observers' descriptions. However, documents have inherent limitations (see Introduction to part III).

7.1.7 Validity and reliability in observation

Findings in an evaluation can be challenged on two counts: whether they are reliable (consistent between occasions or between informants) and whether they are valid (accurate, relevant).

Reliability

One can apply three measures of reliability, following Medley and Mitzel (1963): a stability coefficient, an observer agreement coefficient, and a repeated measure reliability coefficient.

A *stability coefficient* compares measures made by the same observer on different occasions of the same event. It is a measure of intra-observer reliability. It is an appropriate measure in the video-based training of observers because the same recorded class can be observed twice. However, it would not be appropriate for describing a class in a school on different occasions, as these events are not comparable. An educational programme does not remain still so that it can be measured (King et al. 1987). Furthermore, although in training this measure may indicate consistency in judgement (i.e. reliability), it would not necessarily be valid (i.e. the observer may be consistently inaccurate in the completion of a checklist or in coding classroom talk).

In establishing the reliability of observations, it is also usual to give evidence of inter-observer reliability. An *observer agreement coefficient* compares observations made by different observers of the same classroom event, occurring on a single occasion. A high level of agreement indicates inter-observer reliability. Again, however, this measure does not indicate validity (a true representation of what is taking place). Observers may agree but may not necessarily have recorded all the relevant data. It is thus important to take steps to ensure the validity of the measures being used by other means (e.g. prior identification of criterial features by all concerned stakeholders, and prior confirmation that the instrument is actually measuring what it is supposed to measure). Once the evaluators are confident of the validity of their instruments, then it becomes necessary to demonstrate their reliability. An instrument cannot be valid if it cannot be used reliably.

In other fields of enquiry, such as language testing, reliability is often established by administering the same instrument on different occasions to the same person. While a person's language performance may remain constant in the short term between two occasions, a teacher's performance and interaction in the same classroom may vary considerably from occasion to occasion. Therefore, this type of *repeated measure reliability* is not appropriate for use with real-time observational data.

Intra- and *inter-observer* reliability measures would, however, seem to be appropriate in most evaluation contexts, with the former advisable for observer training and the latter the best available means when collecting real-time classroom data. (For one method of calculation see section 7.3, step 8.)

Validity

In order to meet validity criteria, observations should meet the following conditions:

1   Observations provide an accurate record of what took place. This means that observation measures should indicate significant features in behaviour.
2   Observation data are relevant to the characteristic features of the programme.
3   Observation data are complete, in that the whole programme is fairly reflected (Beretta 1986b).

Given that evaluations take place under field conditions, it may be problematic to meet all these criteria. However, it is essential that the evaluator attends to these criteria, takes optimum measures to satisfy them, and provides an account of these measures in the final evaluation report. To meet validity criteria, one has to anticipate and control for sources of bias.

Sources of bias: The observer Observer bias is liable to affect description where observers have a strong stake in findings, or where instruments are unstructured, or where high-inference categories or unstructured instruments are used. Personal interests can affect what observers selectively attend to and how they interpret specific events. Furthermore, high-inference or unstructured instruments are susceptible to divergent interpretation even by disinterested parties (Brown 1975: chapter 1). In summative evaluation for contractual accountability (see chapter 3) or for formal professional accountability (see chapter 4) where it is necessary to control for this source of bias, it is essential to engage neutral observers: people who have nothing to gain from the results of the observation, with no stake in the outcome of the evaluation or the success or failure of the programme under review (King et al. 1987). Equally important as the validity of the data they can provide is the fact that such observers should be *seen* as neutral by stakeholders, who will therefore be less likely to repudiate their findings on grounds of bias in what may be a politically sensitive study.

It does seem that eliminating bias is less critical in insider observations for formative purposes, in the sense that the use of findings is normally within the institution. Nevertheless, the insider observation will be that much more effective if this source of bias can be minimized. This means that the practical expediency of some more informal methods (field notes or hastily and thereby poorly constructed checklists) has to be weighed against potential threats to their reliability and validity. Philpott (1993) and Linder (1991) show how systematic measures can be used by teachers to good effect in insider programme development. As has been shown in the field of action research (Day et al. 1987, Hustler et al. 1986, Roberts 1993) the presence of a critical audience can greatly enhance self-evaluation by motivating a more objective and systematic approach. Having to present your account either verbally or in writing to a 'third party' demands a degree of explicitness and clarity which might otherwise be missing. From our experiences we have come to feel that insider data collection for an outside audience (the external evaluator or the funding agency) may benefit in the same way, particularly where a common set of instruments has been developed.

Sources of bias: The observer effect The presence of an observer will have some initial effects on the behaviour of teachers and learners. This may result from distraction. More significantly, it may result from 'impression management': participants may avoid actions they perceive as risking poor self-presentation, or they may contrive to do what they think is wanted of them. For example, a lesson may be abandoned in favour of an 'all purpose' revision class, or teachers who customarily use mother tongue may not do so when observed. In spite of these strong pressures, classes tend to revert to normal when the observer becomes a familiar presence and when teachers and learners become engaged in their tasks. This is because much classroom discourse is based upon strongly habituated routines followed by both teachers and learners (Doyle 1977). The observer effect can be minimized by:

1 the engagement of neutral observers;
2 training of observers to be as unobtrusive as possible; and
3 making a sufficient number of observations. As a rule of thumb, King et al. (1987) suggest six. However, the number of visits should not be based on a 'magic number' of observations per class but on resources and the known variability between classes.

Sources of bias: Observation instruments With structured methods, the instrument used will pre-determine the nature of the data obtained. Therefore, the instrument itself should not be vulnerable to criticism for inaccuracy or irrelevance. As Davies (1992) suggests, there is a danger of cutting short the time necessary to refine the observation instrument in the breathless pursuit of data. The criticism of irrelevance can be best met by the selection of criterial features that have been validated by insiders (see also section 7.3 and chapter 3). The criticism of inaccuracy can be met in a number of ways.

1 Pilot the instrument sufficiently to ensure that its design does not cause inaccuracies, such as by giving insufficient time to code or make notes, or by requiring too many simultaneous recording processes.
2 Guidelines should be provided which ensure consistent and systematic procedures of observation.
3 Items within the instrument should be capable of cross-referencing so that internal consistency can be taken as evidence of accuracy.
4 Low-inference items should be included in the instrument.
5 All the categories employed should be unambiguous and mutually exclusive (Hook 1981: 51–3).
6 Category definitions and operational descriptions should be available in an observation manual.

7.1.8 Sampling

Observation findings may be challenged because the sampling is perceived as unrepresentative or skewed. To evaluate a programme fairly, one has to try to obtain data subject to the range of variations under which the programme is carried out. There can be extreme variations which should be reflected in sampling: for instance, there are important qualitative differences between urban and rural schooling in some settings. However, some compromise may be demanded by costs, time, and logistics. Some compensation for this problem may be achieved by:

1 Adopting a sampling strategy which can claim validity in its own terms. For example, a study might match relatively small control and experimental samples according to criteria agreed by participants (see chapter 4). Alternatively,

a relatively small selection of schools might be chosen for case study description (Yin 1989).

2 Triangulating observational data with interviews or questionnaires, which can represent a larger sample.

As in other aspects of evaluation method, an explicit description of sampling criteria must be presented in the final report (Joint Committee 1981).

7.1.9 Logistical constraints

Conducting an adequate number of observations often requires a considerable number of observer/man days, particularly if schools are widely scattered. In a study of any size, additional observers may need to be recruited (see chapter 3). This adds greatly to costs and to the demands on evaluators who have to train and monitor these 'technical staff' (King et al. 1987). In some cases, a combination of a lack of resources and poor planning may result in too few observations, or to rushed observations, or to the under-training of technical staff.

The time needed for observations tends to be longer than anticipated. There are usually problems in coordinating the timetables of observers and classes. There are often absences, latenesses, school closures and other last-minute changes which end in a missed observation and a lengthening of the time-scale. These problems have to be anticipated by detailed forward planning informed by those with local knowledge of travel times, local holidays, and other variables unfamiliar to the evaluator. In general, the evaluator has to assess the efficiency of the education system within which he/she is operating and make realistic plans as a result. In disorganized systems, observation plans may have to be driven by access and opportunity. Also, effective planning has to include building some 'slippage' into the schedule, ensuring adequate resources, good advance communication, and obtaining the active support of responsible staff (see section 7.2.7).

7.2 Steps in collecting observational data

The nature of an evaluation is determined by the decision(s) it is designed to inform. If your role is as a summative, accountability-oriented evaluator, acting on behalf of a funding or employing agency, then your brief is likely to include the measurement of the effects of the programme, particularly in terms of the objectives for which funding was initially provided. It is likely that your categories of observation will be led by, if not exclusively determined by, the planned goals of the programme (chapter 3, Lynch 1992, Mitchell 1992). In order to do this, you would precede observation by identifying planned features of the programme as a focus for observational categories (King et al. 1987). This can be defined as an *analytic* approach to programme description. If you feel that this restricts the evaluation too much, it is essential to establish this when you are negotiating your terms of reference (see also chapter 8). If your role is that of a formative evaluator, planned goals are more likely to be seen as open to change or interpretation; learning from implementation will be your main concern, not the hitting of pre-determined information targets based on stated programme goals. In this case a naturalistic approach (Parlett and Hamilton 1977, Patton 1987b) would be appropriate. This would suggest observations focused by the concerns of insiders, rather than exclusively by programme objectives, though these are bound to influence insiders' interest.

The rest of this section describes the stages in preparing for and doing observations in general terms, but cross-referred with the Nepal evaluation when relevant, while analysing the results is discussed in section 7.3 and is directly based upon the work reported in chapter 3. Both sections represent an *analytic* approach as followed in the Nepal study.

7.2.1   Planning: Costings and accountability

Observations are time consuming and expensive and so an adequate budget is essential. Funding will determine the number of observers, the number of observations possible, the possibility of joint observation, the distribution of observation sites, the distribution of observations over time, and the time allowed for training and for the analysis of results.

7.2.2   Planning: Identifying criterial features

When planning observations, the summative evaluator will begin with the task of identifying the programme's key criterial features; and then selecting from them the features that can be best described by observation (see section 3.2.3). Criterial features are the key defining characteristics of a programme as planned. In a teacher training course these features might be identified as follows.

1   In oral practice stages, half the time is taken by student talking time.
2   Teachers give their pupils practice in listening to passages spoken in English.
3   New vocabulary is presented separately from new structures.
4   Teachers encourage pupils to correct each other's written work.
5   Grammatical and word meaning is conveyed by teachers in English through situations and examples.

The purpose of the list of planned features is to identify in detail the intended nature of the programme when it is implemented. The features described might include:

- Materials
- Groupings of students
- Specific exercises/learning activities
- Resources
- Talk categorized according to:

  - types of elicitation
  - types of correction
  - mother tongue/target language
  - by teacher/by student/by students
  - functions used
  - communication strategies used

There are four main sources of information to enable the identification of criterial features: unstructured observation, records; insiders' accounts, and scenarios.

Unstructured observation

Ideally, there should be some direct and unstructured observation at the phase of preparing observation categories (see section 7.1.5). Its value would be to meet the conditions under which summative observations would be made, and also to allow the evaluator to question insiders' perhaps over-optimistic accounts of programme objectives and implementation. If exploratory observation is not possible, the observer has to rely on records and insiders' reports but this is risky and may require adjustments later. This to some degree was the case in the Nepal study (see section 3.8).

Records

Records could give information on plans by means of:

- Project plans
- Course books and other teaching materials
- Syllabus descriptions
- Teacher training manuals
- Teacher assessment instruments

There could also be direct data on current implementation through:

- Tests and examinations
- Students' exercise books
- Project reports
- Internal formative evaluation findings

In the case of the Nepal evaluation, the key document was the detailed training manual prepared for Nepali counterpart trainers. Other documents used were ELTO reports, internal evaluation findings and the original project documents (Burton et al. forthcoming).

Insiders' accounts

To plan summative measures, the evaluator needs the best concrete information on what is intended to take place in classrooms. Consultation with insiders who determine programme objectives will be necessary. Trainers, inspectors and materials writers can provide concrete descriptions of criterial features, and can give their views on the priority of these features in the programme. Once there is a draft list of features, staff must be consulted in order to confirm its fairness to the programme. If the programme is already under way, it is desirable to get feedback from teachers to qualify or perhaps prioritize the criterial features to be described.

The evaluator should be discriminating in using insiders' accounts: they will have their own agendas and good impressions to make. Also, there may be discrepancies between different informants' views of objectives: for example, training staff may tell a somewhat different story from teachers. It is similarly unwise to base a list of criterial features on purely 'official' objectives, important as they are, and so even if there may be resistance to it, the evaluator should try to meet the teachers who are actually 'at the chalk face'. Inputs from formative evaluations, and from staff with direct experience of implementation, are needed to broaden the criterial features list and to get it as close as possible to what is actually taking place.

Scenarios

A scenario is a word picture of a classroom, based on records, staff accounts, and perhaps evaluators' own exploratory observations. Evaluators should prepare scenarios which describe a typical lesson as planned by the programme, and a typical lesson which should not occur (King et al. 1987). The purpose of the scenario is to:

1   elicit from staff the features that are criterial – that is, those that in their view are of the greatest importance to the programme – and
2   confirm with staff that the criterial features of the programme have been properly identified.

Once purposes 1 and 2 are achieved, the evaluator can begin to identify categories for an observation instrument with reasonable confidence. Further uses of scenarios are to:

3   integrate an inventory of behaviours in a way that is coherent and can illuminate the educational rationale for the programme, and
4   contribute to the training of observers.

7.2.3   Design factors

The procedures in 7.2.2 should enable the definition of relevant and fair observation categories. However, the instrument itself must be designed so as to minimize inaccuracies or inter-observer inconsistencies when it is being used. For example, it should be user-friendly and economical in its demands on observers. To meet these criteria, constraints customarily considered once an instrument has been selected should be taken into account *at the planning and design stage* (King et al. 1987). The choice of observers and economy of data are two particularly important factors here.

Observers   If additional staff are engaged it may be necessary to modify the instrument to fit observers' characteristics. For example, one may choose to obtain limited data if that is all you consider observers can safely provide (see section 3.2.3).

Economy   When contracted, the evaluator should determine what resources are available for data analysis, probably in the form of an agreed number of man days paid by the sponsor. Inevitably, this will determine the type of data collected. Where resources are limited, labour-intensive methods such as recording and transcription are likely not to be appropriate. In the same way, naturalistic methods tend to be demanding of analysis time. On the other hand, codings have the advantage of relatively speedy analysis.

'Describability'   There may be criterial features of the programme which the observer is forced to exclude from the final observation instrument, because of the criterion of 'describability'. This would include some features which may be unsuited to reliable description, perhaps because of their highly inferential nature.

7.2.4   Designing the instrument: first steps

Operational descriptions   By this stage the evaluator should have a list of criterial features to use as the basis for the categories in the observation instrument. In the case of ELT classrooms, these will probably apply to talk and to learning activities. The observation categories must be capable of description in 'operational terms' – that is, in terms of observable actions and events. For example, 'Teacher models orally' can be operationally defined as 'Teacher says a sentence, phrase or word while the students listen so that they can hear its correct form. Students subsequently repeat what the teacher says.' Operationally described categories of correction would be, for example, 'Teacher corrects by eliciting the correct or desired utterance from another student.' This procedure of operationalizing is vital, for the following reasons.

1   It leads to the identification of low-inference features which are most suitable for quantification through coding in interaction analysis.
2   It helps identify higher inference features more suited to description by field notes, rating scales, or checklists.
3   It provides a basis for training observers and improving inter-observer reliability.

Methods and units of description   The method used will depend upon the nature of the feature to be described (table 7.1).

Table 7.1 Types of observation instrument

Low-inference features		High-inference features
Pre-selected behaviours	Rating	Unstructured description
Interaction analysis (coding)	Checklist	Field notes
	Rating scales	

Interaction analysis   Where one's aim is to describe talk or behaviour so that an objective basis for contrast in terms of frequency is possible, then interaction analysis systems become appropriate. A small-scale unit of frequency (time segment or category boundary) is applied to segment the stream of classroom behaviour, so enabling quantification and contrast through coding. An example of this is Mitchell's use of thirty-second intervals (a relatively long time interval for interaction analysis that is justified by categories based upon the 'learning segment'; see Mitchell 1992: appendices 2 and 3). Systems may, for example, measure the incidence of contrasted question types or of categories of student talk or procedures such as the presentation of new language. The interaction analysis system was first developed by Flanders (1970), whose FIAC system is lucidly explained in Brown (1975: 81–5). Such instruments should consist of operationalized categories, rules for observation and coding and a standardized format. They should also provide rules for presenting and analysing data. There are hundreds of systems in existence (Galton 1978, Simon and Boyer 1968). The parameters along which they vary are summarized by Galton (1978) as: setting, target of observation, method of data collection, number of live observers, coding unit, number of targets, inter-observer agreement method, applications, focus, subject focus. Systems applied to ELT are summarized and compared in Long (1980) and Malamah-Thomas (1987). An interaction analysis instrument would produce data as appears in figure 7.2 (BIAS system, Brown 1975) reported in Malamah-Thomas (1987: 49–50):

In order to implement the BIAS system, a time-line display sheet is used and marked every three seconds for the duration of the observation. Figure

5 (from Brown 1975) shows an example of a time-line display sheet filled in for the first minute or so of a lesson ... The pictures obtained of [lesson 1 and lesson 2] show the percentages of each lesson taken up by the different categories, and the ratios of the different categories to each other in the lesson. This information is to be seen in the context of the type of lesson being taught, and in relation to its general aims and purposes.

TL = Teacher describes, explains, narrates, directs
TQ = Teacher questions
TR = Teacher responds to pupil's response
PR = Pupil responds to teacher's questions
PV = Pupil volunteers information, comments or questions
 S = Silence
 X = Unclassifiable

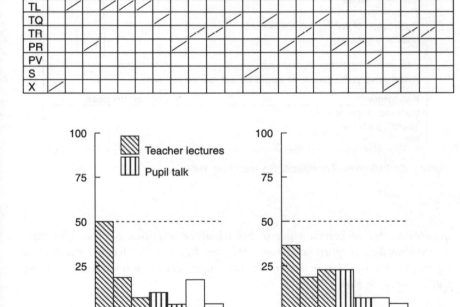

Figure 7.2 Example of interaction analysis. *Source:* Malamah-Thomas 1987: 49–50

Checklists A checklist is a list of observation categories, and is best used to account for activities consisting of complexes of behaviours that are not reducible to a simple frequency unit. It is also suited to recording the simple occurrence or

Behaviour	Skill observed	
	Yes	No
Indicate the map title		
Name the sheet number		
Point out the sheet location diagram		
State the scale of the map		
Point out the key to conventional signs		
Set the map towards magnetic north		
Give written reference for a known location		
Locate an object given the grid reference		

Behaviour	Time interval (minutes)				
	0	5	10	15	18
Personal physical attack					
Taunting/ridicule					
Threatening					
Destruction of another pupil's labours					
Usurping property					
etc.					

Alternatively, the checklist could be set out as follows:

Behaviour	No. of occurrences
Personal physical attack	
Taunting/ridicule	
etc.	

Figure 7.3   Examples of checklists. *Source:* Hook 1981

non-occurrence of certain types of behaviour or activities, but can take many forms according to purpose (Hook 1981; see figure 7.3). Detailed examples of checklists used to describe student activity, input sources and student behaviours can be found in Ross (1992: 172–6).

Rating scales   A checklist can be developed into a rating scale in order to record the observer's judgement either by estimating the frequency of behaviours on a scale (e.g. extremely low – extremely high) or more often by assessing their merit according to qualitative performance criteria (e.g. outstanding–inadequate). They are routinely used for teacher assessment, but have very limited *descriptive* value. In figures 7.4 and 7.5 are fragments of scales according to frequency (Ullman and Geva 1984 in Malamah-Tomas 1987: 117) and merit (from Wallace 1991: 62).

Field notes   Where unanticipated or non-quantifiable pedagogic or contextual features need to be described, then field notes should be used. These may be unstruc-

	extremely low	low	fair	high	extremely high
TEACHER					
Use of L1	0	1	2	3	4
Use of L2	0	1	2	3	4
teacher talk time	0	1	2	3	4
explicit lesson structure	0	1	2	3	4
task orientation	0	1	2	3	4
clarity	0	1	2	3	4
initiate problem solving	0	1	2	3	4
personalized questions and comments	0	1	2	3	
positive reinforcement	0	1	2		
negative reinforcement	0	1			
corrections	0				
pacing					
use of audio-visual aids					
gestures					
humour					
enthusiasm					
STUDENTS					
Use of L1 on task					
Use of L2 on task					
student talk time on task					
initiate problem solving					
comprehension					
attention					
participation					
personalized questions and comments					
positive affect					

Figure 7.4 Rating scale extract (TALOS). *Source:* Malamah-Thomas 1987: 117

tured or may be structured by the use of headings. Field notes are desirable in order to capture qualitative, 'real life' aspects of classes observed so that a more complete account can emerge than the focused and necessarily exclusive record produced by interaction analysis or checklists. Also, notes allow the observer to record factors uniquely relevant to a particular observation: for instance, if there has been a power cut; or if teachers or students have reason to be fatigued; or, as in the writer's case, if there has been a force 6 earthquake halfway through the lesson!

There is no reason why the different observation methods should not be combined in one instrument, so long as the simultaneous demands upon the observer do not become so great as to lead to inaccuracy.

Professional action observation schedule

Trainee's name _____   Class _____

Observer's name _____   School _____

Date _____

Time _____

	Summary grades	Outstanding	Competent	Inadequate	Insufficient information	Trainee's familiarity with class:
PERSONAL QUALITIES						FURTHER COMMENT
1. Presence/style						
2. Voice						
3. Rapport						
PLANNING						
4. Shape and balance of activities						
5. Aims and objectives: specification						
6. Aids/materials/methods: suitability						
7. Anticipation of difficulties						
IMPLEMENTATION						
8. General class management						
9. Introduction and presentation techniques						
10. Questioning techniques						
11. Language skills development						
12. Teaching aids						
13. Teaching materials						
14. Awareness/treatment of error						
5. Smoothness of flow						
·ility to adapt/extemporise						
·d ee model/l·						

Figure 7.5 Rating scale extract. *Source:* Wallace 1991: 62

7.2.5   Further decisions in preparing observation instruments

There are no simple blueprints for the design of observation instruments (though this section is intended to show the steps followed by the authors in the Nepal evaluation). Apart from those already discussed, decisions have to be made about defining categories and category boundaries and about time sampling. In all cases, decisions are led by what it is one wants to describe, what behaviours one wishes to discriminate, and the overall purpose of the description. (A more detailed treatment appears in Hook 1981 and King et al. 1987.)

Integrity of categories

Adequate description depends upon the use of categories that are adequately defined and mutually exclusive. Definition is a matter of operational description. Mutual exclusiveness is an effect of adequate operational description and adequacy when applied in actual description: care must be taken to avoid overlapping categories because they lead to inaccuracy. For example, one action could be coded by different observers as any one of the three categories below.

- Teacher gives directions.
- Teacher talks to pupils.
- Teacher gives information.

Categories must therefore be defined adequately and then piloted in order to test for mutual exclusiveness (Hook 1981).

Sign or category?

In a *category* system, a tally or score is given for each occurrence of a particular category and therefore is dependent upon the observer identifying the point at which one category has ended and another has begun. An adequate category system depends upon consistent and unambiguous identification of the boundaries between its categories. To do this in real time is difficult over the whole length of a lesson, because discourse categories frequently require their whole context to be known before classification is possible. The degree of difficulty is a function of the nature and number of categories employed for the analysis. Where category boundaries are problematic to identify, such 'real time' decisions risk error. It is for this reason that category systems are usually applied to the analysis of recorded and transcribed data (Long 1980), a procedure often impractical in field evaluations unless you are able to work in real time with categories that are clear and are limited in number. In the Nepal study (see chapter 3) the goal was to establish a simple distinction between relative frequency of teacher and student talking time in English and, given the local constraints and restricted time available for training, it offered a more practical (and in the long term more reliable) approach to description than a sign system. Such a compromise was unavoidable, given the length of additional time it would have taken to train the observers in the use of a sign system.

In a *sign* system, an arbitrary time unit is used (e.g. BIAS, see figure 7.2). Talk is coded into one of the set of categories on each time interval (conventionally a short time interval such as three seconds, often over the whole lesson). This approach loses some data but has the advantages of not requiring transcription and of being based upon an objective unit of frequency. It is most suited to systems whose purpose is to show relative proportions of time with which categories occur. The tendency to error in such systems demands relatively large samples of observed time.

Typically, a sign system will use fewer categories than a category system because categories have to be learnt over an extended period of training and also because coding in real time is very demanding even upon the trained observer. Whether a limited set of categories is descriptively adequate depends again on the purpose and priorities of data collection.

Time samples

A further decision will apply to the proportion of class time to be described. A category system can aspire to describe all the talk, if it is based on recordings. A sign system may be used to describe whole lessons, but this procedure is so demanding that larger time units usually have to be used, as in Mitchell's (1992) adaptation of Boydell and Jasman's system, which uses a thirty-second time unit to analyse whole lessons, or extremely well trained personnel have to be employed. If a large number of classes are to be observed, time sampling may be a preferable strategy so that a random proportion of class time is coded. An example would be one-minute coding followed by two minutes' rest as with COLT (Frohlich et al. 1985); or three fixed-time excerpts of five minutes each, as in the Nepal study (chapter 3). In an alternative approach, using a category system, Ross (1992: 175–6) quantified the proportion of total class time devoted to different activity types.

7.2.6   The draft instrument

Once all the categories of description are decided and the above decisions made, a draft instrument can be designed. While it is sensible to study other widely used instruments, one must beware of mere copying, as the purposes of the instrument you have referred to and your own observation purposes may not be the same. The criteria to apply to the design of the instrument are:

1   it enables data recording to be done efficiently;
2   it will allows easy data analysis.

Considerations that come under the first point are the size and layout of the (chapters 1 and 3) instrument, and the facilitation of the observer's task in recording data. For example, it could emerge that there are too many categories in an interaction analysis section, or that there is not enough room to make notes, or that the layout is in some way confusing. Clearly, the instrument itself should not be a cause of confusion or error. Under the second point are such considerations as ease of counting and transferring scores to an array.

When designing the instrument it is essential to anticipate how data will be collated and analysed. It often happens that data are collected, only to find after the event that its analysis is highly problematic. This may be because the data wanted is not there, or that there is too much data, or that it is hard to analyse. For example, an observer may decide to use extensive field notes with verbatim descriptions, but then be quite at a loss as to how to introduce order into a thick pile of non-standardized, narrative descriptions (Patton 1980, 1987b). Therefore, piloting of instruments must include a pilot data analysis.

Piloting

Only piloting under real classroom conditions is an adequate test of an instrument. Also, even if it is only to be used by its designer, it is still highly desirable to have others pilot it too. However carefully it is designed, problems unforeseen by the designer are sure to crop up, so demanding revisions he/she would not have made otherwise. These could be in the layout, or more fundamentally in category definition: ambiguous definitions, category overlaps, or data exclusion. Revision of the instrument may require further piloting, with considerable additional time added to the evaluation process. This must be planned for from the start. The ultimate tests for the completion of piloting are whether:

1 the instrument is judged able to provide reliable data – i.e. whether inter-observer agreement is at an acceptable level (see section 7.3);
2 on analysis the data answer the questions you have asked – i.e. whether they are valid.

A more detailed set of criteria by which to assess an observation instrument is provided in appendix 7.2 (from Boehm and Weinberg 1977).

Triangulation

As the precise nature of the data to be produced by the instrument becomes clearer, so should the identification of information that will be used to corroborate them (see also section 7.1.6). This may take the form of validation checks with insiders, or may require a recording and re-analysis of a sub-sample of classes, or triangulation with documents. The criteria to apply to triangulation are:

1   their relevance to the observation findings;
2   the economy of getting and analysing the triangulation data;
3   the criteria for corroboration chosen.

7.2.7   Preparing school visits

Prepare sampling plan

You should prepare a schedule for the visits you will make, detailing dates, locations, travel method, and times. It is essential to confirm access to classrooms and to anticipate any disruptions to normal schooling (for example, local holidays, examinations, sports days, in-service training days, presidential visits). You must calculate for missed arrangements, illnesses, delayed transport, and so on. The schedule should quantify target observation hours, for subjects and for observers. You should protect anonymity by coding schools and teachers by letter or number and thereafter only by referring to subjects by their codes, keeping a 'key' in a safe place.

Inform schools

To conduct observations without forewarning schools or teachers may have its attractions: there is less possibility of 'impression management' (see section 7.1.7) and so of less skewed description. However, one should avoid teachers' feeling 'ambushed' by unannounced visits. Respect for the rights of teachers improves the possibility of cooperation and of seeing reasonably representative classes. Also, one must ensure that a class is taking place when a visit is made. These considerations favour giving advance information about visits. The exception to this general rule would be where multiple observations are sited in one institution, and a general access agreement has been negotiated with staff. Planned visits have the additional advantage we noted in section 4.3 in motivating internal monitoring prior to the visit.

It is therefore essential to prepare a letter addressed to head teachers, teachers, and others involved, explaining the purpose of observations, how data will be used, and how confidentiality will be observed. This may well need to be supported by a statement from the relevant higher level authorities, to enable access and co-operation. Contacts with administrators and head teachers will then have to be made to ensure access and permissions, and to confirm the feasibility of the schedule. Consideration of the interests and standing of these senior staff is essential. (These issues are developed in chapter 8.)

7.2.8   Select and train observers

Where extra observers are engaged, it is essential to give them sufficient training, and later to monitor their observations in the field (see chapter 3). The goal of observer training is to achieve an acceptable level of inter-observer reliability (see sections 7.1.7 and 7.3). An observers' manual is essential for the training and to maintain reliability in the field. Its main components should be:

1a a description of the instrument and its purpose
 b operational descriptions of categories
 c detailed guidelines for the conduct of observations
2a category recognition tasks (using transcripts and recordings) with feedback
 b use of the instrument with comparison of descriptions and feedback on short samples of the type of classes to be observed (e.g. video or live)
 c full-scale use in representative classrooms, with feedback and inter-observer reliability checks
3 logistical and financial information, detailing equipment, expenses, access, travel, and so on

7.2.9   Conduct of observations

Observers should ensure that all equipment is checked and ready before leaving for schools. They should arrive at school in time to see staff before the observation. They should restate the purpose of the observation and reassure the teacher about confidentiality. If asked to speak to the class, they should explain that they can only do so at the end of the lesson. They should be seated in the classroom away from the sightline between the teacher and the students. They should never interfere in the lesson, whatever cues are given. If doing joint observation, pairs should ensure that their time sampling is synchronized, but should avoid any communication over coding or other descriptions.

Neatness and order are essential in completing the instrument: untidiness can only produce inaccuracy, and wastes time. Immediately after the class, observers should re-read the completed instrument to check for any omissions and errors.

Afterwards, thank the students, teachers, and head teacher and stay for hospitality if it is offered. If asked for feedback about the lesson by anyone, then general positive comments about the pupils are constructive and avoid the observer's being cast in the role of inspector. When contact with the school is completed, one should send a letter of thanks to the head teacher, to be passed on to teachers.

7.3 Steps in analysing observational data

In the rest of this chapter we take the reader through the steps required to analyse and present observational data of the type obtained in the Nepal study (chapter 3), in which one compares quantified observational data of two sub-groups (trained and untrained teachers interacting with pupils). We do not expect readers to do any analysis and at each step examples are provided.

This section is intended to illustrate one procedure for analysis and not to serve as an all-purpose blueprint. These procedures represent a form of analysis for data obtained from an instrument which has been tried and tested in a number of studies overseas. They are a practical series of steps for readers to use as guidelines in analysing their own quantitative data.

Figure 7.6 is a sample instrument based on that used in the Nepal evaluation (see chapter 3). It consists of three pages: the first page is for information on the identity of observers and teacher, the date, location, and lesson taught. Page 2 is for the *coding* data: interaction analysis type coding of talk into eight categories (Teacher English – question; Teacher English – statement; Teacher Nepali – question; Teacher Nepali – statement; Pupil English – question; Pupil English – statement; Pupil Nepali – question; Pupil Nepali – statement). One tally represents one utterance of the category chosen. Coding is taken from three standard time samples of five minutes each. These codings are designed to quantify the relative frequency of the eight categories, since the relative frequency of pupil English as compared with other categories was identified as a criterial feature (see section 3.2.3) of the classroom interaction of trained teachers. On page 3, brief field notes are taken following the time sequence of the coding data on facing page 2. Also on page 3, there is a *checklist* of criterial features to identify the presence or absence of these criterial activities in the classrooms of trained and untrained teachers.

Step 1 'Code name' the observed teachers and assemble the completed observation instruments

Your first step would be to give an anonymous label (e.g. T/1, T/2, etc.) to each teacher and to keep a list for your reference if needed (figure 7.7).

Next, you would sort the instruments into the trained and untrained teacher sets and clearly label each completed instrument with the teacher's code. You could also erase names and schools at this point.

Baseline Study Observation Form

Observer

Teacher

School

Class

Number of pupils present:

Lesson/
Page

Date

Teacher's Lesson Outline

1

Figure 7.6 Observation instrument. *Source:* Weir and Roberts 1990

Lesson start ☐								

	Teacher				Pupil			
	English		Nepali		English		Nepali	
	Q	S	Q	S	Q	S	Q	S
Start ☐								
End ☐								

	English		Nepali		English		Nepali	
	Q	S	Q	S	Q	S	Q	S
Start ☐								
End ☐								

	English		Nepali		English		Nepali	
	Q	S	Q	S	Q	S	Q	S
Start ☐								
End ☐								

Lesson end ☐

2

From	To		
		1	
		2	
		3	

	Teacher explained grammar mainly in Nepali		Pupils produced original sentences in English
	Teacher practised language in situations mainly in English		Pair work or group work used (all class)
	Teacher gave models in English (word or sentence)		Teacher gave extended listening practice
	Oral drills used, in English (more than 1 student)		Extra practice
	Pupils did written exercises by copying		Notes on extra practice:
	Pupils did guided writing exercise not in book		
	Comprehension questions asked in English not in book/some new questions		

3

	Trained Group		
	Name	Code	School
1.	Bhatta, Dambar	T/1	Janata
2.	Poudyal, Nanda	T/2	Adarsha
3.	Thapa, Nirmal	T/3	Mahendra
4.		T/4	
5.		T/5	

Figure 7.7   Partly completed 'code name' list

Step 2 Prepare blank data arrays for coding and checklist totals

An array is a collation of all the data you have obtained. It is a key document and should be presented as neatly and clearly as possible. Figure 7.8 is a fragment of a blank array (with rows for only five teachers for the coding data and one for the checklist data (figure 7.9). Coding (instrument page 2) and checklist scores (instrument page 3) from every completed instrument would be transferred to them. The field notes (page 3) would be used later for triangulation (see step 8).

	Teacher English	Teacher Nepali	Pupil English	Pupil Nepali	
T/1					
T/2					
T/3					
T/4					
T/5					

Figure 7.8   Extract from blank array: Coding totals

Step 3   Add up the interaction analysis tallies

For *each completed observation instrument*, you would add up the raw totals of coding tallies in each column, entering the scores on the form, and totalling all three time samples (see figure 7.10).

	1	2	3	4	5	6	7	8	9	10	11
T/1											
T/2											
T/3											
T/4											
T/5											

Figure 7.9 Extract from blank array: Checklist totals

After this you would work out the percentage proportions of each category. You would add together the tallies for TE, TN, PE, PN as below:

161   3   119   3

___   ___   ___   ___

and then add the category tallies and write in the tally total:

161   3   119   3   286

___   ___   ___   ___   ___

                                                                    Tally total

after which you would calculate the frequency percentage value for each category:

$$\frac{\text{Category total}}{\text{Tally total}} \times 100 = \underline{\quad} \%$$

For example:

$$\frac{161}{286} \times 100 = \underline{56.3\%}$$

$$\frac{119}{286} \times 100 = \underline{41.6\%}$$

Finally, you could write the percentages onto each completed instrument:

161   3   119   3   =   286

56.3%   1%   41.6%   1%

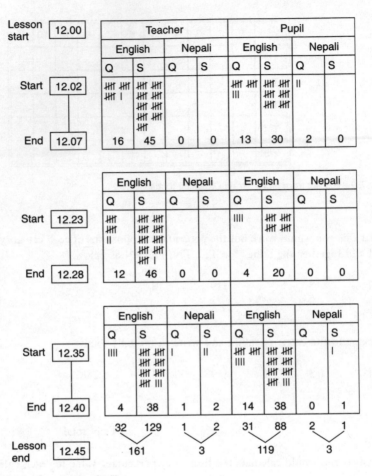

Figure 7.10   Raw totals of tallies

Step 4   Completing the array: Coding

You could then transfer raw tallies and percentages from the instruments to the data array. Figure 7.11 is an example of what the coding section of a completed array (trained group) might look like after three teachers' results have been entered.

Step 5   Completing the array: Checklist

In the same way, the checklist data would be transferred to the array. Observers could be instructed to indicate not only whether a particular feature occurred but

	Teacher English		Teacher Nepali		Pupil English		Pupil Nepali		
	Q	S	Q	S	Q	S	Q	S	
T/1	32	129	1	2	31	88	2	1	= 286
	56.3%		1%		41.6%		1%		
T/2	40	101	0	0	25	83	1	0	= 250
	56.4%		0%		43.2%		0%		
T/3	21	140	4	2	16	77	6	4	= 270
	60%		2%		34.4%		3.1%		

Figure 7.11   Extract from array: Coding totals

they could also be required to indicate its frequency or importance by the rough-and-ready means of giving a three-point positive response: a tick, tick+ or a tick++ ('+' indicates it occurred on more than one occasion during the lesson, '++', that it occured more than once and that this was a significant or marked feature of the class). In completing the array a tick scores 1, tick+ scores 2 and tick++ scores 3 (figures 7.12a and 7.12b). The observer was asked to provide a written description justifying the rating in the space provided under the criterial features.

Step 6   Checking for errors

This is a crucial stage, and should not be omitted. It is almost certain that some errors will occur and so systematic checks would have to be done – for example, on counting up coding totals and on percentages, or on transferring checklist data to the array.

Step 7   Completing totals in the array

This would be the final stage of completing the array.

Coding

You would add up the scores in each column and write the raw total at the foot (see figure 7.14), then calculating an average percentage by dividing this total by the number of scores; For example:

	Teacher explained grammar mainly in Nepali		Pupils produced original sentences in English
√	Teacher practised language in situations mainly in English		Pair work or group work used (all class)
√+	Teacher gave models in English (word or sentence)		Teacher gave extended listening practice
√	Oral drills used, in English (more than 1 student)		Extra practice
√	Pupils did written exercises by copying		Notes on extra practice:
	Pupils did guided writing exercise not in book		
	Comprehension questions asked in English not in book/some new questions		

Figure 7.12a   Sample checklist

	1	2	3	4	5	6	7	8	9	10	11
T/1	0	1	2	1	1	0	0	0	0	0	0
T/2											

Figure 7.12b   Extract from completed array: Checklist

$$\frac{820}{1425} \times 100 = \underline{57.5\%}$$

Alternatively, one would add up the percentage scores for each teacher, and average them; for example:

$$\frac{862.5}{15} \times 100 = \underline{57.5\%}$$

This would be repeated for each column (TE, TN, PE, PN) and written in the array (see figure 7.13).

Checklist

In the same way, you would enter checklist totals and averages for each column to complete the array (see figure 7.14); for example:

$$\frac{16}{118} \times 100 = \underline{13.5\%}$$

	Teacher English Q S	Teacher Nepali Q S	Pupil English Q S	Pupil Nepali Q S	
T/1	32 129 56.3%	1 2 1%	31 88 41.6%	2 1 1%	= 286
T/2	40 101 56.4%	0 0 0%	25 83 43.2%	1 0 0%	= 250
T/3	21 140 60%	4 2 2%	16 77 34.4%	6 4 3.7%	= 270
T/15	18 120 56.3%	0 0 0%	20 85 42.8%	2 0 0.8%	= 245
Total	820	25	530	50	= 1425
Average	57.5%	1.75%	37.2%	3.5%	

Figure 7.13   Extract from a completed coding array

	1	2	3	4	5	6	7	8	9	10	11	12
T/1	1	2	2	1	0	0	0	0	2	0	2	0
T/2	0	2	1	0	0	0	0	0	2	0	1	0
T/15	1	2	1	1	0	0	0	0	1	0	1	0
Total	16	22	20	14	1	2	0	0	18	1	24	0
Average	13.5	18.6	16.9	11.9	1	1.7	0	0	15.2	1	20.3	0

Figure 7.14   Extract from a completed coding array: Checklist

Step 8   Measure inter-observer reliability

To measure the reliability of the observations (very necessary in case findings are challenged, and also to meet data quality standards – see section 1.6) one can calculate inter-observer reliability when *joint* observations have taken place (see section 7.1.7). After Boehm and Weinberg (1977), also in Hook (1981), a simple calculation can be done, as in the following example.

1   You would first count number of tallies for each category (table 7.2).

Table 7.2   Number of tallies for each category

Category	Observer 1	Observer 2
Teacher English	38	45
Pupil English	10	12
Teacher Nepali	0	0
Pupil Nepali	46	43

2   You would then total the number of observation tallies.

Observer 1: 94
Observer 2: 100

3   You would then count the number of agreements in each category and over categories (table 7.3).

Table 7.3   Agreements in each category

Teacher English	38
Pupil English	10
Teacher Nepali	0
Pupil Nepali	43

4   You would then divide the number of agreements by the total number of observations.

$91/194 = .46$

5   You would multiply the resulting figure by the number of observers.

$2 \times .46 = .92$
Rate of agreement $= .92$

The minimum accepted level of observer agreement is usually considered to be .90 (which represents a shared variance of just over 80 per cent). If this figure were not reached, it would indicate either the need for further training or the need to revise the categories being used or to review who was engaged in observation and whether they were a source of bias.

Triangulation: Two examples

If you need to check the accuracy of observations, it can be done by cross-referring data within the instrument, in terms of its logical consistency. This can be done in the case of our example here by cross-checking matching coding scores (page 2 of instrument) and field notes (page 3) to see whether there are any discrepancies, in the sense that coding scores do not fit with the classroom events recorded in the notes. These discrepancies are not objectively defined, but would be based upon knowledge of the classroom.

In the Nepal study, observation scores were also triangulated with teachers' self-report lesson descriptions. The problem with any method that is based on logical consistency (rather than quantified levels of agreement) is that it cannot set a minimum objective standard for agreement levels as in the inter-observer reliability test above.

Example 1 Matching field notes and codings In this form of triangulation, you would read the field notes which describe the lesson then match them with the corresponding coding scores and assess whether the two are consistent. For example, if an oral pattern drill were described in the notes, then a relatively high proportion of pupil English would be scored in the coding. If the field notes reported the teacher giving a grammar explanation, then the codings should show a high proportion of teacher talk as compared with all pupil talk. If discrepancies are not found, it would increase your confidence in the data.

Example 2 Feasibility of coding In a coding time sample (five minutes in the case of our example instrument), there could only be a certain maximum possible number of utterances, given the realities of talking time in an ELT classroom (one hundred or so utterances in five minutes). If there were considerably more than this, one could infer that the observer could have exceeded the time sample period, or could have inflated the score of a particular category. If you found a case like this, you would need to check it against the field notes. If there were discrepancies between field notes or if the number of utterances occurring were unlikely, then that particular observation instrument might have to be excluded from the data.

Step 9   Interpretation and display

If you are analysing observation results, there would be no automatic recourse to parametric statistical analysis. Very often statistical analysis procedures (e.g. correlations) are misused with very small samples. If the sample size were small (usually reckoned at below thirty), then it is unlikely that parametric statistics could be applied. You would be restricted to visual representation and cautious comment on patterns in the results. Your findings would only be suggestive and would require confirmation through data from a larger sample before you could make any generalizations. With small samples, one might simply present tabular data in one of a range of chart types (e.g. block graph, scatter graph, pie diagram) to reveal the patterns in the data, and ensure that the comments that accompany such data make it clear how tentative any 'findings' must be due to the restricted sampling. (It is worth obtaining the advice of a specialist statistician on the types of analysis that are appropriate to your data and also on effective ways of displaying data. There is also computer software available for the production of graphics from tabular data e.g. SlideWrite *Plus*, Advanced Graphic Software Inc.) The examples of visual data presentation in figure 7.15 are drawn from Hook (1981). In each example, Hook begins with tabular data and then shows how different charts can bring out trends in the information.

7.3.1   Statistical analysis

In summative evaluation for contractual accountability using the comparative design described here, the initiator of the evaluation would want to know whether comparative scores (between groups or at different times within the same group) differed significantly or occurred merely by chance (see also chapters 1 and 3). In this case, the significance of the difference refers to a *statistical significance*: the concept that difference between two sets of scores can be expressed numerically to show the likelihood of chance explaining it. If differences are not statistically significant, they can be perceived as of no value as they could have occurred purely as a result of random factors.

However, we should note that statistical significance does not say anything about the meaningfulness of results. Statistical significance may simply result from a large sample size and the observed differences may be relatively unimportant in real terms. Therefore, in educational settings, one should be cautious in the use of statistical significance as it is not necessarily synonymous with educational or personal significance to stakeholders. In spite of these reservations, in summative evaluations measures of statistical significance provide an objective standard of judgement to bring to evaluation findings, and suggest how confidently you may generalise the results from a sample to a larger population. (See Brown 1988 and Hatch and Lazaraton 1991 for accessible guides to the statistical techniques that may be appropriate in observational studies of the type described above.)

7.4   Endnote

We have now considered self-report and observation as two key data collection methods. In part II we have referred to their use in evaluation designs that are summative (chapter 3) and formative (chapters 4 and 5). We are aware that our coverage of methods is not comprehensive and that many procedures are not dealt with in this book, particularly those relevant to formative evaluation (but see section 1.4.6 for an outline and references to other sources).

To conclude this book, we turn finally to more personal dimensions of evaluation:

Pupil's work involvement

Alternative a

Frequency of observed behaviour	1	2	3	Weeks 4	5	6	7	8	9
Off task	44	50	40	32	20	15	11	9	11
On task	14	11	16	26	35	38	45	51	56

Alternative b

Weeks	Off task	On task
1	44	14
2	50	11
3	40	16
4	32	26
5	20	35
6	15	38
7	11	45
8	9	51
9	11	56

Graph displaying pupil's work involvement

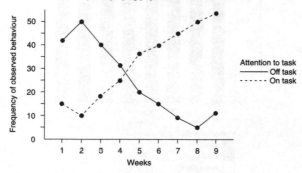

Bar graph contrasting off-task and on-task behaviours

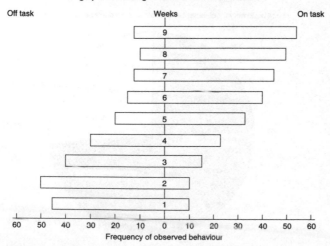

Figure 7.15 Examples of graphics from tables

A social studies teacher's record of pupil behaviours associated with motivation

Weeks	Number of occurrences of pupil behaviour				
	Participation	Attention	Inattention	Obstruction	Total
1	70	30	16	5	121
2	64	42	10	10	126
3	81	33	13	14	141
4	76	29	21	16	142
5	72	32	14	30	148
6	84	36	15	24	159
7	71	26	24	29	150
8	68	34	18	20	140
Mean	73.25	32.75	16.37	18.5	

Graphical representation of pupil behaviour associated with motivation

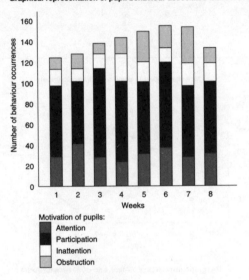

Pupil motivation: individual behaviours as a percentage of total behaviour

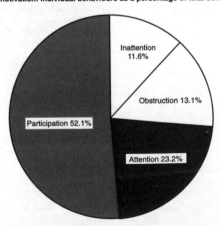

Figure 7.15 (cont.). *Source:* Hook 1981

some less than obvious but very important factors which may affect the conduct and outcomes of an evaluation.

NOTES

1 Useful background ELT publications on classroom observation include Allwright and Bailey (1991), Long (1980), Malamah-Thomas (1987), and Nunan (1989). King et al. (1987) are of particular practical help, while Patton (1987b) provides a detailed account of qualitative data analysis methods. Recent accounts of collecting and analysing observational data for ELT evaluation can be found in Lynch (1992), Mitchell (1992), Philpott (1993), Ross (1992), and Spada (1990).
2 Naturalistic methodology attempts not to intervene in a situation, and to discover relevant categories of description in it (Patton 1980, 1987b: 13).

Part IV Personal Considerations

8 Political and Personal Dynamics of Evaluation

Evaluation in education, like any kind of social research, cannot be value free. An evaluator, like a researcher, has to choose; to choose which data; which interviews; which interpretation. Evaluation is therefore a political activity, since political questions arise when people disagree and a choice has to be made.

Holt, *Evaluating the Evaluators*

The evaluator's autonomy and impartiality are not within the immediate control of the evaluator, but are dependent on the evaluation approach chosen . . . the evaluator has to take into account the forms of management and lines of accountability within the institution, system or project. For the most part those structures already exist before the evaluator begins work and I call these structures the 'preconditions'. How the evaluator establishes and sustains a role within the preconditional structures I think of as part of evaluation procedures. The evaluator ignores preconditions and procedures at his/her peril.

Adelman, *The Politics and Ethics of Evaluation*

8.1 Introductory

Evaluations have political and personal dimensions. The former is concerned with power and decision making while the latter is concerned with the effects of evaluation on individuals. The political nature of evaluation is embodied in the way decisions are made at each of its stages. At the *planning* stage, if stakeholders are excluded from decisions about the purpose, scope and method of the evaluation, they are thereby disempowered. At the *implementation stage,* if any groups are not consulted or their concerns not sufficiently represented, they are similarly disempowered. Finally, *use* of evaluation findings can raise issues of fairness and the rights of stakeholders (see discussion of this in section 1.5); if, for example, administrators fail to act on findings, or if the action is seen as favouring the views and interests of some stakeholders over others. In these ways, an evaluation can take on a political rather than merely technical character, so that its educational content becomes secondary (for example, an evaluation may come to be seen simply as a means for one group's interests to override those of another).

In personal terms, an evaluation can affect participants' self-concept: of their worth, of their standing in an institution, and of their relationships to others in that institution. This will depend upon such factors as the way the process has been conducted – for example, who is or is not consulted at any stage in the evaluation; whether others are seen as acting consistently and honestly; and upon the extent to which individual practice is disclosed and then seen to be subjected to confirmation or disapproval. In all cases, an evaluation is bound to raise the issue of change in collective and individual practice, and hence its worth.

Both dimensions, the political and personal, tend to become enmeshed within institutions, since interpersonal relations are affected by each person's need to defend the interests and autonomy associated with their role within the institution. Furthermore, institutions are characterized by certain internal 'truces', tacit boundaries between individuals or groups that are observed so that day-to-day work can go on. In their account of two institutional evaluations, Adelman and Alexander (1982) show how these truces can be disrupted and personal/role relationships can then be affected, with consequences far beyond the evaluation's original remit. Adelman and Alexander generalize their case studies as follows.

1   The means of conducting the evaluation and reacting to its findings are taken as a demonstration of the political realities of the institution.
2   The evaluation illustrates the effects of institutional structure and previous policy decisions (e.g. delegation of control, specialization, etc.) upon interests of staff and students and on educational management of courses.
3   Evaluation procedures or findings may be deployed as an instrument to settle a previous dispute.
4   Conflict over the control over findings may produce personal tensions between stakeholders.
5   The evaluation of particular courses may widen in scope to issues of the adequacy of managerial responsiveness, the maintenance of agreements, and internal control.

The evaluator will also be subject to pressures, two of which are relevant to institutional dynamics:

6   Where findings are challenging, resistance will take the form of a rejection of the procedures used or the bona fides of the evaluator.
7   Factions within the institution may try to co-opt an evaluator to represent their interests.

Given all these risks, it is clear that care must be taken to follow evaluation procedures that are both ethically and technically right. Next we will consider some of these issues, in terms of two common roles: an external evaluator contracted for purposes of accountability and an insider engaged in a formative evaluation. We have argued for the most constructive possible integration of their respective contributions to an evaluation (see also Alderson and Scott 1992) and we return to this theme at the end of the chapter. However, even in the broader approach to evaluation proposed in this book, which seeks to synthesize insider and outsider contributions, there will always be concerns specific to different roles within the system.

8.2   The external evaluator: Independence and integrity

Externally imposed evaluations for accountability are unambiguously political because their purpose is to inform policy decisions. In this context, the evaluator *has* to employ procedures that are seen to be impartial. If they are not, he/she will be perceived as a mere instrument for pre-determined administrative decisions, and so will lose professional independence and any prospect of serious cooperation from stakeholders. The defence of independence begins with the terms of reference negotiated with the sponsor. It subsequently derives from the principles under which the evaluation is conducted: accuracy in data collection, the identification of all information users; the inclusion of stakeholders as informants; reference to stakeholders to validate findings; observation of confidentiality; an open account of methods used (Joint Committee 1981, Simons 1982c).

8.2.1   Negotiating contracts

In the UK, inexperience in sponsored educational evaluation has tended to lead to a rather loose approach to contract setting. In contrast, in the USA and Canada, sponsored evaluations have for some time been subject to rigorous procedures at the stage of drawing up proposals and agreeing terms of reference (Mackay, forthcoming). As Simons (1984b: 58) summarizes it:

Proposals for funds are subjected to detailed scrutiny in terms of aims, methodology, outcomes and costs and may be quite changed as a result: setting up conditions for fieldwork often involves mandatory negotiations with stakeholding groups including parents, teachers and administrators who are also able to exact changes. Contracts are usually written agreements signed by the appropriate parties acknowledging acceptance of the study under the terms eventually agreed.

It is in the interest of the evaluator, sponsor and stakeholders alike to set contracts on the basis of complete information, and to define unambiguous terms of reference. If this is not done, then misconceptions may persist over the role of the evaluator, lines of accountability, and the range of stakeholders and information users to be consulted. Mitchell (1992) provides an interesting discussion of these issues regarding the Bilingual Education Project, Western Isles, Scotland. If there is contractual ambiguity, the evaluator may be assumed to be an advocate or an adversary by an interest group when he/she is in fact independent. He/She may, in other cases, be perceived as an adviser when in fact he/she is an assessor. In such cases, cooperation may be withheld unnecessarily, or there may be extreme dissatisfaction with an evaluator's report when it fails to meet inappropriate expectations (for example, by identifying problems without suggesting solutions). Problems arising from differential role expectations of external evaluators arose as an issue in section 4.5.

Simons (1984b) describes her experience as an evaluator when engaged under ambiguous terms of reference. She was employed by a teacher training institution to evaluate its programmes, with schools, teachers, administrators, and community as informants. Funds obtained from the EEC were provided by the local education authority (LEA) so that the institution could conduct an ostensibly independent self-evaluation. However, the LEA was also a significant client of the institution's (through secondment) and having negotiated an independent brief with the institution as her employer, Simons subsequently found that other parties had made separate agreements without her knowledge.

1   The LEA had promised blanket confidentiality to teachers.
2   The LEA had arranged a separate agreement with the institution.
3   The LEA expected to have control over the information provided by the evaluator.

Some of the possible consequences for Simons were therefore:

1   she was subject to conflicting demands from two sponsors over the ownership of information;
2   there was uncertainty over which parties would implement the evaluation findings;
3   as regards control over her own evaluation findings, parts of her report might have been integrated into someone else's report, so removing her control over the use and interpretation of her findings but with her personal responsibility still attached to them.

In circumstances like this, where agreements with stakeholders are seen not to be binding and liable to be changed, there is a risk that stakeholders will feel misled over the way information they have provided is eventually used. This would be extremely damaging for the standing of the evaluator. It is essential therefore that the evaluator negotiates the terms of reference in such a way that he/she protects his/her independence and integrity, and also takes into account the significant centres of power and involvement affected by his/her enquiries. If a contract is ambiguous, the evaluator may be faced later with the prospect of resignation, renegotiation, or breaking agreements. Contractual ambiguities will rebound on the evaluator and vitiate the evaluation.

McKay (forthcoming) identifies certain essential elements in contract setting. First, the design of the evaluation cannot be achieved unless information is available on:

- the background to the evaluation
- the purpose of the evaluation
- stakeholders
- the principal information users – i.e. the decision makers with the power to act on the report
- the time frame
- financial resources
- the form of the final report
- circulation of the final report

Mackay argues that if a client cannot give information on these aspects, then the evaluator should propose a feasibility study to obtain it. Once this information is known, a contract can be set, but to enable the evaluator it should contain:

- a clear statement of the authority to undertake the evaluation, with some evidence of cooperation from information sources;
- a clear statement of what the evaluation is intended to achieve and for whom;
- a detailed work plan of the evaluation;
- a description of organizational and reporting conditions, identifying the sponsor's liaison officer *by name*;
- a specification of the resources to be committed to the evaluation;
- an outline of procedures for amending the work plan.

The evaluator should ensure that the contract allows him/her to obtain all information that is salient to his/her purpose, recognizing that data sources cannot be predicted with certainty at the stage of contract setting. It is a further reasonable condition that the agreement reached with the sponsor should be known to all stakeholders. Such care over contractual terms should protect the integrity of both evaluator and evaluation study. In the case of the Nepal study (chapter 3) the evaluators negotiated their terms of reference in that they argued for the case for process data to complement language test data; the ODA also funded a feasibility visit in which the viability of a baseline design was explored and local agreements were negotiated by the evaluators with local staff (The New Era and project staff).

8.2.2 Standards

Standards in ethics and method must be maintained for several reasons: for the evaluator to be seen as credible; for the evaluation findings to be considered in decision making; for the cooperation of important groups of informants; and to escape co-option by any interest group. These standards may be summarized as follows.

1   Terms of reference

    a   Negotiated with sponsor
    b   Insiders informed

2   Method

    c   Fair and impartial (controlled for bias)
    d   Accurate
    e   Economic
    f   Confidential (implies informants' control over obtaining and releasing data as far as they apply to themselves)
    g   Relevant to negotiated purpose
    h   Makes acceptable demands on informants (e.g. in terms of time, the level of self-disclosure)

3   Reporting

    i   Intelligible to audience(s)
    j   Capable of indicating remedies
    k   Enables informed criticism of method and findings

To maintain these standards, many evaluators require the support of procedural guides, such as the Sage Program Evaluation Kit (e.g. King et al. 1987). A fuller description of standards that should apply to an evaluation appears at the end of chapter 1. One should also note that some evaluators (e.g. Simons 1982c) argue that in all school evaluations, there should be negotiation with participants to 'set the boundaries of the study'; that is, that to be effective all school evaluations should be democratic in nature.

In the evaluations reported in part II, the ethical issues which arose reflect their differing purposes and contexts. In the Nepal study (an external summative evaluation; see chapter 3), it was of particular importance to produce accurate, unbiased data, which influenced the decision to engage The New Era, and the care taken to validate test and observation instruments. Also, it was of the greatest importance to ensure confidentiality, and for the teachers in the study to feel confident that they would remain anonymous (Pring 1984). The engagement of The New Era helped with this, as did the procedures of 'code naming' all schools and teachers in the study, and sealing and then mailing all data directly to the evaluators in England without any access by the Nepali Ministry of Education or its employees. In terms of freedom of information, it is worth noting that ODA evaluation reports are released for publication and can be read in the ODA reference library. The authors have also found the ODA happy to permit them to publish the work they have done for them, normal conditions of confidentiality allowed. Chapter 4 describes how, in the formative evaluation of the CALS pre-sessional programme, methods were strongly influenced by the need for economy, and the approach to evaluation was grounded on the principles of staff ownership and the integration of staff development and curriculum development (see section 4.4). Similarly, issues of staff ownership arose in chapter 5 (an external formative project evaluation) as it relates to the readiness of counterparts to sustain the project objectives on departure of the ELTO. Also, to ensure the use of findings, the evaluator chose to produce a discussion paper for use with insiders, which they all had and which became a key section of the report to the funding agency.

8.3 Insider evaluation: Ownership and climate

An evaluation done by an 'inside' member of staff may be initiated by an external agency for accountability/quality control purposes. In this case, the internal evaluator will be subject to external/summative type conditions: he/she will be working on behalf of management or funding agency to apply criteria for quality control and so the considerations discussed in section 8.2 would apply to him/her. Indeed, it is highly likely that the impartiality of the insider evaluator would be even more open to question than that of the external evaluator. This is because he/she will have a personal history, with known preferences and commitments potentially relevant to evaluation issues in hand. Also, he/she is liable to be seen as affiliating with management against peers. For this reason, explicit and agreed criteria and processes have to be employed. If they are not, the evaluator is liable to be rebuffed: his/her impartiality and integrity denied; cooperation withdrawn; findings under attack.

There may still be problems even when administrators (e.g. Directors of Studies) initiate their own evaluation for developmental purposes with no external intervention. In this context, initiation by administrators may confront the internal evaluator with certain obstacles. Apart from meeting universal standards of impartiality and accuracy, he/she will have the task of allaying suspicion over motives: that the goals are genuinely developmental in nature, intended for programme improvement and no other hidden purpose.

Assuming that doubts over the agenda have been resolved, a key task will be to cultivate a climate of *mutual trust* between all participants. This is because the effectiveness of formative evaluation and programme development is determined by the readiness of participants to disclose their concerns, uncertainties and dilemmas to each other (Fullan 1982, Rudduck 1988). By definition, the starting point for self-directed formative evaluation is a gap – the gap between what participants want to achieve and what they see themselves currently achieving. Exploration of this gap entails scrutiny of one's present practice and anticipation of changes in one's teaching role, both of which impact on the whole self (Easen 1985, Fullan 1982, Rudduck 1988). As a result, engagement in formative evaluation can elicit ambivalent personal reactions: the 'stronger self' will confront the prospect of criticism or change and use it rationally, while the 'weaker self' may fear loss of esteem, feel threat and anxiety and as a result might deny or resist the evaluation's procedures and results. The 'weaker self' will certainly get the upper hand if staff have reason to suspect there is a hidden agenda to the evaluation, and that their own concerns and interests are not being adequately considered. As a result, the formative evaluator's aim is not only to conduct a technically proficient evaluation. It is also to foster this climate of trust so that those affected by evaluation will become *involved* in its processes, will be disposed to communicate freely with peers, and so will be more able to engage in self-criticism and rethinking habituated practices.

A sense of being in control of key processes is a prerequisite to self-scrutiny (Rudduck 1988, Scriven 1991: 270–1, Simons 1984a). This climate requires not only trust between individuals, but also that the identification of issues and areas for improvement be done by the participants themselves. There has to be genuine *ownership* by staff of the evaluation and development process, beginning with the crucial phase of responsive needs assessment and problem definition, so that common goals and priorities can be agreed and the development agenda can be directed by participants. Democratic and systematic needs assessment procedures are an important means to the end of ownership. Some of these procedures are outlined in appendix 8.1. (Further detail on needs assessment procedures may be found in Cline et al. 1990, Easen 1985, McMahon et al. 1986, and Simons 1982c.)

Whether the climate of the institution can promote a formative evaluation depends upon a complex of factors (Fullan 1982, 1991), only some of which will be under the evaluator's control (Adelman 1984). National events, such as pay disputes, inflation, or political turmoil, can create external conditions which can vitiate development activities. Internally, management policy, the readiness of staff to share responsibility and the evaluator's own practice will all affect the outcomes of development-oriented, formative evaluation. Management can affect the climate through using explicit and negotiated procedures (McDonald and Roe 1984), delegation of responsibility, and positive resourcing. Staff will have to accept possibly unfamiliar demands and responsibilities while seeing the process through (Easen 1985). The evaluator can foster the right climate by helping structure key development activities (such as needs assessment, problem analysis, and the identification of priorities for action); by ensuring that the purpose and scope of the evaluation is understood by all and kept to by all; by ensuring that the autonomy of participants is further protected by conventions governing confidentiality and the release of evaluation data; and by maintaining a good flow of information and opinion (Joint Committee 1981; also chapters 1, 4 and 5). As Simons (1982c: 289) indicates, when discussing her concept of democratic evaluation of schools for professional accountability: 'The evaluators should negotiate with participants to set the boundaries of the study in terms of accessibility, relevance of issues and feasibility of procedures and approach. They should negotiate clearance of information offered by participants and used as data for the evaluation before distribution to anyone else.'

This strong form of confidentiality is also appropriate to internal evaluations: self-criticism is best enabled where one is in control of the key processes. A weaker form of confidentiality, anonymity, is not sufficient in most institutions because it is usually possible for the source and object of evaluation data to be identified. Therefore, a high degree of control over information should be the right of all participants in an internal formative evaluation. Whether this right is enjoyed will depend on the enlightenment of senior programme staff.

A final observation: the internal evaluator should examine his/her own motives for engaging in the evaluation, and obtaining the power that goes with it. If he/she is merely pursuing a personal hidden agenda, then it will readily be recognized by colleagues, and dissension and bad feeling are likely to arise. The internal evaluator who is open, problem oriented, and motivated by a commitment to the growth of the institution is most likely to achieve success.

8.4 Final reflections

We have learnt about evaluation from a range of sources (see acknowledgements at start of the book and references in the text).

We have learnt that evaluations have to meet the distinctive needs of different players (funding agencies in order to justify the allocation of funds to one group amid the claims of many; managers in order to lead their institution to prosper financially and professionally; staff in order to best meet their clients' educational needs and to feel that they are doing the most professional job they can). Furthermore, we have come to believe that in spite of these distinctive needs, it is possible to integrate the evaluation activities of these players, each making their distinctive contribution to the benefit of the others, and to the overall benefit of the educational activity to which they are committed.

In terms of our central questions – Why, What, Who, When, and How? – our experience suggests a broad view of evaluation design and implementation, drawing on both external accountability-oriented evaluation and internally motivated evaluation for development. In chapter 1 we described this broad view as embracing: a need for both insider and outsider commitment and involvement to ensure adequate evaluation; a central interest in improvement, as well as the demonstration of 'product value'; an associated commitment to a deeper professional understanding of the process of educational change, as well as the results of that change; systematic documentation for evaluation purposes both during implementation and at the beginning and end of a programme or project's life; a willingness to embrace both qualitative and quantitative methodologies as appropriate to the purpose of the evaluation and the characteristics of the context under review.

The bottom line in any evaluation activity is that it must be appropriate to the questions being asked and provide useful information to inform decision making. No two situations are the same and so there can be no one blueprint for evaluation design – therefore there is no single 'best' or 'correct' method of evaluating a project or programme. The strategies used in any evaluation must represent appropriate and defensible choices from a range of options, not simply the ideological preference of the evaluator.

While we know that the collection and analysis of data should meet standards of feasibility and accuracy, we have also learnt that positive interpersonal and institutional relationships *must underpin* technical adequacy, and are at the heart of effective evaluation: this is because relationships of commitment and trust enable the involvement of players in the evaluation process, and the utilization of evaluation findings. We have learnt that the importance of these relationships must be taken into account from the very outset, 'upstream' of technical data collection. Planning in the full awareness of the importance of each player's personal stake in the evaluation can make a constructive outcome far more likely.

These lessons, however, are all based upon a belief which we hope our readers share. *Systematic evaluation (on a scale appropriate to context and purpose) is an essential element in both language curriculum planning and development, and in personal staff development.* This is as true for the staff of a small language school as it is for those of a major project. It is an essential element because it provides the information, some good news and some bad, with which we can make reasoned and responsible judgements about our work so that our clients (pupils, adult learners, trainees, students, funding agencies) can have the best professional service we can offer. It is also essential because it provides information about our learners' experiences and reactions which can lead us to revise our personal perspectives and thereby develop our classroom practice.

Perhaps it is true that in the field of ELT we have not yet developed an occupational culture disposed to systematic evaluation which is perceived by ELT practitioners as a normal part of their responsibilities. Similarly, it appears that many employers are not yet ready to allow for such activities in the conditions of service they offer. This may explain the lack of evaluation of many ELT projects and programmes.

The hallmark of professional activity and professional strength is a readiness to subject one's work to informed, critical, and systematic scrutiny by others. Of course there are obstacles: lack of time, the resistance of others, institutional inertia, and so on. However, we must all ask ourselves if perceived obstacles are not, in truth, convenient alibis which allow us to shirk scrutiny of our work. The ultimate obstacle to scrutiny lies within ourselves. We all have a weaker and a stronger self. Our weaker self will tend to resist scrutiny and change: our fear of bad news can make us prefer no news at all, for reasons of the personal threat that it can represent, so plainly put by Jean Rudduck (1988: 208): 'If we accept that practitioners' own sense of self is deeply embedded in their teaching it should not be surprising to us that they find real change difficult to contemplate and accomplish.'

However, if we give in to our weaker self, we give up an opportunity for personal growth. Given an appropriate climate and a perception of the worth-whileness of evaluation, our stronger self will accept scrutiny, will take the bad news with the good, and in the very process of developing the educational offering we make, will enable us to develop personally too.

Bibliography

Adelman, C. (ed.) 1984 *The Politics and Ethics of Evaluation*. London: Croom Helm.

Adelman, C. and Alexander, R. 1982 *The Self Evaluating Institution*. New York: Methuen and Co.

Ahenakew, F. 1988 'Program Evaluation and Quality Control' in Native Language Education. *TESL Canada Journal*, 5/2: 51–5.

Alatis, J. E. (ed.) 1978 International Dimensions of Bilingual Education. Washington, D.C.: Georgetown University Press.

Alderson, J. C. (ed.) 1985 *Practical Papers in English Language Education. Vol. 6: Evaluation.* Oxford: Pergamon.

Alderson, J. C. 1985 'Is There Life after the Course?' in Alderson, J. C. (ed.) 1985: 129–50.

Alderson, J. C. 1986 'The Nature of Evaluation'. Paper presented at the national seminar on ESP, Embu, Brazil, May. Mimeo.

Alderson, J. C. 1992 'Guidelines for the Evaluation of Language Education' in Alderson, J. C. and Beretta, A. (eds) 1992: 274–305.

Alderson, J. C. and Beretta, A. (eds) 1992 *Evaluating Second Language Education*. Cambridge: Cambridge University Press.

Alderson, J. C. and Scott, M. 1992 'Insiders, Outsiders and Participatory Evaluation' in Alderson, J. C. and Beretta, A. (eds) 1992: 25–60.

Alderson, J. C. and Waters, A. 1982 'A Course in Testing and Evaluation for ESP teachers or, "How bad were my tests?"' in Waters, A. (ed.) 1982: 39–61.

Alderson, J. C., Krahnke, K. and Stansfield, C. W. 1987 *Reviews of English Language Proficiency Tests*. Washington, D. C.: TESOL.

Alkin, M. C. 1969 Evaluation Theory Development. *Evaluation Comment*, 2/1: 2–7.

Alkin, M. C., Daillak, K. and White, P. 1979 *Using Evaluation: Does Evaluation Make a Difference?* Newbury Park, Calif.: Sage.

Allen, P. and Carroll, S. 1987 Evaluation of Classroom Processes in a Canadian Core French Programme. *Evaluation and Research in Education*, 1/2: 49–61.

Allwright, R. 1983 Classroom-centred Research on Language Teaching and Learning: A Brief Historical Overview. *TESOL Quarterly*, 17/2: 191–204.

Allwright, R. 1988 *Observation in the Language Classroom*. London and New York: Longman.

Allwright, R. and Bailey, K. 1991 *Focus on the Language Classroom: An Introduction to Classroom Research for Language Teachers*. Cambridge: Cambridge University Press.

Altrichter, H., Posch, P. and Somekh, B. 1993 *Teachers Investigate Their Work: An Introduction to the Methods of Action Research*. London: Routledge.

Anderson, S. B., Ball, S., Murphy, R. T. and associates (eds) 1973 *The Encyclopedia of*

Educational Evaluation: Concepts and Techniques for Evaluating Education and Training Programs. San Francisco: Jossey-Bass.

Anivan, S. (ed.) 1991 *Issues in Language Programme Evaluation in the 1990's*. Anthology Series 27. Singapore: Regional Language Centre.

Argyris, C. and Schon, D. A. 1976 *Theory in Practice: Increasing Professional Effectiveness*. San Francisco and London: Jossey-Bass.

Asian Development Bank 1986 *Handbook on Management of Project Implementation*. Manila: Asian Development Bank.

Ashton, P. M. E., Henderson, E. S. and Peacock, A. 1989 *Teacher Education through Classroom Evaluation: The Principles and Practice of IT-INSET*. London and New York: Routledge.

Aubrey, C. 1988 Guidelines for an Effective Evaluation. *British Journal of In-Service Education*, 14/3: 140–6.

Bachman, L. 1981 'Formative Evaluation in Specific Purpose Program Development' in Mackay, R. and Palmer, J. (eds) 1981: 106–16.

Bachman, L. 1987 Some Uses of Evaluation in Language Programs. *PASAA*, 17/2: 39–45.

Bachman, L. 1989 'The Development and Use of Criterion-referenced Tests of Language Ability in Language Program Evaluation' in Johnson, R. K. (ed.) 1989: 242–58.

Bachman, L. 1990 *Fundamental Considerations in Language Testing*. Oxford: Oxford University Press.

Bailey, K. M. 1983 'Competitiveness and Anxiety in Adult Second Language Learning: Looking at and through the Diary Studies' in Seliger, H. W. and Long, M. H. (eds) 1983: 67–102.

Bailey, L. G. 1975 An Observational Method in the Foreign Language Classroom: A Closer Look at Interaction Analysis. *Foreign Language Annals*, 8/4: 335–44.

BALEAP 1993 *Handbook: Accreditation Scheme for English Language and Study Skills Courses in Universities and Polytechnics*. Manchester: British Association of Lecturers in English for Academic Purposes.

Bamberger, M. 1991 'The Politics of Evaluation in Developing Countries'. *Evaluation and Program Planning*, 14/4: 325–39.

Barrington, G. V. 1986 Evaluating English as a Second Language: A Naturalistic Model. *TESL Canada Journal*, 3/2: 41–52.

Barrow, R. 1984 *Giving Teaching Back to Teachers*. Brighton: Wheatsheaf Books.

Bastiani, J. and Tolley, H. 1979 *Researching into the Curriculum*. Rediguide 16, Nottingham University.

Becker, A. and MacClure, S. (eds) 1978 *Accountability in Education*. Windsor: NFER Publishing.

Bell, J. 1987 *Doing Your Own Research Project*. Milton Keynes: Open University Press.

Bell, J., Bush, T., Fox, A., Goodey, J. and Goulding, S. (eds) 1984 *Conducting Small-scale Investigations in Educational Management*. London: Harper and Row/Open University.

Bell, L. 1988 *Appraising Teachers in Schools*. London: Routledge.

Bell, M. 1982 *Guidelines for the Evaluation of TAFE Programs*. Australia, Technical and Further Education.

Bensoussan, M. and Ramraz, R. 1984 Helping the Poor to Help Themselves: A Quantitative Re-evaluation of the Outcomes of an Advanced Reading Comprehension Program in English as a Foreign Language. *System*, 12/1: 61 6.

Beretta, A. 1986a A Case for Field Experimentation in Language Teaching Program Evaluation. *Language Learning*, 36/3: 295–309.

Beretta, A. 1986b Program-fair Language Teaching Evaluation. *TESOL Quarterly*, 20/3: 431–44.

Beretta, A. 1986c Towards a Methodology of ESL Program Evaluation. *TESOL Quarterly*, 20/1: 144–55.

Beretta, A. 1987 Evaluation of a language teaching project in South India. Ph.D. thesis, University of Edinburgh.

Beretta, A. 1990 The Program Evaluator: The ESL Researcher without Portfolio. *Applied Linguistics*, 11/1: 1–15.

Beretta, A. 1992 'What Can Be Learned from the Bangalore Evaluation' in Alderson, J. C. and Beretta, A. (eds) 1992: 250–74.

Beretta, A. and Davis, A. 1985 Evaluation of the Bangalore Project. *English Language Teaching Journal*, 39/2: 121–7.

Berk, R. A. and Rossi, P. H. 1990 *Thinking about Program Evaluation*. London: Sage Publications.

Berkowitz, L. and Donnerstein, E. 1982 External Validity Is More Than Skin-deep: Some Answers to Criticisms of Laboratory Experiments. *American Psychologist*, 37/3: 245–57.

Bernhard, E. B. and Hammadou, J. 1987 A Decade of Research in Foreign Language Teacher Education. *Modern Language Journal*, 7/1: 301–6.

Beveridge, W. E. 1968 *Problem Solving Interviews*. London: Allen and Unwin.

Bickley, V. (ed.) 1987 *Future Directions in English Language Teacher Education*. Hong Kong: Institute of Language in Education, Education Department.

Biggs, J. B. and Collis, K. F. 1982 *Evaluating the Quality of Learning*. New York: Academic Press.

Bloom, B. S., Hastings, J. T. and Madaus, G. F. 1971 *Handbook on Formative and Summative Evaluation of Student Learning*. McGraw Hill.

Blue, G. (ed.) 1993 *Language Learning and Success Studying through English*. Basingstoke: Modern English Publications.

Boehm, A. E. and Weinberg, R. A. 1977 *The Classroom Observer: A Guide for Developing Observation Skills*. New York: Teachers College Press.

Borg, W. R. and Gall, M. D. 1989 *Educational Research*. New York: Longman.

Borich, G. (ed.) 1974 *Evaluating Educational Products*. Englewood Cliffs, N.J.: Educational Technology Press.

Borich, G. D. and Klinzing, G. 1984 Some assumptions in the observation of classroom process with suggestions for improving low inference measurement. *Journal of Class Interaction*, 20/1: 36–44.

Bowers, R. 1980 Verbal Behaviour in the Language Teaching Classroom. Ph.D. thesis, University of Reading.

Bowers, R. 1983 'Project Planning and Performance' in Brumfit, C. (ed.) 1983: 99–120.

Bowers, R. (ed.) 1987 *Language Teacher Education: An Integrated Programme for ELT Teacher Training*. Modern English Publications.

Boydell, D. 1983 *The Pupil and Teacher Record: A Manual for Observers*. Leicester: ORACLE Project, School of Education, University of Leicester.

Bracht, G. H. and Glass, G. V. 1986 The External Validity of Experiments. *American Educational Research Journal*, 5/4: 437–74.

Bradburn, N. M. and Sudman, S. 1982 *Asking Questions: A Practical Guide to Questionnaire Design*. San Francisco: Jossey-Bass.

Bramley, P. 1986 *Evaluation of Training: A Practical Guide*. London: British Association for Commercial and Industrial Education.

Braskamp, L. A. and Brown, R. D. 1980 *New Directions for Program Evaluation: Utilization of Evaluation Information*. San Francisco: Jossey-Bass.

Breen, M. P. 1989 'The Evaluation Cycle for Language Learning Tasks' in Johnson, R. K. (ed.) 1989: 187–206.

Breen, M. P. and Candlin, C. 1987 'Which Materials?: A Consumer's and Designer's Guide' in Sheldon, L. E. (ed.) 1987: 13–28.

Briggs, C. L. 1986 *Learning How to Ask*. Cambridge: Cambridge University Press.

Brindley, G. 1987 Assessing Achievement in a Learner Centred Curriculum. Paper presented at the annual conference of Teachers of English of Speakers of Other Languages, New York. Mimeo.

Brindley, G. 1990 Defining Language Ability: The Criteria for Criteria. McQuarie University, Australia: NCELTR. Mimeo.

British Council 1981 *Dunford House seminar report 1980: Design, Evaluation and Testing in English Language Projects*.

British Council 1989 *Dunford House seminar report 1988: ELT in Development Aid – Defining Aims and Measuring Results*. British Council.

British Council 1990 *Dunford House seminar report 1989: Managing ELT Aid Projects for Sustainability*. British Council.

British Council 1991 *Dunford House seminar report 1990: Training for Sustainability of ELT Aid Projects*. British Council.

British Council 1992 *Dunford House seminar report 1991: The Social and Economic Impact of ELT in Development*. British Council.

British Council and ARELS-FELCO 1991 *Handbook: Accreditation Scheme*. Manchester: British Council.

Brittan, D. 1985 Teacher Training in ELT, Parts 1 and 2. *Language Teaching*, 18/2: 112–28, 18/3: 220–38.

Broadfoot, P. 1986 *Profiles and Records of Achievement: A review of Issues and Practice*. London: Cassel.

Bromme, R. 1987 'Teachers' Assessments of Students' Difficulties and Progress in Understanding in the Classroom' in Calderhead, J. (ed.) 1987: 125–46.

Brown, G. 1975 *Microteaching*. London: Methuen.

Brown, J. D. 1988 *Understanding Research in Second Language Learning*. Cambridge: Cambridge University Press.

Brown, J. D. 1989 Language Programme Evaluation. A Synthesis of Existing Possibilities. Paper delivered at the Seminar on Evaluation and Testing, Bangkok, December 1986. Reprinted in Johnson, R. K. (ed.) 1989: 222–41.

Brumfit, C. (ed.) 1983 *Language Teaching Projects for the Third World*. ELT Documents 116. Pergamon/British Council.

Brumfit, C. J. 1984a *Communicative Methodology in Language Teaching: The Roles of Fluency and Accuracy*. Cambridge: Cambridge University Press.

Brumfit, C. J. 1984b The Bangalore Procedural Syllabus. *English Language Teaching Journal*, 38/4: 233–41.

Brumfit, C. J. (ed.) 1984c *Language Issues and Education Policies*. ELT Documents: 119. Pergamon.

Brumfit, C. J. and Mitchell, R. 1990 *Research in the Language Classroom*. ELT Documents 133. MEP/British Council.

Buckby, M. 1981 Graded Objectives and Tests for Modern Languages: An Evaluation. *British Journal of Language Teaching*, 19/1: 13–14.

Budd, R. W., Thorp, R. K. and Donoghew, L. 1967 *Content Analysis of Communication*. New York: MacMillan.

Burgess, R. (ed.) 1985a *Field Methods in the Study of Education*. London: Falmer Press.

Burgess, R. (ed.) 1985b *Issues in Educational Research: Qualitative Methods*. London: Falmer Press.

Burton, J. and Mickan, P. 1993 'Teachers' Classroom Research: Rhetoric and Reality' in Edge, J. and Richards, K. (eds) 1993: 113–21.

Burton, J., Weir, C. J. and Roberts, J. R. (forthcoming) *Evaluation of a Baseline Study: English Teaching Nepal* Evaluation Department, Overseas Development Administration, London.

Bynner, J., McCormick, R. and Nuttall, D. 1982 *Organisation and the Use of Evaluation*. Milton Keynes: Open University Press.

Byrne, H. and Canale, M. (eds) 1986 *Defining and Developing Proficiency: Guidelines, Implementations, and Concepts*. Lincolnwood, Ill.: National Textbook.

Calderhead, J. (ed.) 1987 *Exploring Teachers' Thinking*. London: Cassell Educational.

Calderhead, J. (ed.) 1988 *Teachers' Professional Learning*. Lewes: Falmer Press.

Calderhead, J. 1990 Conceptualising and Evaluating Teachers' Professional Learning. *European Journal of Teacher Education*, 13/3: 153–60.

Campbell, D. A. and Fiske, D. W. 1959 Validation by the multitrait multimethod matrix. *Psychological Bulletin*, 56/2: 81–105.

Campbell, D. T. and Stanley, J. C. 1963 'Experimental and Quasi Experimental Designs for Research in Teaching' in Gage, N. L. (ed.) 1963: 171–246.

Campbell, D. T. and Stanley, J. C. 1966 *Experimental and Quasi Experimental Designs for Research*. Chicago: Rand McNally.

Candlin, C. N. and Breen, M. P. 1979 *Evaluating and Designing Language Teaching Materials*. Practical Papers in English Language Education 2. Lancaster: University of Lancaster.

Candlin, C. N. and Murphy, D. 1987 *Language Learning Tasks*. Englewood Cliffs, N.J.: Prentice-Hall.

Caro, F. G. (ed.) 1971 *Readings in Evaluation Research*. New York: Russell Sage Foundation.

Case, R., Werner, W., Onno, E. and Daniels, L. 1985 *Evaluation for Development Education: An Introduction*. Vancouver: Center for the Study of Curriculum and Instruction, University of British Columbia.

Celani, M. A. A., Holmes, J. L., Ramos, R. C. G. and Scott, M. R. 1988 *The Brazilian ESP Project: An Evaluation*. Centro de Pesquisas, Recursos e Informacao e Leitura de Sao Paulo, Brazil. Sao Paolo; Editora de PUC.-SP.

Chambers, F. and Erith, P. 1990 On Justifying and Evaluating Aid-based ELT. *ELTJ*, 44/2: 138–43.

Charters, W. W. and Jones, J. 1973 On the Risks of Appraising Non-events in Program Evaluation. *Educational Researcher*, 2/11: 5–7.

Chastain, K. D. and Woerdehoff, F. J. 1968 A methodological study comparing the audio-lingual habit theory and the cognitive code-learning theory. *Modern Language Journal*, 52/5: 268–79.

Chatfield, C. and Collins, A. J. 1980 *Introduction to Multivariate Analysis*. London: Chapman and Hall.

Cheung, N.-L. 1985 *Varying Interpretation: A Pilot Study Using a Triangulated Procedure*. Working Papers in Linguistics and Language Teaching 7: 56–73. University of Hong Kong Language Centre.

Churchman, D. 1979 A New Approach to Evaluating the Implementation of Innovative Education Programs. *Educational Technology*, 19/1: 25–8.

Clarke, D. 1988 The Project Approach to Bilateral Aid ELT Programmes. *ETIC*, 22/1: 25–9.

Clift, P., Nuttall, D. L. and McCormick, R. (eds) 1987 *Studies in School Self Evaluation*. Lewes: Falmer.

Cline, T., Frederickson, N. and Wright, A. 1990 *Effective In-Service Training: A Learning Resource Pack*. University College London.

Cohen, A. D. and Hosenfeld, C. 1981 Some Uses of Mentalistic Data in Second Language Research. *Language Learning*, 31/2: 285–313.

Cohen, L. and Manion, L. 1980 *Research Methods in Education*. London: Croom Helm.

Cohen, L. and Manion, L. 1984 'Action Research' in Bell, J. et al. (eds): 41–57.

Coladarci, T. and Gage, N. L. 1984 Effects of a Minimal Intervention on Teacher Behavior and Student Achievement. *American Educational Research Journal*, 21/3: 539–55.

Coleman, G. 1986 The Logical Framework Approach. Paper presented at the Overseas Development Administration Logical Framework Workshop, University of East Anglia, 19 December.

Coleman, G. 1987 Project Planning: Logical Framework Approach to the Monitoring and Evaluation of Agricultural and Rural Development Projects, *Project Appraisal*, 2/4: 251–9.

Coleman, H. 1985 'Evaluating Teachers' Guides: Do Teachers' Guides Guide Teachers?' in Alderson, J. C. (ed.) 1985: 83–96.

Coleman, H. 1992 'Moving the Goalposts: Project Evaluation in Practice' in Alderson, J. C. and Beretta, A. (eds) 1992: 222–49.

Cook, T. D. and Campbell, D. T. 1976 'The Design and Conduct of Quasi-experiments and True Experiments in Field Settings' in Dunnette, M. D. (ed.) 1976: 223–327.

Cook, T. D. and Campbell, D. T. 1979 *Quasi-experimentation: Design and Analysis Issues for Field Settings*. Chicago: Rand McNally.

Cook, T. D. and Reichardt, C. (eds) 1979 *Qualitative and Quantitative Methods in Evaluation Research*. California: Sage Publications.

Cooper, K. 1976 Curriculum Evaluation: Definitions and Boundaries in Tawney, D. (ed.): 1–11.

Cracknell, B. E. (ed.) 1984 *The Evaluation of Aid Projects and Programmes*. London: Overseas Development Administration.

Cronbach, L. J. 1963 'Course Improvement through Evaluation' *Teachers College Record*, 64: 672–83.

Cronbach, L. J. 1982 *Designing Evaluations of Educational and Social Programs* San Francisco: Jossey-Bass.

Cronbach, L. J. and Snow, R. E. 1981 *Aptitudes and Instructional measures* (2nd edn) New York: Irvington.

Cronbach, L. J., Rajaratnam, M. and Gleser, G. 1963 Theory of Generalisability: A Liberation of Reliability Theory. *British Journal of Statistical Psychology*, 16/2: 137–63.

Cronbach, L. J., Ambron, S. R., Dorubusch, S. M., Hess, R. D., Hornik, R. C., Phillips, D. C., Walker, D. F. and Weiner, S. S. 1980 *Towards Reform of Program Evaluation*. San Francisco: Jossey-Bass.

Cumming, A. 1987 What Is a Second-Language Program Evaluation? *Canadian Modern Language Review*, 43/4: 678–99.

Cunningsworth, A. 1984 *Evaluating and Selecting EFL Teaching Materials*. London: Heinemann.

Daillak, R. H. 1983 Evaluators in an Urban School District: Organisational Constraints upon Evaluation Influence. *Studies in Education Evaluation*, 9/1: 33–46.

Davies, A. 1992 Book Review. Alderson, J. C. and Beretta, A. 1992 *Evaluating Second Language Education*. *Language Testing*, 9/2: 207–9.

Davies, I. K. 1976 *Objectives in Curriculum Design*. London: McGraw Hill.

Davis, E. 1981 *Teachers as Curriculum Evaluators*. Sydney, London and Boston: George Allen and Unwin Australia.

Day, C., Whitaker, P. and Wren, D. 1987 *Appraisal and Professional Development in Primary Schools*. Milton Keynes: Open University Press.

Delamere, T. 1986 On the Supervision and Evaluation of Instruction. *System*, 14/3: 327–33.

Delamont, S. and Hamilton, D. 1976 'Classroom Research: A Critique and a New Approach' in Stubbs, M. and Delamont, S. (eds) 1976: 3–20.

Dick, W. 1982 Evaluation in Diverse Educational Settings. *Viewpoints in Teaching and Learning*, 58/3: 84–9.

Dijkstra, W. and Vanderzouwen, J. (eds) 1982 *Response Behaviour in the Surrey Interview*. London: Academic Press.

Dodd, W. A. 1986 'Evaluation: A Few Heretical Thoughts' in *Proceedings of* the 25th Annual Conference of *The Association of Teachers of Overseas Education*. 1–2. London: Garnett College.

Dove, L. 1986 *Teachers and Teacher Education in Developing Countries*. Beckenham, Kent: Croom Helm.

Doyle, W. 1977 Learning the Classroom Environment: An Ecological Approach. *Journal of Teacher Education*, 28/6: 51–5.

Dubin, F. and Wong, R. 1990 'An Ethnographic Approach to Inservice Preparation: The Hungary File' in Richards, J. C. and Nunan, D. (eds) 1990: 282–92.

Dunnette, M. D. (ed.) 1976 *Handbook of Industrial and Organizational Psychology*. Chicago: Rand McNally.

Easen, P. 1985 *Making School Centred Inset Work*. Beckenham, Kent: Croom Helm.

Ebel, R. L. 1951 Estimation of the Reliability of Ratings. *Psychometrika*, 16: 407–24.

Ebel, R. L. 1991 *Essentials of Educational Measurement*. (5th edn). Englewood Cliffs, N.J.: Prentice-Hall.

Ebbutt, D. 1985 'Educational Action Research' in Burgess, R. (ed.) 1985b: 152–74.

Edge, J. and Richards, K. (eds) 1993 *Teachers Develop Teachers Research: Papers on Classroom Research and Teacher Development*. Oxford: Heinemann International.

Eisner, E. W. 1979 *The Educational Imagination: On the Design and Evaluation of School Programs*. New York: Macmillan.

Eisner, E. W. 1984 Can Educational Research Inform Educational Practice? *Phi Delta Kappa*, 65/7: 447–52.

Eisner, E. W. 1985 *The Art of Educational Evaluation: A Personal Review*. Lewes: Falmer Press.

Elley, W. B. 1989 'Tailoring the Evaluation to Fit the Context' in Johnson, R. K. (ed.) 1989: 270–85.

Elliot, J. 1979 'Implementing School-based Action Research: Some Hypotheses' in Bell et al. (eds) 1984: 58–71.

Ellis, R. and Robinson, E. 1981 A Reassessment of Lesson Evaluation in ELT. *System*, 9/1: 5–10.

Entwistle, N. J. and Nisbet, J. D. 1972 *Educational Research in Action*. London: University of London Press.

Eraut, M. 1982 What Is Learned In-service Education and How? A Knowledge in Perspective? *British Journal of In-Service Education*, 9/1: 6–14.

Eraut, M., Goad, L. and Smith, G. 1975 *The Analysis of Curriculum Materials*. Occasional Paper 9, University of Sussex Education Area.

Fenstermacher, G. D. 1979 A Philosophical Consideration of Recent Research on Teacher Effectiveness. *Review of Research in Education*, 6: 157–85.

Fenstermacher, G. D. 1982 On Learning to Teach Effectively from Research on Teacher Effectiveness. *Journal of Classroom Interaction*, 17/2: 7–12.

Fetterman, D. M. 1988 Qualitative Approaches to Evaluating Education. *Educational Research*, 17: 17–23.

Findley, C. and Nathan, L. 1980 Functional Language Objectives in Competency Based ESL Curriculum. *TESOL Quarterly*, 14/2: 221–31.

Fink, A. and Kosecoff, J. 1985 *How to Conduct Surveys: A Step by Step Guide*. Beverley Hills, Calif.: Sage.

FitzGibbon, C. T. and Morris, L. L. 1987a *How to Analyze Data*. Newbury Park, Calif.: Sage.

FitzGibbon, C. T. and Morris, L. L. 1987b *How to Design a Program Evaluation*. Newbury Park, Calif.: Sage.

Flanagan, J. C. 1954 The Critical Incident Technique. *Psychological Bulletin*. 51: 327–58.

Flanders, N. A. 1970 *Analyzing Teaching Behaviour*. Cambridge, Mass.: Addison-Wesley.

Flowerdew, J., Brock, M. and Hsia, S. (eds) 1992 *Second Language Teacher Education*. City Poly-technic of Hong Kong.

Fowler, F. J. (1989) *Survey Research Methods* (2nd edn). Newbury Park, Calif.: Sage.

Fowler, F. J. and Mangione, T. W. (1990) *Standardized Survey Interviewing: Minimizing Interviewer Related Error*. Newbury Park, Calif.: Sage.

Fraser, B. J. 1984 Directions in Curriculum Evaluation. *Studies in Educational Evaluation*, 10: 125–34.

Freedman, E. S. 1979 Valid Research into Foreign Language Teaching: Two Recent Projects. *System*, 7/3: 187–99.

Freedman, E. S. 1982 Experimentation into Foreign Language Teaching Methodology: The Research findings. *System*, 10/2: 119–33.

Frick, T. and Semmel, M. I. 1978 'Observer agreement and reliabilities of classroom observational measures'. *Review of Educational Research*, 48/1: 157–84.

Frohlich, M., Spada, N. and Allen, P. 1985 Differences in the Communicative Orientation of L2 Classrooms. *TESOL Quarterly*, 19/1: 27–57.

Fullan, M. G. 1982 *The Meaning of Educational Change*. New York: Columbia University Teachers College Press.

Fullan, M. G. 1983 Evaluating Program Implementation: What Can Be Learned from Follow Through. *Curriculum Inquiry*, 13/2: 215–27.

Fullan, M. G. 1986 Improving the Implementation of Educational Change. *School Organisation*, 6/3: 321–6.

Fullan, M. G. 1991 *The New Meaning of Educational Change*. London: Cassell.

Fullan, M. G. and Pomfret, A. 1977 Research on Curriculum and Instruction Implementation. *Review of Educational Research*, 47/1: 335–97.

Fuller, F. F. and Manning, B. A. 1973 Self-confrontation Reviewed: a Conceptualization for Video Playback in Teacher Education. *Review of Educational Research*, 43/4: 469–528.

Gage, N. L. (ed.) 1963 *Handbook of Research on Teaching*. Chicago: Rand McNally.

Gaies, S. J. 1983 The Investigations of Language Classroom Processes. *TESOL Quarterly*, 17: 205–17.

Galton, M. 1978 *British Mirrors: A Collection of Classroom Observation Systems*. Leicester University School of Education.

Galton, M. and Moon, B. (eds) 1983 *Changing Schools... Changing Curriculum*. London: Harper and Row.

Garfinkel, H. 1967 *Studies in Ethnomethodology*. New Jersey: Prentice Hall.

Gebhard, J. 1990 Interaction in a Teaching Practicum in Richards, J. C. and Nunan, D. (eds) 1990: 118–31.

Gibbs, G. and Haigh, M. 1983 *Alternative Models of Course Evaluation: Examples for Oxford Polytechnic*. Occasional Paper No. 13, Standing Conference on Educational Development. Oxford Polytechnic.

Gibbs, G. and Haigh, M. 1984 *A Compendium of Course Evaluation Questionnaires*. Occasional Paper No. 17, Standing Conference on Educational Development. Oxford Polytechnic.

Gitlin, A. and Smyth, J. 1989 *Teacher Evaluation: Educative Alternatives*. Lewes: Falmer Press.

Glaser, R. 1963 Instructional Technology and the Measurement of Learning Outcomes. *American Psychologist*, 18: 510–22.

Golby, M., Greenwald, J. and West, R. (eds) 1975 *Curriculum Design*. London: Croom Helm/Open University.

Goodlad, J. I. and Klein, M. F. 1974 *Looking behind the Classroom Door*. Worthington, Ohio: CA Jones.

Green, D. R. 1983 Content Validity of Standardized Achievement Tests and Test Curriculum Overlap. Paper presented at the annual meeting of the National Council on Measurement in Education, Montreal, March (ERIC Document Reproduction Service No. ED 235 237).

Greenwood, J. 1985 Bangalore Revisited: A Reluctant Complaint. *ELTJ*, 39/4: 268–73.

Gronlund, N. E. and Linn, R. L. 1990 *Measurement and Evaluation in Teaching*. New York: Macmillan.

Guba, E. G. 1978 *Toward a Methodology of Naturalistic Inquiry in Educational Evaluation*. Monograph Series in Evaluation No. 8. Los Angeles: Center for the Study of Evaluation, UCLA.

Guba, E. G. 1981 The Paradigm Revolution in Inquiry: Implications for Vocational Research and Development. Paper presented at the National Center for Research in Vocational Education Staff Development Seminar, Columbus, Ohio (ERIC Document Reproduction Service No. ED 212 829).

Guba, E. G. and Lincoln, Y. S. 1983 *Effective Evaluation: Improving the Usefulness of Evaluation Results through Responsive and Naturalistic Approaches*. San Francisco: Jossey-Bass.

Guba, E. G. and Lincoln, Y. S. 1989 *Fourth Generation Evaluation*. Newbury Park, Calif.: Sage.

Hall, G. E. and Loucks, S. F. 1977 A Developmental Model for Determining Whether the

Treatment Is Actually Implemented. *American Educational Research Journal*, 14/3: 263–76.

Hall, G. E. and Rutherford, W. W. 1983 *Client Concerns: A Guide to Facilitating Institutional Change*. Austin, Texas: Research and Development Center for Teacher Education, University of Texas (ERIC Document Reproduction Service No. ED 251 728).

Hall, G. E., George, A. and Rutherford, W. W. 1977 *Measuring Stages of Concern about the Innovation: A Manual for the Use of the SoC Questionnaire*. Austin, Texas: Research and Development Center for Teacher Education, University of Texas (ERIC Document Reproduction Service No. ED 147 342).

Hambleton, R. K., Swaminathan, H., Algina, J. and Coulson, D. B. 1978 Criterion Referenced Testing and Measurement: A Review of Technical Issues and Developments. *Review of Educational Research*, 48/1: 1–47.

Hamilton, D. 1976 *Curriculum Evaluation*. London: Open Books.

Hamilton, D., Jenkins, D., King, C., McDonald, C. and Parlett, M. (eds) 1977 *Beyond the Numbers Game*. Basingstoke: Macmillan.

Hanson, R. A. and Bailey, J. D. 1983 *Program-fair Educational Evaluation and Empirical Curriculum Inquiry*. Los Alamitos, Calif.: Southwest Regional Laboratory for Educational Research and Development (ERIC Document Reproduction Service No. ED 251 505).

Harlen, W. (ed.) 1981 *Evaluation and the Teacher's Role*. London: Macmillan Educational Schools Council Research Studies.

Harlen, W. and Elliott, J. 1982 'A checklist for planning or reviewing an evaluation' in McCormick, R. et al. 1982 (eds): 296–304.

Harper, W. M., Blake, M. J. and Weissberg, R. C. 1981 A Performance Evaluation of an Alternative Approach to English Language Training. *System*, 9/1: 23–8.

Harris, A., Laurie, M. and Prescott, W. 1975 *Curriculum Innovation*. London: Croom Helm/Open University.

Harris, P. R. and Moran, R. T. 1987 *Managing Cultural Differences* (2nd edn). London: Gulf Publishing.

Harrison, M. 1991 An investigation of the usefulness of collection and provision of baseline data on education systems prior to beginning ELT aid projects overseas. MATEFL diss., CALS, University of Reading.

Harrison, M. I. 1987 *Diagnosing Organisations: Methods, Models and Processes*. London: Sage.

Harwood, D. 1989 The Nature of Teacher–Pupil Interaction in the Active Tutorial Work Approach: Using Interaction Analysis to Evaluate Student-centred Approaches. *British Educational Research Journal*, 15/2: 177/194.

Hatch, E. and Lazaraton, A. 1991 *The Research Manual: Design and Statistics for Applied Linguistics*. New York: Newbury House.

Hatch, J. 1983 Applications of Qualitative Methods to Program Evaluation in Education. *Viewpoints in Teaching and Learning*, 59/1: 1–11.

Hatta, G. 1989 An Evaluation of an INSET Course. *British Council University/College Teachers of English Alumni Association (BCTEA) Bulletin* (British Council, Japan), no. 3: 1–4.

Havelock, R. 1971 The Utilization of Educational Research and Development. *British Journal of Educational Technology*, 2/2: 84–97.

Havelock, R. G. and Huberman, A. M. 1977 *Solving Educational Problems: The Theory and Reality of Innovation in Developing Countries*. Paris: UNESCO.

Hayes, A. 1983 'Planning a Project: The KELT Project, Sierra Leone' in Brumfit, C. (ed.) 1983: 15–27.

Heaton, B. (ed.) 1982 *Language Testing*. Oxford: Modern English Publications.

Heaton, B. and Adams, P. 1991 *Sociocultural Problems in English for Academic Purposes*. London: Macmillan.

Henderson, E. S. 1976 'Attitude Change in-Service Training' in *British Journal of In-Service Education*, 2/2: 113–16.

Henderson, E. S. 1978 *The Evaluation of In-Service Teacher Training*. London: Croom Helm.

Henerson, M. E., Morris, L. L. and Fitzgibbon, C. T. 1987 *How to Measure Attitudes*. Newbury Park, Calif.: Sage Publications.

Henning, G. 1975 Measuring Foreign Language Reading Comprehension. *Language Learning*, 25/1: 109–14.

Henning, G. 1986 Quantitative Methods in Language Acquisition Research. *TESOL Quarterly*, 20/4: 701–8.

Henry, C. and Kemmis, S. 1985 A Point by Point Guide to Action Research for Teachers. *The Australian Administrator* (Deakin University Press), 6/4: 1–4.

Herbert, J. and Attridge, C. 1975 A Guide for Developers and Users of Observation Systems and Manuals. *American Educational Research Journal*, 12/1: 1–20.

Herman, J. L., Morris, L. L. and Fitzgibbon, C. T. 1987 *Evaluator's Handbook*. Newbury Park, Calif.: Sage Publications.

Hodgson, F. and Whalley, G. 1985 Evaluation of In-Service Education: The Question of Criteria. *British Journal of In-Service Education*, 12/1: 44–7.

Hofstede, G. 1980 *Culture's Consequences: International Differences in Work-related Values*. Beverly Hills, Calif.: Sage.

Holliday, A. 1983 'Research into Classroom Culture as a Necessary Input into Syllabus Design' in Swales, J. and Mustafa, H. (eds) 1983.

Holliday, A. and Cooke, T. M. 1982 'An Ecological Approach to ESP' in Waters, A. (ed.): 123–43.

Holsti, O. (1969) *Content Analysis for the Social Sciences and Humanities*. Reading, Mass.: Addison Wesley.

Holt, M. 1981 *Evaluating the Evaluators*. London: Hodder and Stoughton.

Hook, C. 1981 *Studying Classrooms*. Deakin University Press.

Hopkins, D. 1985 *A Teacher's Guide to Classroom Research*. Milton Keynes: Open University Press.

Hopkins, D. (ed.) 1986 *Inservice Training and Educational Development*. London: Croom Helm.

Hopkins, D. 1989 *Evaluation for School Development*. Milton Keynes: Open University Press.

Horgan, C. 1988 Evaluation: A case study of the Reading presessional course. MATEFL diss., University of Reading.

Horngren, C. T. 1977 *Cost Accounting: A Managerial Emphasis* (4th edn). London: Prentice Hall.

Horst, D. P., Tallmadge, G. K. and Wood, C. T. 1975 *A Procedural Guide for Validating Achievement Test Gains in Educational Projects*. Mountain View, Calif.: RMC Research Corporation.

House, E. R. (ed.) 1973 *School Evaluation: The Politics and Process*. Berketey, Calif.: McCutchan.

House, E. R. 1980 *Evaluating with Validity*. Beverley Hills, Calif.: Sage Publications.

House, E. R. (ed.) 1986 *New Directions in Educational Evaluation*. Lewes: Falmer Press.

House, E. R., Thurston, P. and Hand, J. 1984 Evaluation Reflections: The Adversary Hearing as a Public Forum. *Studies in Educational Evaluation*, 10: 111–23.

Hudson, T. 1989 'Mastery Decisions in Program Evaluation' in Johnson, R. K. (ed.) 1989: 259–69.

Hughes, A. (ed.) 1988 *Testing English for University Study ELT Documents 127.* Oxford: Modern English Press.

Hundleby, S. and Breet, F. 1988 Using Methodology Notebooks on In-service Teacher Training Courses. *English Language Teaching Journal,* 42/1: 34–6.

Hustler, D., Cassidy, T. and Cuff, T. (eds) 1986 *Action Research in Classrooms and Schools.* London: Allen and Unwin.

Hutchinson, B., Hopkins, D. and Howard, J. 1988 The Problem of Validity in the Qualitative Evaluation of Categorically Funded Curriculum Development Projects. *Educational Research,* 30/1: 54–64.

Hutchinson, T. and Waters, A. 1987 *ESP: A Learning Centred Approach.* Cambridge: Cambridge University Press.

Iredale, R. 1989 The Economic Benefits of English Language Teaching. Keynote address at the Dunford House Seminar in British Council 1989. Reprinted in British Council 1992: 8–10.

Iredale, R. 1990 International Agencies: Learning How to Identify and Meet Needs. *International Journal of International Development,* 10/2, 3: 163–8.

Jacobsen, P. L. H. 1982 Using Evaluation to Improve Foreign Language Education. *Modern Language Journal,* 66/3: 284–91.

Jafarpur, A. 1987 Are Standardised Tests Sensitive to ESL Students' Growth? *Regional English Language Centre Journal,* 18/2: 74–87.

James, M. 1982 *Approaches to Evaluation: Institutional Self-Evaluation.* Milton Keynes: Open University Press.

Jansen-Strasser, E. 1989 Joint Course-provider/Client Evaluation of Short EFL Courses. MATEFL diss., University of Reading.

Jarvis, G. A. 1968 A Behavioral Observation System for Classroom Foreign Language Skill Acquisition Activities. *Modern Language Journal,* 52/6: 335–41.

Jarvis, J. 1992 Using Diaries for Teacher Reflection on In-Service Courses. *English Language Teaching Journal,* 46/2: 133–43.

Jenkins, D. and Shipman, M. D. (eds) 1976 *Evaluation on the Run: A Curriculum Reader.* Basingstoke: Macmillan.

Johnson, R. K. (ed.) 1989 *The Second Language Curriculum.* Cambridge: Cambridge University Press.

Joint Committee on Standards for Education a Evaluation 1981 *Standards for Evaluations of Educational Programs, Projects and Materials.* New York: McGraw Hill.

Kagan, D. M. 1992 Professional Growth among Preservice and Beginning Teachers. *Review of Educational Research,* 62/2: 129–69.

Katamba, F. (ed.) 1982 *Methods and Problems in Doing Applied Linguistics Research.* Lancaster: IELE, University of Lancaster.

Kelly, A. V. 1982 *The Curriculum* (2nd edn). London: Harper and Row.

Kemmis, S. 1986 'Seven Principles for Programme Evaluation in Curriculum Development and Innovation' in House, E. R. (ed.) 1986: 117–40.

Kemmis, S. and McTaggart, R. (eds) 1982a *The Action Research Planner.* Waurn Ponds, Victoria: Deakin University Press.

Kemmis, S. and McTaggart, R. (eds) 1982b *The Action Research Reader.* Waurn Ponds, Victoria: Deakin University Press.

Kennedy, C. 1985 Formative Evaluation as an Indicator of Students Wants and Attitudes. The ESP *Journal*, 4/2: 93–100.

Kennedy, C. 1987 Innovating for a Change: Teacher Development and Innovation. *English Language Teaching Journal*, 41/3: 163–70.

Kennedy, C. 1988 Evaluation of the Management of Change in ELT Projects. *Applied Linguistics*, 9/4: 329–42.

Kincheloe, J. 1991 *Teachers as Researchers: Qualitative Inquiry as a Path to Empowerment*. London: Falmer Press.

King, J. A. 1982 Studying the Local Use of Evaluation: A Discussion of Theoretical Issues and an Empirical Study. *Studies in Educational Evaluation*, 8: 175–83.

King, J. A., Morris, L. L. and Fitz-Gibbon, C. T. 1987 *How to Assess Program Implementation*. Newbury Park, Calif.: Sage.

Knop, C. K. and Nerenz, A. G. 1982 A Time-based Approach to Study of Teacher Effectiveness. *Modern Language Journal*, 66/3: 243–53.

Koehler, V. 1978 Classroom Process Research: Present and Future. *Journal of Classroom Interaction*, 13/2: 3–11.

Kouraogo, P. 1987 Curriculum Renewal and INSET in Difficult Circumstances. *English Language Teaching Journal*, 41/3: 171–8.

Krasnick, H. 1991 The Use of the Concept of Cultural Sensitivity in Teacher Evaluation: A Case Study. *TESOL Quarterly*, 25/1: 195–200.

Krijcie, R. V. and Morgan, D. W. 1970 Determining Sample Size for Research Activities. *Educational and Psychological Measurement*, 30/4: 607–10.

Kyriacou, C. 1985 Conceptualising Research on Effective Teaching. *British Journal of Educational Psychology*, 55: 148–55.

Kyriacou, C. 1991 *Essential Teaching Skills*. Oxford: Blackwell.

Kyriacou, C. and Newson, R. 1982 Teacher Effectiveness: A Consideration of Research Problems. *Educational Review*, 34: 3–12.

Laaksonen, J. 1987 Life after the Course: An 'Illuminative' Evaluation Study. MA in Applied Linguistics project, University of Reading.

Labaw, P. J. 1980 *Advanced Questionnaire Design*. Mass.: Abt Books.

Lacey, C. and Lawton, D. (eds) 1981 *Issues in Evaluation and Accountability*. London: Methuen.

Langford, A. (forthcoming) A tracer study of students attending the presessional EAP course at CALS, University of Reading. MATEFL diss., University of Reading.

Lawton, D. 1980 'The Politics of Curriculum Evaluation' in McCormick, R. et al. (eds) 1982: 169–84.

Lecomte, B. J. 1986 *Project Aid: Limitations and Alternatives*. Paris: Development Centre of the Organisation for Economic Cooperation and Development.

Lee, Y. P., Fok, A. C. Y. Y., Lord, R. and Low, G. D. (eds) 1985 *New Directions in Language Testing*. Oxford: Pergamon.

Leinhardt, G. 1980 Modelling and Measuring Educational Treatment in Evaluation. *Review of Educational Research*, 50/3: 393–420.

Leithwood, K. A. and Montgomery, D. J. 1980 Evaluating Program implementation. *Evaluation Review*, 4: 193–214.

Levin, H. 1983 *Cost Effectiveness: A Primer*. Newbury Park, Calif.: Sage.

Leviton, L. C. and Hughes, E. F. X. 1981 Research on the Utilisation of Evaluations: A Review and Synthesis. *Evaluation Review*, 5: 525–48.

Lewkowicz, J. and Moon, J. 1985 'Evaluation: A Way of Involving the Learner' in Alderson, J. C. (ed.) 1985: 45–80.

Lewy, A. 1990 'Formative and Summative Evaluation' in Walberg, H. J. and Haertel, G. D. (eds) 1990: 26–8.

Lincoln, Y. S. and Guba, E. E. 1985a *Naturalistic Inquiry*. Newbury Park, Calif.: Sage.

Lincoln, Y. S. and Guba, E. E. 1985b *Research, Evaluation, and Policy Analysis: Heuristics for Disciplined Inquiry* (ERIC Document Reproduction Service No. ED 252 966).

Linder, P. 1991 Collaborative Action Research into Mixed Ability Communicative EFL Teaching. MATEFL diss., University of Reading.

Littlejohn, A. and Melouk, M. (eds) 1987 *Research Methods and Processes*. Lancaster: Department of Linguistics, University of Lancaster.

Livingston, S. A. and Zicky, M. J. 1982 *Passing Scores: A Manual for Setting Standards of Performance on Educational and Occupational Tests*. Princeton, N.J.: Educational Testing Service.

Long, M. H. 1980 Inside the 'Black Box': Methodological Issues in Classroom Research on Language Learning. *Language Learning*, 30/1: 1–42.

Long, M. H. 1984 Process and Product in ESL Program Evaluation. *TESOL Quarterly*, 18/3: 409–25.

Loucks, S. F. 1983 Defining Fidelity: A Cross-study Analysis. Paper presented at the annual meeting of the American Educational Research Association, Montreal, April (ERIC Document Reproduction Service No. ED 249 659).

Loucks, S. F., Newlove, B. W. and Hall, G. E. 1975 *Measuring Levels of Use of the Innovation: A Manual for Trainers, Interviewers and Raters*. Austin, Texas: The Research and Development Centre for Teacher Education, University of Texas.

Love, A. J. 1991 *Internal Evaluation: Building Organisations from Within* Newbury Park, Calif.: Sage.

Low, G. D. 1987 The Need for a Multi-Perspective Approach to the Evaluation of Foreign Language Teaching Materials. *Evaluation and Research in Education*, 1/1: 19–30.

Low, G. D. 1988 The Semantics of Questionnaire Rating Scales. *Evaluation and Research in Education*, 2/2: 69–79.

Low, G. D. 1991 'Talking to Questionnaires: Pragmatic Models in Questionnaire Design' in Heaton, B. and Adams, P. 1991: 118–34.

Lynch, B. K. 1990 A Context-Adaptive Model for Program Evaluation. *TESOL Quarterly*, 24/1: 23–42.

Lynch, B. K. 1992 'Evaluating a Program Inside Out' in Alderson, J. C. and Beretta, A. (eds) 1992: 61–95.

MacCabe, C. 1987 The External Evaluator-Inspector or Management Consultant. *Evaluation and Research in Education*, 1/1: 1–8.

McCall, G. J. and Simons, J. L. (eds) 1969 *Issues in Participant Observation: A Text and Reader*. Reading, Mass., Menlo Park, Calif., and London, Ontario:. Addison-Wesley.

McCormick, R. and James, M. 1983 *Curriculum Evaluation in Schools*. Beckenham, Kent: Croom Helm.

McCormick, R., Byrner, J., Clift, P., James, M. and Brown, C. M. (eds) 1982 *Calling Education to Account*. London: Heinemann/Open University.

McDonald, R. and Roe, E. 1984 *Reviewing Departments: HERDSA Green Guide 1*. Kensington, NSW: Higher Education Research and Development Association of Australia.

McGinley, K. 1986 Coming to Terms with Evaluation. *System*, 14/3: 335–41.

Mackay, R. J. 1981 Accountability in ESP Programs. *ESP Journal*, 1/2: 107–21.

Mackay, R. J. 1988 Position Paper: Program Evaluation and Quality Control. *TESL Canada Journal*, 5/2: 33–41.

Mackay, A. 1989 The eliability of assessments of teaching performance. MATEFL diss., University of Reading.

Mackey, R. J. 1991 How Program Personnel Can Help Maximise the Utility of Language Program Evaluations' in Anivan, S. (ed.) 1991: 61–71.

Mackay, R. J. (forthcoming) *Evaluation: A Course in Self-Defence for Program Personnel.*

Mackay, R. J. and Mountford, A. 1978 *English for Specific Purposes.* London: Longman.

Mackay, R. J. and Palmer, J. 1981 *Language for Specific Purposes: Program Design and Evaluation.* Rowley, Mass.: Newbury House.

McMahon, A., Bolam, R., Abbott, R. and Holly, P. 1986 *Guidelines for Review and Development in Schools: Secondary School Handbook.* York: Schools Council Publications/ Longman.

McNiff, J. 1988 *Action Research: Principles and Practice.* Basingstoke: MacMillan Educational.

Madaus, G. F., Scriven, M. S. and Stufflebeam, D. L. (eds) 1983 *Evaluation Models: Viewpoints on Educational and Human Services Evaluation.* Boston, Mass. and Lancaster: Kluwer Nijhoff.

Mager, F. F. 1962 *Preparing Instructional Objectives.* Belmont, Calif.: Fearon.

Mahoney, M. J. 1978 Experimental Methods and Outcome Evaluation. *Journal of Consulting and Clinical Psychology*, 46/4: 660–72.

Malamah-Thomas, A. 1987 *Classroom Interaction.* Oxford: Oxford University Press.

Mann, S. J. 1988 Issues in Doing Evaluation: An Account from Practice. Paper presented at Centre for British Teachers Seminar on Evaluation in Educational Projects Overseas, London, July.

Marsh, I. 1987 Teachers' Perceptions of an In-service Course: You Can't Please All the People All the Time. *British Journal of In-service Education*, 14/1: 56–60.

Marston, D., Deno, S. and Tindal, G. 1983 *A Comparison of Standardised Achievement Tests and Direct measurement Techniques in Measuring Pupil Progress.* Minneapolis, Minn.: University of Minnesota, Institute for Research on Learning Disabilities (ERIC Document Reproduction Service No. ED 236 198).

Martin, M. and Norwich, B. 1991 The Integration of Research Findings on Classroom Management into a Programme for Use in Teacher Education. *British Educational Research Journal*, 17/4: 333–51.

Master, P. 1983 The Etiquette of Observing. *TESOL Quarterly*, 17/3: 497–501.

Matthews, A. 1985 'Choosing the Best Available Textbook' in A. Matthews, Spratt, M. and Dangerfield, L. (eds) 1985: 202–6.

Matthews, A., Spratt, M. and Dangerfield, L. (eds) 1985 *At the Chalkface.* London: Edward Arnold.

Medley, D. M. 1977 Future Directions for Process-product Research. *Journal of Classroom Interaction*, 13/1: 3–8.

Medley, D. M. 1978 Research in Teacher Effectiveness: Where It Is and How It Got There. *Journal of Classroom Interaction*, 13/2: 16–21.

Medley, D. M. and Mitzel, H. E. 1963 'Measuring Classroom Behaviour by Systematic Observation' in Gage, N. L. (ed.): 247–328.

Medley, D. M., Soar, R. and Coker, H. 1983 The Minimum Conditions for Valid Evaluation of Teacher Performance. *Journal of Classroom Interaction*, 19/1: 22–7.

Middleton, D. n.d. The Nominal Group Technique. Mimeo.

Miles, M. B. and Huberman, A. M. 1984 *Qualitative Data Analysis A Sourcebook of New Methods*. Beverly Hills, Calif. and London: Sage.

Millar, R., Crute, V. and Hargie, O. 1992 *Professional Interviewing*. London: Routledge.

Millman, J. and Darling Hammond, L. 1990 *The New Handbook of Teacher Evaluation*. London: Sage Publications.

Mitchell, R. 1992 'The "Independent" Evaluation of Bilingual Primary Education: A Narrative Account' in Alderson, J. C. and Beretta, A. (eds) 1992: 100–41.

Mitzel, H. E. (ed.) 1982 *Encyclopedia of Educational Research* (5th edn). New York: The Free Press.

Molenaar, N. J. 1982 'Response-effects of "formal" characteristics of question' in Dijkstra, W. and van der Zouwen, J. (eds) 1982: 49–90.

Mook, D. J. 1983 In Defense of External Invalidity. *American Psychologist*, 38/4: 379–87.

Moore, A. 1987 Educational Project Evaluation and the KELT scheme. MA in Applied Linguistics project, University of Reading.

Morris, L. L. and Fitz-Gibbon, C. T. 1978a *How to Deal with Goals and Objectives*. Newbury Park, Calif.: Sage.

Morris, L. L. and Fitz-Gibbon, C. T. 1978b *How to Measure Achievement*. Newbury Park, Calif.: Sage.

Morris, L. L. and Fitz-Gibbon, C. T. 1978c *How to Measure a Program Implementation*. Beverly Hills, Calif.: Sage.

Morris, L. L., Fitz-Gibbon, C. T. and Freeman, M. E. 1987 *How to Communicate Evaluation Findings*. Newbury Park, Calif.: Sage.

Moser, C. A. and Kalton, G. 1971 *Survey Methods in Social Investigation*. London: Heinemann.

Moskowitz, G. 1976 The Classroom Interaction of Outstanding Foreign Language teachers. *Foreign Language Annals*, 9/2: 135–43, 146–57.

Murphy, D. F. 1981 *Developing Secondary Teachers' Evaluation of Their Work*. Practical Papers in English Language Education 4: 107–33. University of Lancaster.

Murphy, D. F. 1985 'Evaluation in Language Teaching: Assessment, Accountability and Awareness' in Alderson, J. C. (ed.) 1985: 1–16.

Murphy, D. F. 1990 'Principles and Practice in an Evaluation Project' in Anivan, S. (ed.) 1991: 26–34.

Murphy-O'Dwyer, L. 1985 'Diary Studies as a Method for Evaluating Teacher Training' in Alderson, J. C. (ed.) 1985: 97–128.

Murphy, R. and Torrance, H. (eds) 1987 *Evaluating Education: Issues and Methods*. London: Harper.

Murray, G. 1987 English language projects in aid contexts: design, implementation and evaluation. MATEFL diss., CALS, University of Reading.

Nevo, D. 1983 The Conceptualisation of Educational Evaluation: An Analytical Review of the Literature. *Review of Educational Research*, 53/1: 117–28.

Nevo, D. 1985 Face Validity Revisited. *Journal of Educational Measurement*, 22/4: 287–93.

Nicholls, A. 1983 *Managing Educational Innovations*. London: Unwin Educational Books.

Nisbet, J. 1975 'Innovation: Bandwagon or Hearse?' in Harris, A. et al. (eds): 1–14.

Nisbet, J. and Watt, J. 1984 'Case study' in Bell, J. et al. (eds) 1984: 72–92.

Nunan, D. 1986 *Does Instruction Make a Difference?* National Curriculum Resource Centre, Adelaide, S. Australia. Mimeo.

Nunan, D. 1989 Language Inservice Program for Teachers: A Case Study. Paper presented at the annual conference of Teachers of English for Speakers of Other Languages, San Antonio, Texas.

Nunan, D. 1989 *Understanding Language Classrooms: A Guide for Teacher-initiated Action.* New York, London, Toronto, Sydney, Tokyo, Singapore: Prentice-Hall.

Nuttall, D. (ed.) 1986 *Assessing Educational Achievement.* London: Falmer Press.

Nuttall, D. L. and Bynner, J. 1982 *Accountability and Evaluation.* Milton Keynes: Open University Press.

O'Keefe, M. 1984 The Impact of Evaluation of Federal Education Program Policies. *Studies in Educational Evaluation,* 10/1: 61–74.

Open University 1979 *Observing Classroom Language. PE 232–5.* Milton Keynes: Open University.

Open University 1980 *Curriculum in Action: Block(s) 1.* Milton Keynes: Open University Press.

Oppenheim, A. N. 1992 *Questionnaire Design, Interviewing and Attitude Measurement.* London: Pinter.

Oskarsson, M. 1982 *Self-Assessment in Foreign Language Learning* (Contract 20/81). Götebarg: Language Teaching Research Centre.

Overseas Development Administration 1987 *The Lessons of Experience: Evaluation Work in ODA.* London: ODA.

Overseas Development Administration 1988 *Guidelines for the Preparation of Evaluation Studies.* London: ODA.

Owens, T. R. 1973 'Educational Evaluation by Adversary Proceedings' in House, E. R. (ed.) 1973: 295–305.

Oxfam 1988 *Overseas Division. Field Directors' Handbook.* Oxford: Oxfam.

Parlett, M. 1975 'Evaluating Innovations in Teaching' in Golby, Greenwald and West (eds) 1975: 414–24.

Parlett, M. R. 1982 'The New Evaluation' in McCormick, R. et al. (eds) 1982: 185–91.

Parlett, M. R. and Hamilton, D. 1977 *Evaluation as Illumination: A New Approach to Innovatory Programmes.* Occasional Paper No. 9, Centre for Research in the Educational Services, University of Edinburgh.

Parsons, C. 1976 'The New Evaluation: A Cautionary Note' in McCormick, R. et al. (eds) (1982): 192–210.

Patton, M. Q. 1980 *Qualitative Evaluation Methods.* Beverly Hills, Calif.: Sage.

Patton, M. Q. 1982 *Practical Evaluation.* Beverly Hills, Calif.: Sage.

Patton, M. Q. 1986 *Utilization-focused Evaluations.* Newbury Park, Calif.: Sage.

Patton, M. Q. 1987a *Creative Evaluation* (2nd edn). Beverly Hills: Sage.

Patton, M. Q. 1987b *How to Use Qualitative Methods in Evaluation.* Beverly Hills, Calif.: Sage.

Patton, M. Q. 1990 *Qualitative Evaluation and Research Methods* (2nd edition). London: Sage.

Pennington, M. and Young, A. 1989 The Concept of Method, Interested Knowledge and the Politics of Language Teaching *TESOL Quarterly,* 23/4: 589–618.

Perkins, K. and Angelis, P. J. 1985 Some Considerations for ESL Program Evaluation. *RELC Journal,* 16/2: 72–92.

Perren, G. (ed.) 1974 *Teaching Languages to Adults for Special Purposes.* CILT Report No. 11. London: CILT.

Peterson, D., Micceri, T. and Smith, B. O. 1985 Measurement of Teacher Performance: A study in Instrument Development. *Teaching and Teacher Education,* 1/1: 63–77.

Phillips, D. C. 1981 Toward an Evaluation of Experiment in Educational Contexts. *Educational Researcher*, 10/6: 13–20.

Phillips, R. D. and Owens, L. 1986 The Transfer of Teaching and Classroom Observation Skills across Cultures: A Case Study. *International Journal of Educational Development*, 6/4: 223–231.

Philpott, P. 1993 Seating Patterns in Small Language Classes: An Example of Action Research. *British Educational Research Journal*, 19/2: 191–210.

Pilliner, A. E. G. 1974 'The Evaluation of Programmes' in Perren, G. (ed.) 1974: 39–46.

Pilliner, A. E. G. 1982 'Evaluation' in Heaton, B. (ed.): 97–101.

Plomp, T., Huijsman, H. and Kluyfhout, E. 1992 Monitoring in Educational Development Projects: The Development of a Monitoring System. *International Journal of Educational Development*, 12/1: 65–73.

Politzer, R. L. 1970 Some Reflections on 'Good' and 'Bad' Language Teaching. *Language Learning*, 20/31: 31–43.

Popham, W. J. 1975 *Educational Evaluation*. Englewood Cliffs, N.J.: Prentice-Hall.

Popham, W. J. 1981 *Modern Educational Measurement*. Englewood Cliffs, N.J.: Prentice-Hall.

Poster, C., Poster, D. and Benington, M. 1991 *Teacher Appraisal*. London: Routledge.

Potts, P. J. 1985 'The Role of Evaluation in a Communicative Curriculum, and Some Consequences for Materials Design' in Alderson, J. C. (ed): 19–44.

Powney, J. and Watts, M. 1987 *Interviewing in Educational Research*. London: Routledge and Kegan Paul.

Pring, R. 1984 'The Problems of Confidentiality' in Skilbeck, M. (ed.): 38–43.

Rea, P. M. 1981 Formative Assessment of Student Performance: The Role of Self Appraisal. *Indian Journal of Applied Linguistics*, 7/1 and 2: 66–88.

Rea, P. M. 1983 'Evaluation of Educational Projects with Special Reference to English Language Instruction' in Brumfit, C. (ed.) 1983: 85–98.

Rea, P. M. 1987 'Communicative Curriculum Validation: A Task Based Approach' in Candlin, C. N. and Murphy, D. F. (eds) 1987: 147–165.

Rea-Dickins, P. and Germaine, K. 1992 *Evaluation*. Oxford: Oxford University Press.

Reason, P. and Rowan, P. (eds) 1981 *Naturalistic Enquiry: A Sourcebook for New Paradigm Research*. Chichester: Wiley.

Rice, E. G. and Higgins, N. 1982 *The Role of Standardised Testing in the Teacher's Evaluation Strategy*. Paper presented at the annual meeting of the National Council on Measurement in Education, New York, March (ERIC Document Reproduction Service No. ED 222 498).

Richards, J. C. 1984 The Secret Life of Methods. *TESOL Quarterly*, 18/1: 7–23.

Richards, J. C. and Crookes, G. 1988 The Practicum in TESOL. *TESOL Quarterly*, 22/1: 9–27.

Richards, J. C. and Nunan, D. (eds) 1990 *Second Language Teacher Education*. Cambridge: Cambridge University Press.

Roberts, G. W. 1985 A Framework for a Language Simulation Evaluation Checklist. *System*, 13/3: 273–7.

Roberts, J. R. 1993 Evaluating the Impacts of Teacher Research. *System*, 21/1: 1–19.

Robinson, P. C. 1991 *ESP Today: A Practitioner's Guide*. Englewood Cliffs, N.J.: Prentice-Hall.

Rodwell, S. 1988 International Assistance to Third World Educational Management Training:

A Critical Examination of Alternative Strategies. *International Journal of Educational Development*, 8/2: 117–28.

Rosenshine, B. V. 1971 *Teaching Behaviour and Student Achievement*. Slough: NFER.

Rosenshine, B. V. and Furst, N. F. 1971 'Research on Teacher Performance Criteria' in Smith, B. O. (ed.) 1971: 50–9.

Ross, S. 1992 'Program-defining Evaluation in a Decade of Eclecticism' in Alderson, J. C. and Beretta, A. (eds) 1992: 167–95.

Rossi, P. H. and Freeman, H. E. 1985 *Evaluation: A Systematic Approach* (3rd edn). Newbury Park, Calif.: Sage.

Rowley, C. D. 1971 *The Politics of Educational Planning in Developing Countries*. Paris: UNESCO.

Rowntree, D. 1982 *Educational Technology in Curriculum Development* (2nd edn). London: Harper.

Rudduck, J. 1981 *Making the Most of the Short In-Service Course*. London: Methuen.

Rudduck, J. and Stenhouse, L. 1979 A Study in the Dissemination of Action Research. SSRCF Final Report HR 34831, November.

Rudduck, J. 1988 'The Ownership of Change as a Basis for Teachers' Professional Learning' in Calderhead, J. (ed.) 1988: 205–22.

Ruscoe, G. C. 1969 *The Conditions for Success in Educational Planning*. Paris: UNESCO.

Rutman, L. (ed.) 1984 *Evaluation Research Methods: A Basic Guide* (2nd edn). Beverly Hills, Calif.: Sage.

Rutman, L. and Mowbray, G. 1983 *Understanding Program Evaluation*. Beverly Hills, Calif.: Sage.

Salmon, A. (ed.) 1981 *The Evaluation of In-Service Education and Training of Teachers*. Council of Europe.

Sanders, J. and Cunningham, S. 1974 'Techniques for Formative evaluation' in Borich, G. (ed.) 1974.

Sanders, J. R. 1992 *Evaluating School Programs: An Educator's Guide*. Newbury Part, Calif.: Corwin Press.

Sanderson, D. 1982 *Modern Language Teachers in Action*. NFER/University of York.

Schatzman, L. and Strauss, A. L. 1973 *Field Research*. Englewood Cliffs, N.J.: Prentice-Hall.

Scriven, M. S. 1967 'The Methodology of Evaluation' in State, R. E. (ed.) 1967: 38–89.

Scriven, M. S. 1991 *Evaluation Thesaurus* (4th edn). Beverly Hills, Calif.: Sage.

Seliger, H. W. and Long, M. H. 1983 *Classroom-oriented Research in Second Language Acquisition*. New York: Newbury House.

Shadish, W. R. and Reichardt, C. S. 1987 *Evaluation Studies: Review Annual*, Vol. 12. Beverly Hills, Calif.: Sage.

Shapiro, E. 1973 Educational Evaluation: Rethinking the Criteria of Competence. *School Review*, 81/4: 523–49.

Sharp, A. 1990 Staff/student Participation in Course Evaluation: A procedure for Improving Course Design. *English Language Teaching Journal*, 44/2: 132–7.

Sharp, R. and Green, A. 1975 *Education and Social Control*. London: Routledge and Kegan Paul.

Sheal, P. 1989 Classroom Observation: Training the Observers. *English Language Teaching Journal*, 43/2: 92–104.

Sheldon, L. E. (ed.) 1987 *ELT Textbooks and Materials: Problems in Evaluation and Development*. ELT Documents 126. London Modern English Publications/British Council.

SIDA 1987 *Guidelines For Project Support: From Idea to Evaluation*. Stockholm: SIDA.

Siedow, M. D., Memory, D. and Bristow, P. S. 1985 *Inservice Education for Content Area Teachers*. Newark, Del.: International Reading Association.

Simon, A. and Boyer, E. G. 1968 *Mirrors for Behaviour: An Anthology of Classroom Observation Instruments*. Philadelphia: Research for Better Schools.

Simons, H. 1982a 'Conversation Piece: The Practice of Interviewing in Case Study Research in McCormick, R. et al. (eds) 1982: 239–46.

Simons, H. 1982b 'Process Evaluation in Schools' in McCormick, R. et al. (eds) 1982: 119–32.

Simons, H. 1982c 'Suggestions for a School Self-evaluation Based on Democratic Principles' in McCormick, R. et al. (eds) 1982: 286–96.

Simons, H. 1984a 'Ethical Principles in School Self-evaluation' in Bell, J. et al. (eds) 1984: 123–32.

Simons, H. 1984b 'Negotiating Conditions for Independent Evaluations' in Adelman, C. (ed.) 1984: 56–68.

Simons, H. 1984c 'Guidelines for the Conduct of an Independent Evaluation' from Adelman, C. (ed.) 1984: 87–92.

Simons, H. 1987 *Getting to Know Schools in a Democracy: The Politics and Process of Evaluation*. Lewes: Falmer Press.

Skilbeck, M. (ed.) 1984 *Evaluating the Curriculum in the '80's*. London: Harper and Row.

Slembrouck, S. 1987 'Questions and Questionnaires, Answers and Answerraires' in Littlejohn, A. and Melouk, M. 1987: 76–90.

Smith, B. O. (ed.) 1971 Research on Teacher Education: A Symposium. Englewood Cliffs, N.J.: Prentice-Hall.

Smith, H. J. 1989a ELT AID and the Project Approach. CALS, University of Reading. Photocopy.

Smith, H. J. 1989b ELT Aid Projects should be run by managers not ELT experts. CALS, University of Reading. Photocopy.

Smith, H. J. 1989c ELT Project Success and the Management of Innovation. CALS, University of Reading. Photocopy.

Somekh, B. 1993 'Quality in Educational Research: The Contribution of Classroom Teachers' in Edge, J. and Richards, K. (eds) 1993: 26–38.

Spada, N. 1987 Relationship between Instructional Differences and Learning Outcomes: A Process-Product Study of Communicative Language Teaching *Applied Linguistics*, 8/2: 137–61.

Spada, N. 1990 'Observing Classroom Behaviours and Learning Outcomes in Different Second Language Programs' in Richards, J. C. and Nunan, D. (eds) 1990: 293–310.

Stake, B. 1986 'Evaluating Educational Programmes' in Hopkins, D. (ed.) 1986: 245–53.

Stake, R. E. 1967a The Countenance of Educational Evaluation. *Teachers' College Record*, 68/4: 523–40.

Stake, R. E. 1967b Towards a Technology for the Evaluation of Educational Programs' in Tyler, R. (ed.) 1967.

Stake, R. E. (ed.) 1967 *Perspectives in Curriculum Evaluation*. AERA Monograph Series on Curriculum Development No. 1. Chicago: Rand McNally.

Stake, R. E. 1975 *Evaluating the Arts in Education: A Responsive Approach*. Columbus, Ohio: Charles E. Merrill.

Stake, R. E. 1986 'An Evolutionary View of Educational Improvement' in House, E. R. 1986: 89–102.

Steadman, S. 1981 'Evaluation Techniques' in McCormick, R. et al. (eds) 1982: 211–23.

Steiner, F. 1975 *Performing with Objectives*. Rowley, Mass.: Newbury House.

Stenhouse, L. 1975 *An Introduction to Curriculum Research and Development*. London: Heinemann.

Stodolsky, S. S. 1984 Teacher Evaluation: The Limits of Looking. *Educational Researcher*, 13/9: 11–18.

Stones, E. 1975 *How Long Is a Piece of String?* London: Society for Research into Higher Education.

Stubbs, M. and Delamont, S. 1976 'Classroom Research: A New Critique and a New Approach' in Stubbs, M. and Delamont, S. (eds) 1976: 3–20.

Stubbs, M. and Delamont, S. (eds) 1976 *Explorations in Classroom Observation*. Chichester: Wiley.

Stufflebeam, D. L. 1985 'Coping with the Point of Entry Problem in Evaluating Projects. *Studies in Educational Evaluation*, 11/2: 123–9.

Stufflebeam, D. L. 1990 'Professional Standards for Educational Evaluation' in Walberg, H. J. and Haertel, G. D. (eds) 1990: 94–106.

Stufflebeam, D. L. and Webster, W. J. 1980 An Analysis of alternative approaches to evaluation. *Educational Evaluation and Policy Analysis*, 2/3: 5–20.

Swain, M. 1984 A Review of Immersion Education in Canada: Research Evaluation Studies. ELT *Documents* 119 (Language Issues and Educational Policies): 35–51. London: British Council.

Swain, M. and Lapkin, S. 1982 *Evaluating Bilingual Education: A Canadian Case Study*. Clevedon, Avon: Multilingual Matters.

Swales, J. and Mustafa, H. (eds) 1983 *English for Specific Purposes in the Arab World*. Birmingham: Aston University Language Studies Unit.

Taba, H. 1962 *Curriculum Development: Theory and Practice*. New York: Harcourt Brace and World.

Talmage, H. 1982 'Evaluation of Programs' in Mitzel, H. E. (ed.) 1982: 592–611.

Tawney, D. (ed.) 1976 *Curriculum Evaluation Today: Trends and Implications*. London: Macmillan Educational.

Thompson, A. R. 1985 Evaluation in Overseas Education: Some Parameters and Priorities. *International Journal Educational Development*, 5/3: 227–33.

Thompson, P. 1989 Oral Presentations in an Academic context. MATEFL diss., CALS, University of Reading.

Thornbury, S. 1991 Watching the Whites of Their Eyes: The Use of Teaching Practice Logs'. *English Language Teaching Journal*, 45/2: 140–6.

Thorndike, R. L. and Hagen, E. 1969 *Measurement and Evaluation in Psychology of Education*. New York: John Wiley.

Tonkyn, A. P. C., Robinson and Furneaux, C. 1993 'EAP Teacher: Prophet of Doom or Eternal Optimist? EAP Teachers' Predictions of Students' Success' in Blue, G. (ed.) 1993: 37–49.

Trethowan, D. 1987 *Appraisal and Target Setting: A Handbook for Teacher Development*. London: Harper Education Series.

Tucker, G. R. and Cziko, G. A. 1978 'The Role of Evaluation in Bilingual Education' in Alatis, J. E. (ed.) 1978: 423–46.

Turkewych, C. 1986 Evaluation Strategies for EWP Programs: A Marketing Perspective. *TESL Talk*, 16/1: 34–41.

Turney, C., Cairns, L. G., Eltis, K. J., Hatton, N., Thew, D. M., Towler, J., Wright, R. 1982a *The Practicum in Teacher Education*. Sydney: Sydney University Press.

Turney, C., Cairns, L. G., Eltis, K. J., Hatton, N., Thew, D. M., Towler, J. and Wright, R. 1982b *Supervisor Development Programmes: Role Handbook*. Sydney: Sydney University Press.

Tyler, R. 1949 *Basic Principles of Curriculum and Instruction*. Chicago: University of Chicago Press.

Tyler, R. W. (ed.) 1967 *Perspectives on Curriculum Evaluation*. Chicago: Rand McNally.

Ullman, R. and Geva, E. 1984 'Approaches to Observation in Second Language Classes' in Brumfit, C. J. (ed.) 1984c: 113–28.

Valette, R. M. 1966 Evaluating the Objectives in Foreign Language Teaching. *International Review of Applied Linguistics*, 4/2: 131–9.

Valette, R. M. 1969 The Pennsylvania Project, Its Conclusions and Its Implications. *Modern Language Journal*, 53/6: 396–404.

Valette, R. M. 1973 Developing and Evaluating Communicative Skills in the Classroom. *TESOL Quarterly* 7: 407–24.

van Lier, L. 1982 'Ethnographic Monitoring and Classroom research' in Katamba, F. (ed.) 1982: 59–71.

van Lier, L. 1988 *The Classroom and the Language Learner: Ethnography and Second Language Classroom Research*. London: Longman.

von Elek, T. 1985 'A Test of Swedish as a Second Language: An Experiment in Self-assessment' in Lee, Y. P., Fok, A. C. Y. Y. Lord, R. and Low, G. D. (eds) 1985: 47–57.

Vulliamy, G. and Webb, R. 1992 The Influence of Teacher Research: Process or Product? *Educational Review* 44: 41–58.

Wajnryb, R. 1986 Learning to Teach: The Place of Self-evaluation. *TESL Reporter*, 19/4: 69–73.

Walberg, II. J. (ed.) 1974 *Evaluating Education Performance: A Sourcebook of Methods, Instruments and Examples*. Berkeley, Calif.: McCutchan.

Walberg, H. J. and Haertel, G. D. 1990 *The International Encyclopedia of Educational Evaluation*. Oxford: Pergamon Press.

Wales, M. L. 1987 Programme Evaluation: Some Problems from English in the Workplace in Australia. *Evaluation and Research in Education*, 1/2: 107–112.

Walker, R. (ed.) 1985 *Applied Qualitative Research*. Brookfield, Vt.: Gower.

Walker, R. 1989 *Doing Research: A Handbook for Teachers*. London: Routledge.

Walker, R. and Adelman, C. 1975 *A Guide to Classroom Observation*. London: Methuen.

Wallace, M. 1991 *Training Foreign Language Teachers: A Reflective Approach*. Cambridge: Cambridge University Press.

Wang, M. C., Nojan, M., Strom, C. D. and Walberg, H. J. 1984 The Utility of Degree of Implementation Measures in Program Implementation and Evaluation Research. *Curriculum Inquiry*, 14/3: 249–86.

Waters, A. (ed.) 1982 *Issues in ESP*. Lancaster Practical Papers in English, Vol. 5, Pergamon.

Waters, A. 1987 Participatory Course Evaluation in ESP. *English for Specific Purposes*, 6/1: 3–12.

Watts, A. 1985 The Role of the Outside Adviser In School Teacher Education. Paper presented at the International Seminar on Language Teacher Education: Future Directions, Institute of Language in Education, Department of Education, Hong Kong, 16–18 December.

Webb, E. J., Campbell, D. T., Schwarz, R. D. and Sechrest, L. 1966 *Unobtrusive Measures: Non-reactive Research in the Social Sciences.* Chicago: Rand McNally.

Weir, C. J. 1983 Identifying the language needs of overseas students in tertiary education in the United Kingdom. Ph.D. thesis, University of London.

Weir, C. J. 1988 'The Specification, Realization and Validation of an English Language Proficiency Test' in Hughes, A. (ed.) 1988: 45–111.

Weir, C. J. 1990 *Communicative Language Testing.* Hemel Hempstead Prentice-Hall.

Weir, C. J. 1993 *Understanding and Developing Language Tests.* Hemel Hempstead: Prentice-Hall.

Weir, C. J. and Burton, J. (forthcoming) *The Guinea Baseline Study.* London: Evaluation Department, Overseas Development Administration.

Weir, C. J. and Roberts, J. 1990 Evaluating a Teacher Training Project in Difficult Circumstances. Paper delivered at the Regional English Language Centre seminar on Testing and Evaluation, April 1990; published in Anivan, S. (ed.) 1991: 91–109.

Weiss, C. H. 1972 *Evaluation Research: Methods of Assessing Programm Effectiveness.* Englewood Cliffs, N.J.: Prentice-Hall.

Weiss, C. H. 1984 'Increasing the Likelihood of Influencing Decisions' in Rutman, L. (ed.) 1984: 159–91.

Weiss, C. H. 1986 'Towards the Future of Stakeholder Approaches in Evaluation' in House, E. R. (ed.): 186–200.

Welch, W. W. 1983 Experimental Inquiry and Naturalistic Inquiry: An Evaluation. *Journal of Research in Science Teaching,* 20/2: 95–103.

White, R. 1988 *The ELT Curriculum: Design, Innovation and Management.* Oxford: Blackwell.

White, R., Martin M., Stimson, M. and Hodge, R. 1991 *Management in English Language Teaching.* Cambridge: Cambridge University Press.

Wideen, M. F. and Andrews, I. 1987 *Staff Development for School Improvement.* Lewes, Sussex: Falmer Press.

Wiener, H. S. 1986 Collaborative Learning in the Classroom: A Guide to Evaluation. *College English,* 48/1: 52–61.

Wiggins, S. 1985 *The Management of Rural Development Projects in Developing Countries* Reading: Department of Agriculture and Horticulture and Department of Agricultural Economics and Management, University of Reading.

Wiseman, S. and Pidgeon, D. 1970 *Curriculum Evaluation.* Slough: NFER.

Wolf, R. L. 1975 Trial by Jury: A New Evaluation Method. 1: The Process. *Phi Delta Kappan,* 57/3: 185–7.

Wolf, R. L. (ed.) 1987 Educational Evaluation: The State of the Field. *International Journal of Educational Research,* 11/1: 1–143.

Wood, C. M. 1982 *The Role of Standardised Achievement Tests in the Management of Instruction: A Survey of Teacher and Administrator Practices and Attitudes* (ERIC Document Reproduction Service No. Ed 219 446).

Woods, A., Fletcher, P. and Hughes, A. 1986 *Statistics in Language Studies.* Cambridge: Cambridge University Press.

Woods, D. 1991 Teachers' Interpretations of Second Language Teaching Curricula. *RELC Journal,* 22/2: 1–18.

Worthen, B. R. and Sanders, J. R. 1987 *Educational Evaluation: Alternative Approaches and Practical Guidelines.* New York: Longman.

Wragg, E. C. 1980 *Conducting and Analysing Interviews.* Rediguide 11. University of Nottingham School of Education.

Wragg, E. C. 1987 *Teacher Appraisal: A Practical Guide*. Basingstoke: Macmillan Education.

Wright, G. and Fowler, C. 1986 *Investigating Design and Statistics*. Harmondsworth: Penguin.

Yin, R. K. 1989 *Case Study Research Design and Methods*. Newbury Park, Calif., London and New Delhi: Sage.

Youngman, M. B. 1986 *Analysing Questionnaires*. University of Nottingham School of Education.

Zeichner, K. M., Tabachnik, B. R. and Densmore, K. 1987 'Individual, Institutional, and Cultural Influences on the Development of Teachers' Craft Knowledge' in Calderhead, J. (ed.) 1987: 21–59.

Appendices

The ODA's

1.1 Project framework approach

1.1.1 Project framework

Project narrative	Indicators of achievement	Means of verification	Important assumptions
Wider objectives What are the wider (national) objectives or problems which the project will help to resolve?	What are the quantitative or qualitative ways of assessing whether wider objectives have been achieved?	What sources of information exist or can be provided cost-effectively?	What conditions, external to the project, are necessary if the project's immediate objectives are to contribute to the wider objectives?
Immediate objectives (project purpose) What are the intended benefits and changes which the project will bring about?	What is the quantitative evidence or qualitative evidence by which effects and benefits will be judged?	What sources of information exist or can be provided cost-effectively? Does provision for collection need to be made under inputs/outputs?	What are the factors outside the control of the project authorities which, if not present, are liable to restrict progress from outputs to achievement of immediate objectives?
Outputs What outputs (kind, quantity and by when) are to be produced by the project in order to achieve the immediate objectives?		What are the sources of information?	What external factors must be realized to obtain planned outputs on schedule? What risks have been considered? Are any conditions attached to improve prospects of success?
Inputs What services (personnel, training, etc.) or equipment/ materials are to be provided, at what cost and over what period by: donor, other donors, recipient?		What are the sources of information?	What decisions or actions, outside control of the donor, are necessary for inception of the project?

Source: British Council 1990: 16–17, 45–6

1.1.2   Project structures (The ODA project framework: typical paradigms)

	Vocational/ professional training	Teacher-trainer training	Institutional development	Research
Wider objectives	Sectoral effect, e.g. improved industry, agriculture, management	Sectoral effect, e.g. improved teacher performances	Sectoral effect, e.g. improved performance in sector of institution	Sectoral effect, application of research conclusions
Immediate objectives	Function/work/ roles being fully undertaken by those trained	Function/role fully undertaken by those trained, e.g. the training of teachers	Function/role of institution being fully performed, achievement of manage-ment, behavioural tasks	Hypothesis of research proved or otherwise, research conclusions
Outputs	Trained staff in job	Trained teacher trainers/ trainers in their posts	Agreed policy changes, programme of institutional activity, development	Research results, data obtained
Inputs	Equipment, courses, workshops, training	Equipment, courses, workshops, training for teacher trainers or trainer trainers	Consultancy	Equipment, training, research link arrangements, consultancy

1.1.3   Examples of the approach

	Indicators of achievement	How assessed	Assumptions
Wider objectives			
To improve the standard of English amongst university entrants to contribute to Nigeria's development in science and technology	Improved levels at university entrance Improved levels of subject attainment through better English during university course	University entrance exam results in English Exam results and survey of subject specialist departments	English remains language of instruction Universities function Exams and entrance requirements remain constant Cooperation of departments on evaluation
Immediate objectives			
To improve in-service training of English teachers at junior secondary school level	Numbers of courses run and numbers of teachers attending Competent training Competent teaching Improved levels of English at end of junior secondary school	Statistics from inspectorate, etc. Observation and report, evaluation by trainees Observation by trainers, inspectors, etc. Exam results at junior secondary school	Trainers stay in jobs Trainers initiate Resources provided and continued Incentives provided Trainees can attend Evaluation valid
Outputs A cadre of trained teacher trainers		Project reports including end-of-course assessment	Trainees turn up Resources provided Existence of local administrative structures
Inputs Consultancy, workshops, materials, personnel, training		Project reports	Various parties agree Recruitment of ELTOs Trainers stay in jobs Resources provided and continued Incentives provided Trainees can attend

	Indicators of achievement	How assessed	Assumptions
Wider objectives			
To raise the standard of English in secondary schools	National exam results in schools affected	WAEC results	Political/economic stability Exam system remains and is reliable
Immediate objectives			
To produce more effective English teacher training at secondary level To produce more effective English teaching at secondary level	Evaluations by: inspectors, deans of admission, heads of departments, headmasters, pupils, tutors/trainees	Seminar reports Ministry of Education official reports	Continuity of policy commitment despite post changes
Outputs			
Teacher trainers Days' training		Project reports Ministry of Education reports Evaluation Unit reports	Trainees remain available No ethnic/religious/gender obstruction
Inputs			
Number of trainers Days' training at £ cost (including residential/travel costs for producing more effective teacher training and English teaching at secondary level)		Project reports ELT profile	Host ministries release and pay local teachers and provide resources Suitable teacher training available when needed Teachers given status/recognition Institutional link possible

Source: British Council 1989

1.2 Taxonomy of classroom research techniques

Technique	Advantages(s)	Disadvantage(s)	Use(s)
Field notes	Simple; on going; personal; *aide memoire*	Subjective; needs practice	• Specific issue • Case study • General impression
Audio tape recording	Versatile; accurate; provides ample data	Transcription difficult; time consuming; often inhibiting	• Detailed evidence • Diagnostic
Pupil diaries	Provides pupils' perspective	Subjective	• Diagnostic • Triangulation
Interviews and discussions	Can be teacher–pupil, observer–pupil, pupil–pupil	Time consuming	• Specific in depth information
Video tape recorder	Visual and comprehensive	Awkward and expensive; can be distracting	• Visual material • Diagnostic
Questionnaires	Highly specific; easy to administer; comparative	Time consuming to analyse; problem of 'right' answers	• Specific information and feedback
Sociometry	Easy to administer; provides guide to action	Can threaten isolated pupils	• Analyses social relationships
Documentary evidence	Illuminative	Difficult to obtain; time consuming	• Provides context and information
Slide/Tape photography	Illuminative; promotes discussion	Difficult to obtain; superficial	• Illustrates critical incidents
Case study	Accurate; representative; uses range of techniques	Time consuming	• Comprehensive overview of an issue • Publishable format

Source: Hopkins 1985: 82–3

1.3 Hierarchy of evaluation accountability: Evaluating evaluation

HIERARCHY OF UTILIZATION QUESTIONS

7. PROGRAMME AND DECISION IMPACTS — 7. To what extent and in what ways was the programme improved? To what extent were informed, high-quality decisions made?

6. PRACTICE AND PROGRAMME CHANGE — 6. To what extent did intended use occur? Were recommendations implemented?

5. STAKEHOLDER KNOWLEDGE & ATTITUDE CHANGES — 5. What did intended users learn? How were users' attitudes and ideas affected?

4. STAKEHOLDER REACTIONS — 4. What do stakeholders think about the evaluation? What's the evaluation's credibility? believability? relevance? accuracy? potential utility?

3. STAKEHOLDER PARTICIPATION — 3. Who was involved? To what extent were key stakeholders and primary decision makers involved throughout?

2. EVALUATION ACTIVITIES — 2. What data were gathered? What was the focus, the design, the analysis? What happened in the evaluation?

1. INPUTS — 1. To what extent were resources for the evaluation sufficient and well managed? Was time sufficient?

EVALUATION ACTION HIERARCHY

Source: Patton 1986: 173

3.1 Non-equivalent control group, pre-test/post-test design

Diagram	Time	
	1 (pre)	2 (post)
Experimental group	O X	O
Control group	O	O

Summary

Two groups which are similar, but which were *not* formed by random assignment, are measured both before and after one of the groups gets the programme or the experimental treatment.

The essential steps in implementing Design 3

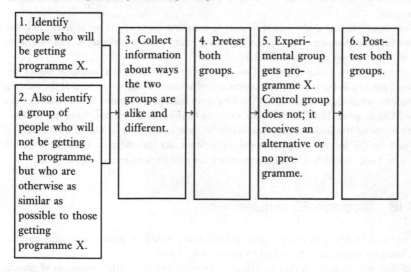

1. Identify people who will be getting programme X.

2. Also identify a group of people who will not be getting the programme, but who are otherwise as similar as possible to those getting programme X.

3. Collect information about ways the two groups are alike and different.

4. Pretest both groups.

5. Experimental group gets programme X. Control group does not; it receives an alternative or no programme.

6. Post-test both groups.

Source: Fitz-Gibbon and Morris 1987b: 86

3.2 Test instruments used in the Nepal study

Part IA Selective Deletion Gap Filling 100 items 1 hour

Passages were selected and reconstructed from the grade 7 and 8 textbooks used in Nepal. They were rewritten taking care to employ only those structures and lexical items occurring in these course books. Items were then deleted from these passages to sample as far as possible the range of structural items in the national curriculum for these grades. The task for students was to repair the deleted items by writing the missing word on an answer sheet provided.

The properties of many realizations of this test method are high correlations with other general proficiency measures and with tests of reading comprehension in particular. We wanted to have a large number of items with a wide range of difficulty because the test might have to show improvement over a period from one to three years. The problem with the more familiar, passage plus comprehension question format is that the number of items that can be set is restricted. By using a gap-filling test it is possible to create a far greater number of items which we thought would demonstrate development in linguistic competence.

It was hoped that students would be able to complete some of the items learnt in grade 7 in the first administration and by the end of the year it was hoped they would be able to score on those set on the year 8 syllabus.

The experimental group might well be expected to outperform the control group on this section of the test as the training course was aimed at improving the teaching of the existing materials in the grade 8 reader and in the long term raising the number of successful passes in the SLC in grade 10. The ability of students to produce structural items was an anticipated result of the trainees' implementation of their training. It would still, however, be a fair test for the control group, as it did not contain any structures or lexis that were not present in books 7 and 8. Gap-filling exercises are also present in the course books.

Part IB Dictation 30 minutes

This was a forty-item test, again of general proficiency, based on sentences (mainly imperatives, instructions and directions) taken from books 7 and 8.

It differs from test 1A in that as well as correlating well with other measures of general proficiency it has a good record of correlating highly with other measures if listening ability.

It was felt that if this test was to be readministered in 1989 and 1990 then it obviously must not be too easy to start with or otherwise a ceiling effect might negate the possibility of measuring achievement and identifying any increase in scores in either of the two groups over the period of the study.

As with the gap-filling test, the purpose was to determine whether the experimental group performance would outdistance the control group, particularly as the trained teachers were trained to use more English than Nepali in the classroom and a number of the activities in the training manual encouraged this. So once again this measure of general proficiency was designed to reflect the main purpose of the training course, namely to enable the teachers to improve the effectiveness of their teaching.

As tests of general language proficiency, both dictation and gap filling can still be considered fair to the control group as they do not contain any language extraneous to the course materials and to a lesser or greater extent dictation and gap filling will occur in the lessons of both groups. Dictation is advocated in the national curriculum which states that at the end of lower secondary level the student will be able to 'take a dictation from any of the prescribed materials in the text book'.

To summarize, the expectation was that with improved teaching methods and a greater use of English in the classroom the experimental group would improve at a greater rate and that eventually performance in the SLC would reflect this.

Part II

Another purpose of the discussions with the trainers during the first visit was to identify criterial, behavioral differences that might be expected to emerge in students' performances as a result of this short in-service training programme.

The training team's view was that it was in the skill of writing that clear differences and new behaviours were likely to occur. The experimental students were more likely to be able to create meaningful new sentences and to execute controlled writing tasks. The control group were more likely to copy from the board and memorize and reproduce paradigms provided by the teacher. They also felt that there might be increased oral interaction among students as a result of the training. However, the considerable difficulties and vast expense of conducting spoken language exams precluded their use under the conditions obtaining in Nepal.

We restricted ourselves to trying to establish whether any differences in written production occurred through employing test tasks to reflect these activities in Part II of the battery.

During our first visit in November 1988 we had asked trainers and trainees to write a short essay on a topic that would be familiar and accessible to their students in year 8 and also to prepare a framework for a cued writing task on the subject. We thus had thirty-five examples to provide us with an idea of levels, topic areas and content. This enabled us to produce four cued writing tasks from which we selected the final two used in the battery after trialling in Katmandhu in December 1988.

3.3 Observation instruments used in the Nepal study

On page 1 of the schedule details of the school, observer, teacher, class and lesson are recorded. On page 2 the observer must code three five-minute samples of classroom talk into categories of: teacher and pupil talk; use of English and Nepali; use of questions as contrasted with all other forms. The samples are selected according to strict time criteria. These data give an indication of the proportion of English used in class, who uses it and to what extent, questions are used by either teachers or pupils. On page 3, the observer is provided with a checklist of classroom activities, to indicate if an activity has occurred, irrespective of duration. For each activity identified, a short illustrative note is required. These data should indicate the occurrence of activity types which discriminate trained and untrained teachers. Also, the observer writes unstructured notes to describe the whole lesson in terms of teacher and student activities, including those in progress during coding. While these notes are unstructured, they are based on a previously identified lexicon of appropriate action verbs. These notes provide a 'thumbnail sketch' of the observed lessons which can also be cross-referred with checklist and coding data.

On page 4, the observer is required to estimate overall talking time in the lesson and the respective proportions of English and Nepali used by teachers and pupils (see chapter 6 for more details).

3.4 Sampling in the Nepal study

Location

The design of the study was heavily influenced by the serious problems of communication and information gathering in Nepal. Most schools do not have telephones and postal delivery is highly unreliable. Telegrams can take up to six weeks to arrive and the only means of ensuring messages getting through is by personal delivery. These problems were compounded in November 1989 by India's obstruction of key Nepali imports, notably petrol, which made all travel extremely difficult. District education office files often do not contain complete or up-to-date information, such as lists of school staff. Without actually visiting the schools, it is not possible to ascertain whether particular teachers are still teaching there or not. As a result a large-scale study of a widely dispersed sample of teachers was always out of the question. These factors also indicated the need to employ experienced field workers through the local New Era research organization rather than ELT subject specialists with no fieldwork experience.

Kathmandhu valley would have been by far the most convenient place to conduct the study, but it is evident that it is quite unlike any other region of Nepal, and would not have provided representative sample schools, particularly since most of the training took place outside Kathmandhu valley.

Pokhara region was chosen after discussions with the project leader during the summer of 1988. It was considered to be a fair representation of rural regions outside Kathmandhu, where the main training effort has been going on. Ninety-seven per cent of Nepal is rural and six districts are contained in the Pokhara region and it includes many quite remote schools. It has relatively good road communications and some of the best contacts with schools and regional directorate of education were in that region. Access to sample schools was possible within a day (if public transport could get fuel), thereby greatly reducing the cost of employing technical staff and limiting the overall time spread of test administration. (Given the limited time span of the study, the longer it took to administer the baseline tests, the less comparable would be the results of the study.)

Selection of teachers

The project leader in consultation with other training staff was asked during the first visit to select sixteen teachers who had been trained in either the past or current Pokhara Inset courses.

The main selection criteria we required were:

1 The teachers were thought to be likely to implement their training, in its key characteristics.
2 The teachers did not work in a school known to be exceptionally different from other sample schools.

The trainers were also asked to select sixteen untrained teachers, with the aim of providing a roughly comparable control group. Initial selection was done according to best available local knowledge of the trainers and the local regional education office.
Further selection criteria for both groups were:

1 Pupils and teachers in control (C) and experimental (E) groups should be as equivalent as possible in terms of language ability. Methods to ensure this as follows:

  a Pupil equivalence:
    SLC results of C and E schools should be compared and schools with equivalent scores included in the study.
  b Teacher equivalence:
    The part 1 language test designed for the baseline study was administered to the teachers during the SEPELT trainers' initial visit in January. Teachers with widely disparate language levels were at this stage dropped from the study. This resulted in reducing the n in each group from 16 to 12. This obviously meant that we were reducing the potential effect of improved English arising out of the training because our main concern in this study was to see if improved teaching methods made any difference to pupil language scores.

2 There should be no special features in the school intakes which would bias the sampling, e.g. extreme variations in parental income, rural versus urban settings, etc.
3 Access to the schools by technical staff should be both possible and welcome.
4 The teachers should remain with their grade 8 class throughout grade 8 and should be likely to continue with the same pupils through grade 9.
5 There should be equivalent stability in pupil population in both C and E group schools; that is, attrition rates should not differ markedly.
6 All schools in the study should be well enough organized and run to ensure the efficient collection of test and observational data.
7 There should be adequate facilities for testing, to minimize student copying.
8 As far as possible, C group teachers should not receive informal 'secondary training' during the period of the study, e.g. by contact with trained teachers.
9 It was essential that C teachers should not attend a training until late 1990.
10 Reaching each school should be possible in the period of the study, and very remote schools were to be excluded.

As far as possible an initial selection of sixteen untrained and sixteen trained teachers was made on the basis of these criteria, with the expectation that there would be some scaling down in sample size because much of the information necessary was simply not available in a documented form. The initial selection had to be made based on the best available knowledge of the trainers and the regional education office staff.
Because of the difficulties involved in selecting the sample, we built an initial visit in January 1989 into the study in which the trainers were asked to collect data to determine the extent to which the above criteria were met. As a result, the sample was cut down to twelve

in the control and twelve in the experimental group. Two teachers subsequently left their posts and we thus finished up with a sample of eleven trained and eleven untrained teachers whose conditions are roughly comparable and on whom the study could be based.

A more careful screening of the schools as originally envisaged would obviously have been preferable. However, given the constraints in Nepal this was never feasible. In particular, the need to move the study forward at very short notice from its planned start date in March to January 1989 made these arrangements the best that could have been achieved.

3.5 Establishing the language level of teachers in the Nepal study

We managed to conduct tests on 18 of the 24 teachers in the study during the course of our visit. During the subsequent programme of visits, the New Era staff administered all the tests with the exception of the oral to those not attending.

Method

Teachers (with the exception of the six not attending) were individually assessed on the basis of their performance in interviews, using the British Council's nine-band oral assessment checklist. To further determine their ability to teach English in the secondary system, all teachers were given the students' tests which are based on grade 7 and 8 textbooks (the dictation and the gap filling). They were given an additional MCQ grammar test designed for University Entrance Language Proficiency screening in the UK.

In terms of their command of the structures and lexis in the books, there was little to choose between the two groups, as was clearly shown in the dictation and gap-filling tests. At this level they were both displaying a similar competence in the language. This is borne out by the *t*-tests carried out on this data, where no significant difference can be shown between the control and experimental group teachers on the gap-filling and dictation tests. Both groups exhibited a high degree of competence in these textbook-based tests.

In the analysis done on the students' test scores, teachers' scores on which we had complete data were taken into account when assessing the students' improved performance from February to November.

In the statistical analysis we looked at the contribution of the teacher language level to student test performance and found there to be a negligible effect. There is no indication that teachers' language ability had any noticeable effect on students' language scores.

In terms of the student samples we have to accept the non-equivalence of the two groups on the basis of their initial test scores but note that the differences are not large. In any case, the General Linear Models Procedure (GLIM analysis) we used to analyse the data took these differences into account.

In terms of size of class, school results and the number of hours spent, there are small differences between the control and experimental groups but these are not statistically significant. Size of class, number of hours' tuition, school SLC results (both general and in English) made insubstantial contributions to test scores.

3.6 An example of a self-report lesson description

What I did in the lesson.

In the lesson No 7. Before Midnight. I took a reading passage. I read the passage twice. Then, I explained the meaning of some words with action. It was very interesting. Then, the turn of reading from the boys came. They read in individual's. I asked some questions from the passage. The pupils replied it correctly. I made them ask the same questions to their colleagues. They did the work nicely. It took more than 30 minutes. After this Simple Past, I made a substitution of the 'used to + V'. I pinned a chart on 'used to + V'. There were 8 sentences. I asked the pupils to read the sentences for example:-

(i) I ate an apple.
    she cooked rice.

(ii) I had a pen.
     she book etc.

(iii) s. used to + V
      I   play   clues
      she live   in Kath
      Ide   etc.

I then gave cue words.
The students did it well
At last — I gave them 20 sentences for home.
This did in the lesson.

What the pupils did in the lesson?   Class - 8

The pupils read the passage, individually as I pointed them out. They did it well. They asked the questions to one another each other. The performance of the students involve this. The performance was good enough. After this, on this substitution tables, they read the sentences. They made their sentences on the chart, which I had pinned on the flannel board. On the 'used to + V' applied cue words. The pupils frequently fluently made the correct sentences. They had no problem in the performance. It took 15 minutes. They took down the assignment for the following day.

Date 6/7/20

4.1   Guidelines for the BALEAP code of practice

5.   CRITERIA FOR ASSESSMENT

5.1   THE PRINCIPLES

5.1.1   The overriding principles upon which accreditation is based are to be found in the BALEAP Code of Practice for Courses in English for Academic Purposes.

5.1.2   It is the duty of the assessors to ascertain whether or not the institution seeking accreditation is following the Code of Practice and to report to the BASC in detail on the extent to which the criteria set out below are met.

5.1.3   It is important that all aspects of the course are seen to be operating in accordance with the Code of Practice as interpreted below. Where there is a departure from the Code of Practice, this should be fully justified.

5.2   MANAGEMENT AND ADMINISTRATION

5.2.1   There should be a clear management structure for the course made known to both students and staff.

5.2.2   There should be effective lines of communication and support between the course, the member institution and the university in which the course is taking place.

5.2.3   The Course Director and staff members delegated by the Course Director should be familiar with the overall structure of the university and in active liaison with relevant departments, student bodies and welfare services of the university, so that students can be assisted with integration and so that courses can be developed that are in all ways appropriate to the students' academic and social needs.

5.2.4   There should be arrangements for adequate liaison between staff and between staff and management.

5.2.5   The responsibilities of the Course Director and of teaching staff and support staff should be specified clearly. Part-time and temporary staff should be effectively integrated into the staffing structures.

5.2.6   Procedures for the operation of the course should be carried out efficiently and with sensitivity to the needs of students and staff alike.

5.2.7   For the purpose of assessment, the administrative and management procedures should be clearly designated in writing so that it is clear to the assessors who is responsible for which duties, including such areas as staff recruitment, staff induction/training, course planning, timetabling, provision of materials, provision and administration of tests, allocation of classrooms, student recruitment, student allocation to classes, social events, student welfare, and so on.

5.3 STAFFING

5.3.1 QUALIFICATIONS

Course organisers and teachers will have professional qualifications and experience appropriate to the teaching of English for Academic Purposes to students in Higher Education.

5.3.2 The course will be taught by graduates with recognised English language teaching qualifications. At the present time approved qualifications are:

– MA in Applied Linguistics or English Language Teaching (or equivalent)*
– Postgraduate Certificate in Education with TEFL/TESL
– Postgraduate Diploma in TEFL/TESOL (or equivalent), e.g. RSA or Trinity College Diploma
– 4 year B Ed with Qualified Teacher Status in language teaching (with EFL experience).

*Graduand status need not preclude the appointment of an otherwise suitably qualified/experienced teacher, provided all course work has been satisfactorily completed.

5.3.3 All teachers will have relevant experience in teaching English as a foreign or second language, and the Director or Course Co-ordinator will have a minimum of five years' relevant teaching experience, which will include EAP work in higher education in Britain. At least half the teaching staff will have overseas teaching experience.

5.3.4 CONDITIONS OF SERVICE The terms and conditions of service will be such as to encourage continuity of staffing and commitment of the staff to the course.

5.3.5 The Course Director and/or the Course Co-ordinator will normally be employed as permanent staff of the institution. In no case should the person directly responsible for the course be employed on a contract of less than one calendar year, initially renewable for at least two further years.

5.3.6 The majority of the course hours should be taught by teachers who are full-time employees of the university for at least the duration of the course.

5.3.7 Academic staff salaries will be based on a standard agreed university teaching scale.

5.3.8 NON-ACADEMIC STAFF Non-academic staff will be available as appropriate to deal with secretarial and clerical support and with matters relating to the administration of the course, student welfare, social activities, and teaching equipment or other resources. The role of non-academic staff in the running of the course will be clearly understood by all members of the course.

5.4   RESOURCES AND FACILITIES

5.4.1   Courses will take place in the usual premises of the university.

5.4.2   Students will have access to the life and work of the university as a whole and to relevant learning resources within the university. This will include the main library, and, where applicable, specialist subject libraries, and computer facilities.

5.4.3   The course will be well resourced in terms of learning materials and facilities.

5.4.4   Students will have access to a language laboratory and/or self-access facilities. In addition, supplementary materials for private study will be available. Advice will be given on the use of these resources.

5.4.5   Each classroom will have adequate space for the classes which use it, and will be furnished appropriately for the type of lessons that take place there. Heating, lighting and ventilation will conform to acceptable norms for educational buildings.

5.4.6   Teachers will have the use of standard teaching equipment including an overhead projector, a cassette tape recorder/player, and a video-cassette recorder and monitor.

5.4.7   Teachers will have the use of a staffroom or offices.

5.5   COURSE DESIGN

The course will be well planned, according to explicit principles founded in good practice, and will incorporate a syllabus or outline plan for each component appropriate to the preparation of students for academic work and life in Britain.

5.5.1   The principles on which the course is based should be made known to the teachers and understood by them.

5.5.2   Each component of the course will have explicit aims relating to the preparation of the students for life and work in an English language academic environment.

5.5.3   Each component of the course will have a syllabus or outline plan designed to support these aims. Some components of the syllabus may be negotiated with the students, but in most cases it will be planned before the start of the course on the basis of the students' needs, established where possible by liaison with the receiving department and/or students' sponsors.

5.5.4   The course will include an introduction to the use of the library.

5.5.5   Materials will be selected or prepared to achieve the aims of the course. These materials will, at least in part, be clearly based on the language and activities likely to be experienced by the students in their academic studies. To this end, the staff involved in their selection and preparation will be familiar with the nature of the work in relevant university departments and have strong contacts with those departments.

5.6   TEACHING

The teaching will be supported by the efficient management of the course in terms of class organisation. Classes will be organised, timetabled and of a size to ensure reasonable attention to each student and balance between continuity and variety in teacher–student contact (See sections 5.6.1 and 5.6.4 below).

The teaching will be professional, efficient and informed by sound methodological principles. The teaching approaches will take into account both the cultural and educational backgrounds of the students and their academic needs.

The Code of Practice of BALEAP does not seek to lay down any specific methodo-logical approach since it is appreciated that, at the present time, alternative, equally acceptable methods are available, and scope must be allowed for research and innovation in such a rapidly developing field as teaching English for Academic Purposes.

Nevertheless, the teaching will display the general characteristics outlined in 5.6.5 to 5.6.10 below.

5.6.1   The class size will not exceed 16 students and should not normally be more than 12. However, for certain activities the class size may be in excess of these numbers as, for example, when giving students experience of working in the lecture mode.

5.6.2   Provision will be made for regular individual consultations or tutorials.

5.6.3   Main course teachers will not normally be changed during a university term (on all year courses) or a programme block (on pre-sessional courses).

5.6.4   Students will be taught by a reasonable number of different teachers during the week. The number will depend on the length, size and intensity of the course, but a guide would be that, for a course with more than 20 hours a week class contact, there would be a minimum of three teachers and a maximum of six.

5.6.5   Lessons will be carefully prepared. The preparation will include:

          – the specification of clear aims
          – the choice of materials and teaching aids appropriate to the aims of the lesson

and to the students' language learning needs in relation to their academic studies.

5.6.6   Lessons will be well organised. The organisation will include:

– a clear introduction (where appropriate)
– a well-timed, orderly progression of activities
– good management of physical resources, teaching aids and materials.

5.6.7   Lessons will be responsive to students' academic, personal and linguistic needs. This will be demonstrated in the execution of the lesson by:

– choice of appropriate teaching techniques
– checking of students' grasp of concepts and language items and provision of helpful feedback (especially via the setting and marking of appropriate assignments)
– the active involvement of students at all stages of the lesson

5.6.8   The wider context of each individual lesson will be recognised by the teacher. This will be shown by the teacher's awareness of the links between the lesson and the aims of the course and of the relationship between the lesson and the syllabus.

5.6.9   The teaching will draw on the professional expertise of the teacher, which should include a good knowledge of English phonology, syntax, lexis and text structure as well as an understanding of the varieties of English and the skills required by the students in their academic work.

5.6.10   Teaching methods and materials will not be regarded as static, but will be subject to regular revision and adaptation. To achieve this, the Course Director will have regular contact with the students, possibly by also being a teacher.

5.7   ASSESSMENT

5.7.1   The use of tests and other methods of assessment will vary according to the type and length of the course, but it will be recognised that students need regular feedback on their progress and on their strengths and weaknesses.

5.7.2   Where tests are used for student placement or final assessment, every attempt will be made to ensure that they are valid and reliable.

5.7.3   Students will be informed in advance of assessment procedures to be used on the course.

5.7.4   On intensive courses of more than one month, assessment of students' progress will be carried out at regular intervals and appropriate reporting procedures adopted and records kept.

5.7.5 Information on well-established external examinations in English for Academic Purposes will be available for students who wish to take such an examination. Students requiring external certification of general English Language Proficiency will be able to receive advice regarding availability of such tests.

5.8   STUDENT WELFARE

5.8.1 On all accredited courses, it will be the responsibility of the staff to draw students' attention to the full range of welfare services and facilities available to them. Additionally, students will be informed of channels of communication to do with aspects of welfare.

5.8.2 The course staff will take reasonable steps to assist students to adjust to life in the UK and to integrate into university life by directing them to the appropriate services as required.

5.8.3 Attention to matters of welfare will be a necessary aspect of the roles of the staff connected with the course, in addition to the duties of any specifically designated welfare officer.

5.8.4 Students on courses held during the academic year will be fully registered students of the university.

5.8.5 With full registration, EAP students will have the same access to the university services as any other graduate or undergraduate. These services comprise in particular health and personal counselling, but students will also have access to the usual range of university services in respect of accommodation, catering, recreation facilities, careers counselling and Student Union membership.

5.8.6 It is recognised that full registration may not apply in some universities outside the academic year. Nevertheless, pre-sessional students will have access to such services and facilities as are provided by the university at the time of their course. Pre-sessional staff will ensure access to catering, health and welfare provision, paying particular attention to areas where the university's normal services are not in operation. Staff will know the procedure to be followed in emergencies.

5.8.7 On pre-sessional courses, a social and excursion programme will normally be arranged. Outside visits and excursions should be properly organised and adequately insured.

5.8.8 Accommodation will be arranged in principle by the university according to the normal parameters for students. EAP course staff will be familiar with their own institution's procedures concerning accommodation and the appropriate channels for queries and problems.

5.8.9 Students will additionally be provided with information about welfare, financial and recreational facilities available in the local area.

5.8.10 Students will receive general orientation to British culture and help in complying with official regulations relating to their residential status in Britain.

5.9 COURSE EVALUATION

5.9.1 Provision will be made for on-going course evaluation by both teachers and students and for improvements to be made to the course in the light of any shortcomings revealed by the evaluation. To this end, regular staff meetings will be held.

5.9.2 A mechanism will exist to enable both students and staff to provide regular feedback on all aspects of the course. In appropriate cases, an end-of-course questionnaire and/or an evaluation session will be conducted to provide feedback on the course for all concerned.

5.9.3 As far as possible, there should be follow-up of students who have finished EAP courses. Not only should their subsequent academic achievement be compared with their performance on EAP courses, but attempts should be made to ascertain the degree of usefulness and relevance of the EAP course to their academic studies. Such a follow-up exercise should be undertaken at regular intervals (at least once every three years).

5.9.4 As far as possible, the teaching of all newly-appointed staff will be observed by the Course Director. The staff will be given the opportunity to discuss their teaching methods and use of materials after the observation.

5.10 PUBLICITY

All statements made in publicity materials will accurately reflect the nature of the course and of associated services, facilities and resources.

CHECKLIST OF DOCUMENTATION

NOTES

To facilitate the accreditation procedure, it is essential that the assessors receive, in advance, certain information from the member institution concerning its courses and their management. This will assist the assessors in their preparation for a visit.

The purpose of this checklist is to help the institution gather together the sort of information that will be useful. It is, of course, not an exclusive list, and if institutions wish to offer any further evidence, or documentation in support of an application for accreditation, they are welcome to do so. One such item would be a 'policy statement', outlining the current position of the institution/courses, any recent/planned developments, any particular difficulties overcome/currently faced, any outstanding achievements, and so on. This might also include an account of any reasoned departure from the Code of Practice (See 4.3.9 and 5.1.3). In brief, in addition to giving the institution the opportunity to provide any relevant information not allowed for in the list that follows, this statement would serve to further contextualise the visit for the assessors.

It is appreciated that not all the items listed here may be available. Moreover, in some cases, certain items may be irrelevant. Institutions should, therefore, use their discretion in following this list.

The BASC will be pleased to receive comments on this list from assessors and institutions since it is intended to review the checklist regularly.

INFORMATION AND DOCUMENTATION TO BE SENT BEFORE THE ACCREDITATION VISIT

Each institution applying for course accreditation will be asked to submit a set of papers providing the information outlined below *for each of the courses seeking accreditation*. Where a course is divided into blocks, the information should be provided for each block. For ease of reference, the documentation is listed under the relevant Assessment Criterion (See Section 5).

1. PROFILE

1.1 See Appendix 8a, CL1a and b

1.2 Class lists of students, with information on any streaming, setting, or sub-groupings.

2. MANAGEMENT AND ADMINISTRATION

2.1 Information showing position of the member institution in the structure of the university (e.g. membership of Faculty or School).

2.2 A diagram showing the management structure of the member institution with names of post holders.

2.3 Information about the management of the courses applying for accreditation; for example, job descriptions of relevant staff, positions of responsibility, allocation of administrative duties. This should include such areas as staff recruitment, course planning, timetabling, provision of materials, provision and administration of tests, resources (including staff and student access), allocation of classrooms, student recruitment, student allocation to classes, social events, student welfare, and so on.

3. STAFFING

3.1 An accurate and up-to-date CV for each member of the academic staff, giving (at least) qualifications and relevant experience (including any overseas experience) (See CL2). Each CV should also include the date the teacher took up the present post.

3.2   Details of terms and conditions for both permanent and temporary staff (See CL3).

3.3   The number of part-time and full-time staff teaching on each course with details of number of hours taught by each staff member (See CL3).

3.4   The number of new staff members in the current year teaching on the courses applying for accreditation.

3.5   Statement and documentation on any staff development policy practised by the member institution including, for example, information about internal briefing or staff development sessions, etc, support for staff members to attend professional conferences and/or courses (and a record of attendance during recent years).

3.6   Statement of any research and development policy practised by the member institution including, for example, time allowed for individual research and preparation, any materials or test development related to the courses applying for accreditation, any study leave allowance, or relevant research conducted in the department.

4.   RESOURCES AND FACILITIES

4.1   A map of the premises, indicating offices and classrooms for the relevant courses.

4.2   Information on access to the premises, public transport and car parking facilities.

4.3   Lists of available resources, e.g. course books, supplementary materials, reference materials, self-access materials, hardware. Information on how these resources are accessed by staff and, where applicable, by students.

4.4   Information on library availability and access for students.

4.5   Copies of any information sheets given to students on the use of resources such as self-access centres or libraries.

5.   COURSE DESIGN

5.1   Statement of principles of course design.

5.2   Component syllabuses/outline plans.

5.3   Timetables for the course showing tutors' names, group (class) and room numbers (to be used by the assessors to devise an observation timetable).

5.4   Information on the introduction to the use of the library.

6.   TEACHING

6.1   Number of teachers per group (this should be clear from the timetables).

6.2   Number of students per group (class) (See CL1b).

7.   ASSESSMENT

7.1   Information on entrance requirements for course(s) to be accredited.

7.2   Information on placement procedures and assessment procedures (including any testing).

7.3   Account of procedures for record keeping, reporting to sponsors, departments, etc.

7.4   Sample of test reports or certificates (if any) that are given to students.

7.5   Information regarding any external examinations for which students are entered, including examination results for recent years.

8.   STUDENT WELFARE

8.1   Statement of the extent of welfare provision, including student counselling provision.

8.2   Statement of provision for assisting students with finding accommodation, availability of on-campus accommodation, and any special facilities for host-family accommodation (including any forms/information sent to host families).

8.3   Information about student access to catering facilities.

8.4   Statement concerning health care facilities and how information is provided for students on medical provision.

8.5   Information about student access to general facilities: for example, Students' Union activities, sports facilities, religious and cultural facilities, in or near the institution. Include information on how students are briefed about these facilities, together with any leaflets or information sheets.

8.6   Statement concerning the dissemination of any information provided for students concerning living in Britain: for example, on banking, shopping, legal and cultural issues.

8.7   Information about any social activities/excursions organised during the course.

9.   EVALUATION

9.1   Information on evaluation procedures (including teacher appraisal).

9.2   Sample of any questionnaires used (including student questionnaires on resources and facilities, and welfare).

10.   PUBLICITY

10.1   Any general brochures or Yearbooks of the university that include information relating to the member institution.

10.2   Publicity (brochures, leaflets, etc) for the member institution.

10.3   Any leaflets or brochures for the courses that are applying for accreditation.

Source: Handbook of the British Association of Lecturers in English for Academic Purposes, June 1993

4.2   Oral presentation

4.2.1   Criteria of assessment – Presentation skills and content

Evidence of preparation

0   No evidence of preparation. The speaker gives the impression that s/he is approaching the subject or thinking about the talk for the first time.
1   Some evidence of preparation but the talk is very rough. There may be contradictions, overlaps or gaps, giving a general impression of a lack of competence or assurance, or a lack of familiarity with the subject matter.
2   Generally the talk is executed fairly well. There may be evidence of a lack of adequate rehearsal but this does not detract from an overall impression of competence and assurance.
3   The talk has been well prepared and rehearsed. It is presented in a smooth, flawless way without appearing laboured.

Use of visual aids

0   Visual aids are completely inappropriate to the information being presented (e.g. they are unnecessary or simply a 'visible verbal').
1   Appropriate use of visual aids but visuals have deficiencies in content or are difficult to interpret (e.g. visually overcrowded, lacking in colour, etc.).
2   Use of visual aids appropriate, but presenter shows a lack of competence in their use (e.g. obstruction of audience's vision, exposed to audience too long/short, not enough explanation, etc.).
3   Appropriate and adequate use of visual aids.

Clarity of presentation

0   Presentation lacks any clear structure. Talk is almost impossible to follow.
1   Overall structure of the talk is clear but the individual stages are indistinguishable. No clear logical development.

2 Overall structure and individual stages are clear, but there is a lack of intermediate summaries and signposts.

3 Information is presented in a clear, logical, sequential order.

Delivery

0 Speaker is virtually inaudible.

1 Speaker is loud enough but the speed is inappropriate so that the talk sounds gabbled or slow and disjointed, and is difficult to follow.

2 Speaker talks clearly and at an appropriate speed but there are some failings e.g. a lack of enthusiasm or sincerity.

3 Talk is delivered in a clear and interesting way so that audience's attention is maintained.

Appropriateness of material to audience

0 Speaker has not considered the needs of his audience at all (i.e. he tells his audience what he wants to say, not what they want to hear).

1 Speaker has given some thought to his audience's needs in terms of subject matter but a clear reason why the audience should be interested does not emerge early enough in the talk.

2 Speaker has thought about his audience's needs and interest level but fails to take into account their level of knowledge and understanding.

3 Speaker has thought carefully about his audience and leaves them with the feeling that the talk was not only informative but worthwhile.

Relevance and adequacy of content

0 Response irrelevant to the task set; totally inadequate response.

1 Response of limited relevance to the task set; possibly major gaps and/or pointless repetition.

2 Response for the most part relevant to the task set, though there may be some gaps or redundancy.

3 Relevant and adequate response to the task set.

Source: Thompson 1989

4.2.2   Criteria of assessment – Language (TEEP)

Appropriateness

0 Unable to function in the spoken language.

1 Able to operate only in a very limited capacity; responses characterized by sociocultural inappropriateness.

2 Signs of developing attempts at response to role, setting etc. but misunderstandings may occasionally arise through inappropriateness, particularly of sociocultural convention.

3 Almost no errors in the sociocultural conventions of language; errors not significant enough to be likely to cause social misunderstanding.

Adequacy of vocabulary for purpose

0 Vocabulary inadequate even for the most basic parts of the intended communication.
1 Vocabulary limited to that necessary to express simple elementary needs; inadequacy of vocabulary restricts topics of interaction to the most basic; perhaps frequent lexical inaccuracies and/or excessive repetition.
2 Some misunderstandings may arise through lexical inadequacy or inaccuracy; hesitation and circumlocution are frequent, though there are signs of a developing active vocabulary.
3 Almost no inadequacies or inaccuracies in vocabulary for the task. Only rare circumlocution.

Intelligibility

0 Severe and constant rhythm, intonation and pronunciation problems cause almost complete unintelligibility.
1 Strong interference from L_1 in rhythm, intonation and pronunciation; understanding is difficult, and achieved ? after frequent repetition.
2 Rhythm, intonation and pronunciation require concentrated listening, but only occasional misunderstanding is caused or repetition required.
3 Articulation is reasonably comprehensible to native speakers; there may be a marked 'foreign accent' but almost no misunderstanding is caused and repetition required only infrequently.

Fluency

0 Utterances halting, fragmentary and incoherent.
1 Utterances hesitant and often incomplete except in a few stock remarks and responses. Sentences are, for the most part, disjointed and restricted in length.
2 Signs of developing attempts at using cohesive devices, especially conjunctions. Utterances may still be hesitant, but are gaining in coherence, speed and length.
3 Utterances, whilst occasionally hesitant, are characterized by an evenness and flow hindered, very occasionally, by groping, rephrasing and circumlocutions. Inter-sentential connectors are used effectively as fillers.

Source: Weir 1990

Overall assessment of presentation: Impression marking

Assessment scale

Band

7 Excellent presentation, command of subject matter, organization and use of language.
6 Very good presentation, command of subject matter and organization despite some linguistic deficiencies.
5 Well presented, good command of subject matter despite possible deficiencies in organization and/or language.

4 Quite well presented, adequate command of subject matter but the talk may be lacking organization and/or may show inadequate use of language.
3 Satisfactory presentation despite weak command of subject matter. Talk may also show poor organization and/or very limited range of language.
2 Unsatisfactory presentation, possibly with poor command of subject matter and/or bad organization.
1 Very poor presentation, extremely limited command of subject matter and/or complete lack of organization. Talk is very difficult to follow.
0 Talk is virtually incomprehensible.

4.2.3 Assessment marking sheet

Month..........

Teacher..........

	Criteria of assessment										Overall assessment
	1. Presentation skills					2. Relevance and adequacy of content	3. Language				
Student name	a Evidence of preparation	b Use of visual aids	c Clarity of presentation	d Delivery	e Appropriateness of material to audience		a Appropriateness	b Adequacy of vocabulary for purpose	c Intelligibility	d Fluency	
1.											
2.											
3.											
4.											
5.											
6.											
7.											
8.											
9.											
10.											
11.											
12.											
13.											
14.											
15.											
16.											
17.											
18.											
19.											
20.											

4.3 CALS suggested marking scheme (writing skills)

The following is a revised version of a marking scheme that was used successfully on the Pre-sessional Course at Reading. Teachers may feel they want to make slight adaptations for their own use. The band descriptors should be treated as guidelines rather than being rigidly prescriptive. To be placed in a particular band, a student's work need not meet all the criteria assigned to the band.

In assessing content, the problem of teachers being unfamiliar with students' subject matter may arise. It is not always possible to match teachers of English for Academic Purposes with students in a subject area in which the former have some background or interest. Moreover, it is unrealistic to assume the same degree of subject familiarity as the student's even if this does happen. This does not preclude the assessment of content with a possible high degree of 'impression-marking'.

The marks given in the right-hand columns are the maximum to be allotted for each band. There is a considerable difference between marks allotted for content in marking the unit 5 and unit 6 essays. This is designed to reflect the importance of emphasizing non-content features in the students' first extended essay.

	Marks allotted (max.)	
	Unit 5	Unit 6
Content		
EXCELLENT VERY GOOD Appears relevant to topic, thorough in coverage and wide in scope	5	20
GOOD ADEQUATE Appears relevant but may be a little limited in scope; possibly too detailed in places or too long	4/3	15
FAIR INADEQUATE Appears partly irrelevant (despite possible high language proficiency); may be very limited in scope	2	10
POOR COMPLETELY INADEQUATE Clearly unable to deal with topic competently; may be largely irrelevant or too brief to assess	1/0	5
Use of source material		
EXCELLENT VERY GOOD Source material satisfactorily incorporated; quotations used judiciously; complete absence of plagiarism; adequate bibliography	30	25
GOOD ADEQUATE Adequate reference to source material though there may be minor errors; absence of plagiarism though possible over-use of quotations; bibliography may be incomplete, or inadequate in minor ways	22	16
FAIR INADEQUATE Inadequate reference to source material – quotations incorporated wrongly; some plagiarism in evidence; several types of error in bibliography	14	10

	Marks allotted (max.)	
	Unit 5	Unit 6

POOR TOTALLY INADEQUATE Largely or wholly plagiarized; no quotations or reference to sources; no bibliography or very inadequate one — 7 | 4

Organization

EXCELLENT VERY GOOD Outline of main ideas easily intelligible to reader (even to a non-specialist); sections and paragraphs clearly marked; clear, thorough introduction and conclusion — 15 | 15

GOOD ADEQUATE Some incompleteness or lack of clarity in the whole; sections and paragraphs not divided perfectly; introduction and conclusion not perfectly related to main body — 12 | 12

FAIR INADEQUATE Outline of main ideas difficult to establish; sections and paragraphs sometimes inadequately divided; introduction and/or conclusion inadequate — 8 | 8

POOR TOTALLY INADEQUATE Lack of organization makes reading very difficult; little or no division into sections and/or paragraphs; poor introduction and/or conclusion or none — 4 | 4

Cohesion

EXCELLENT VERY GOOD Close, intelligible relationship between one sentence and another; satisfactory use of connectives — 10 | 10

GOOD ADEQUATE Relationship between sentences may occasionally lack smoothness; some misuse of connectives — 7/8 | 7/8

FAIR INADEQUATE Unsatisfactory cohesion may make comprehension of parts difficult; many connectives misused or repeated too often — 4/5 | 4/5

POOR TOTALLY INADEQUATE Cohesion almost totally absent – writing so fragmentary that comprehension is very difficult; very limited command of connectives — 2 | 2

Presentation

EXCELLENT VERY GOOD Clear and legible (if handwritten); includes contents page; correct spacing and/or indentation of paragraphs; any tables or figures well presented — 10 | 10

GOOD ADEQUATE May be lacking in one of the above — 7/8 | 7/8

FAIR INADEQUATE Presentation makes reading arduous; contents page may be missing; cramped text; tables or figures incomplete or unclear — 4/5 | 4/5

	Marks allotted (max.)	
	Unit 5	Unit 6
POOR TOTALLY INADEQUATE Partly or wholly illegible; may lack margin and contents page; badly spaced	2	2

Language

EXCELLENT VERY GOOD Very few language errors	20	15
GOOD ADEQUATE Some language errors evident but these rarely impede comprehension	15	12
FAIR INADEQUATE Frequent language errors, sometimes impeding comprehension	10	8
POOR TOTALLY INADEQUATE Number and type of error make comprehension frequently or totally impossible	5	4

Mechanical accuracy

EXCELLENT VERY GOOD Virtually no errors of punctuation, spelling or capitalization	10	5
GOOD ADEQUATE Occasional errors in above but these rarely impede comprehension	7/8	4/3
FAIR INADEQUATE Frequent errors in above causing occasional incomprehension	4/5	2
POOR TOTALLY INADEQUATE Errors in almost every sentence	2	1

4.4 Course feedback questionnaires

Centre for Applied Language Studies University of Reading
Pre-sessional course

4.4.1 Spoken Language Classes

Your subject _____

Level (Please tick one box):   Preparatory course   ☐

Undergraduate   ☐

Postgraduate: Diploma   ☐

M.A./M.Sc.   ☐

M.Phil./Ph.D.   ☐

Approximate length of Pre-sessional Course taken: Please tick *one* box.
One month (i.e. September) ☐   Two months (i.e. August & September) ☐
Three months (i.e. July, August & September) ☐

My teacher for the *Spoken Language* Class (Block 2a and 3 intake: 9.15–10.45
                                              Block 2b intake: 11.15–12.45)
was (Please give first name *and* surname if possible):

_____

We would be grateful if you would fill in the attached questionnaire to help us to revise and improve next year's course.

Thank you for your help.

A. P. TONKYN
J. TRZECIAK   Course Directors
C. J. WEIR

Please read the following questions/statements and put an X in the appropiate box. Below is an example.

Example

I think my English has improved.

Strongly agree 5	Agree 4	Not sure 3	Disagree 2	Strongly disagree 1
			X	

(This example shows that the person does not agree with the statement.)

1. *Speaking*

   1.1 Speaking: General improvement

   My speaking ability has improved because of the course.

Strongly agree 5	Agree 4	Not sure 3	Disagree 2	Strongly disagree 1

Comments _____

_____

   1.2 Speaking: Specific improvements

   My speaking has improved in the following areas:

Areas	Strongly agree 5	Agree 4	Not sure 3	Disagree 2	Strongly disagree 1
Asking questions					
Discussing					
Presenting information					
Pronunciation					
Grammar					
Vocabulary					
Others (Please specify) _____ _____					

1.3. Speaking: Practice

How much speaking practice did you get in the following areas?

Areas	None	Not enough	The right amount	More than I wanted
Student presentations				
Discussions				
Asking questions				
Pronunciation				
Grammar				
Vocabulary				

2. *Listening*

2.1 Listening: General improvement

My general listening comprehension has improved because of the course.

Strongly agree 5	Agree 4	Not sure 3	Disagree 2	Strongly disagree 1

2.2 Listening: Specific improvement

The course has helped me to improve my listening comprehension in the following areas:

Areas	Strongly agree 5	Agree 4	Not sure 3	Disagree 2	Strongly disagree 1
Understanding lectures					
Understanding native speakers					
Understanding fellow students					
Taking notes from spoken lectures					

Comments _____

_____

2.3 *Listening*: Practice

I received the following amount of listening practice in the following areas.

Areas	None	Not enough	The right amount	More than I wanted
Lectures				
Discussion				
Taking notes from spoken lectures				

Speaking/Listening: Materials/Activities
The following materials and activities were useful to me. (If you did not use certain materials or do an activity, please write 'N/A'.)

Material/Activity	Strongly agree 5	Agree 4	Not sure 3	Disagree 2	Strongly disagree 1
'Study Speaking' Seminar strategies					
Making oral presentations to the whole class					
Exchanging information in pairs (e.g. personal information, directions, etc.)					
Grammar practice					
Pronunciation practice (e.g. in lab.)					
The Pre-sessional Listening course (lecture-based)					
'Study Listening'					
Tutorials with Spoken Language teacher					
Others (Please specify) _____ _____					

If you are willing to give your *name*, please write it clearly below

_____

Thank you for your help!

Centre for Applied Language Studies
University of Reading

Pre-sessional course

4.4.2 Written Language Classes

Your subject _____

Level (Please tick one box): Preparatory course   [ ]
                                   Undergraduate   [ ]
                   Postgraduate: Diploma   [ ]
                              M.A./M.Sc.   [ ]
                              M.Phil./Ph.D.   [ ]

Length of Pre-sessional Course taken: Please tick *one* box.
One month (i.e. September) [ ]   Two months (i.e. August & September) [ ]
        Three months (i.e. July, August & September) [ ]

My teacher for the *Written Language Class* (July and September intake: 11.15–12.45
                                       (August intake: 9.15–10.45)
was: (Please give first name *and* surname if possible)

_____

We would be grateful if you would fill in the attached questionnaire to help us to revise and improve next year's course.

Thank you for your help.

               A. P. TONKYN
               J. S. TRZECIAK   Course Directors
               C. J. WEIR

3. *Writing*
    3.1   Writing: General improvement
    My writing ability has improved because of the course.

Strongly agree	Agree	Undecided	Disagree	Strongly disagree
5	4	3	2	1

    3.1.1.   In what ways has your writing *most* improved?

        _____

        In what ways has your writing *least* improved?

        _____

3.2   Writing: Practice

How much practice do you get in the following areas in class?

	None	Not enough	The right amount	More than I wanted
Evaluating and revising my writing				
Evaluating other students' writing				
Organizing/planning my writing				
Developing vocabulary				
Grammar revision				
Punction				
Spelling				

3.3   Writing: Course content

3.3.1   Are there any things you have *not* done in the writing class that you would have liked to have done? (Please circle one answer.)

NO

YES What? _____

_____

3.3.2   Were there any things that you think were *not* necessary in the writing class?

NO
YES What? _____

_____

3.3.3   Do you have other comments on the materials you used in the writing classes?

_____

_____

4. Reading
4.1 Reading: General improvement
My reading ability has improved because of the course.

Strongly agree	Agree	Undecided	Disagree	Strongly disagree
5	4	3	2	1

4.1.1 In what ways has your reading *most* improved?

In what ways has your reading *least* improved?

4.2 Reading: Practice
How much practice did you get in class in the following?

	None	Not enough	The right amount	More than I wanted
Reading quickly				
Understanding the main points of text				
Understanding the details of a text				
Guessing unknown words in a text				
Understanding text organization				
Understanding formal style and language use				
Understanding a writer's attitude and purpose				

4.3.   Reading: Course content

4.3.1   Are there any things which you haven't done in the reading class that you would have liked to have done?

NO

YES What? _____

_____

4.3.2   Were there any things that you think were *not* necessary in the reading class?

NO

YES What? _____

_____

4.3.3   Do you have any other comments or questions on the materials you used in the reading classes?

_____

_____

_____

If you are willing to give your name, please write it clearly below:
_____

Thank you for your help! (ᴧ!ᴧ)

Centre for Applied Language Studies
University of Reading   Pre-sessional course

4.4.3 Project classes/Administration

Your subject _____

Level (Please tick one box): Preparatory course   [ ]
                             Undergraduate   [ ]
                     Postgraduate: Diploma   [ ]
                                M.A./M.Sc.   [ ]
                               M.Phil./Ph.D.   [ ]

Length of pre-sessional course taken: Please tick *one* box.
One month (i.e. September) [ ]   Two months (i.e. August and September) [ ]
        Three months (i.e. July, August and September) [ ]

My teacher for the afternoon *Project* class was: (Please give first name *and* surname if possible)

_____

We would be grateful if you would fill in the attached questionnaire to help us to revise and improve next year's course.

Thank you for your help.

>   A. P. TONKYN
>   J. S. TRZECIAK   Course Directors
>   C. J. WEIR

Please read the following question/statements and put a X in the appropriate box.

5. *Project*
   5.1 Project: General improvement
   My ability to write extended academic essays using relevant data has improved.

Strongly agree 5	Agree 4	Undecided 3	Disagree 2	Strongly disagree 1

5.2 Project: Course content
5.2.1 The following parts of the project course were useful:

Areas	Strongly agree 5	Agree 4	Not sure 3	Disagree 2	Strongly disagree 1
Surveying a book					
Library work					
Compiling a bibliography					
Note taking					
Summarizing					
Writing introductions and conclusions					
Writing references and quotations					
Synthesizing information from more than one text					
Extended writing Task: Project 5 (July and August students)					
Project 6 (July, August and September students)					

5.2.2 How useful did you find being in a group with other students specializing in your subject or broadly related subjects?

Very useful	Moderately useful	Not useful at all

5.2.3 Are there any things which you haven't done in the project class that you would like to do?
NO
YES What? _____

5.2.4　Are there any things that you think are *not* necessary in the project class?
　　　　NO
　　　　YES What? _____

　　　　_____

5.2.5　Have you got any other comments on the materials you used in the project class?

　　　　_____

　　　　_____

　　　　_____

6.　*Administration/ Social life/ Welfare*
　　6.1　Please comment on the satisfactoriness of the following aspects of the course administration by ticking in the relevant box.

	Very satisfactory 5	4	3	2	Very unsatisfactory 1
The trips					
The course welfare officer's handling of accommodation matters					
Evening entertainment					

If you wish, please make additional comments or suggestions below on these matters:

a)　Trips _____

　　_____

　　Where else would you like to have gone on trips? (e.g. markets, historical towns, seaside resorts, big cities)_____

　　_____

How long would you prefer journey times for trips to be? Indicate *one* time.	1 hour	2 hours	3 hours	Not important

b)　Handling of future accommodation_____

　　_____

288 Appendices

c) Evening entertainment _____

_____

d) What sort of sports would you have been interested in doing? _____

_____

6.2 *Frequency of trips*: How frequent do you feel the trips should be? (please tick)
One a week (as now)   [ ]
One every two weeks   [ ]
Less often than one every two weeks   [ ]

6.3 *Health Centre*:
    6.3.1 Did you use the University Health Centre during the course?
        YES   [ ]
        NO   [ ]
    6.3.2 If YES, (a) was it difficult to get an appointment at a time to suit you?
        YES   [ ]
        NO   [ ]
        (b) How many times did you use the Health Centre?
           Once   [ ]
           Twice   [ ]
           Three times   [ ]
           More than three times [ ]

6.4 Do you have any further comments/suggestions regarding the administration of the course, and social and welfare provision?

_____

_____

6.5 Wells Hall
How would you rate the following?

	Good	Fair	Poor	Very poor
Food				
Cleanliness				
Staff helpfulness				
Facilities				

If you need to add anything to your ratings above, please write it below.

_____

_____

_____

_____

Have you any further comments or suggestions about Wells Hall? _____

_____

Would you have preferred self-catering accommodation? _____

Would you have preferred not to have lunch in Wells Hall? _____

Would you be willing to pay more for better facilities (e.g. wash basins in rooms)? (Please note that any accommodation would still be student accommodation.) _____

If you are willing to give your *name*, please write it clearly below:

_____

Thank you for your help! (^!^)

4.5 Reading skills questionnaire

Dear colleague,

We want to establish (1) what the most important reading skills for your course are and (2) the difficulties you *still* have in reading. To help us, please fill out this short questionnaire according to your own experience after the pre-sessional reading course last year. *All information will be treated in the strictest confidence.* Please send the questionnaire back through the internal mail in the envelope provided *as soon as possible.* Thank you very much for your help.

Your department _____ Your course _____

Part 1 Please think about the reading skills required in the course you study.

1. Please tick in the boxes below how important it was for you to perform each skill.
1 = Very important
2 = Important
3 = Not important
N = Not sure

2. Please tick in the boxes below how difficult it was for you to perform each skill.
1 = Very difficult
2 = Difficult
3 = Not difficult
N = Not sure

1	2	3	N	Reading skills	1	2	3	N
				1. Skimming: reading a text *quickly* in order to *establish* a general idea of the content, e.g. to determine what part, or whether part or whole, is relevant to an established purpose and should be read again more carefully				
				2. Scanning: looking through a text *quickly* in order to *locate* specific information, e.g. to check a date, a figure in a graph or a key word in the text				
				3. Reading a text or parts of a text more *slowly* and *carefully* to *extract* all the relevant information, e.g. to carry out written assignment such as an essay, dissertation or examination				
				4. Understanding unknown words in the text				
				Please specify any other reading skills you use. 5.				
				6.				

Part II

Please answer the following questions according to your own experience.

1. Please describe any problems you *still* have in your academic reading.

2. Do you think the presessional reading course can be *improved* to prepare you better for your academic reading? Please tick. Yes ☐   No ☐
   If Yes, please explain how.

Source: Li Ying Cheng 1993

5.1 Evaluation activities

Week 1

Monday

1 Meetings at the Embassy (Ambassador, Cultural Attaché, Aid Officer) for background to project and provision of Embassy backup
2 Discussion with ELTO to review the timetable and objectives of the visit
3 Meetings at College with administrative staff (course coordinator and administrative officer) and counterparts
4 Observe three Certificado classes
5 Attend reception for chairman of the local 'Anglo'

Tuesday

1 Meet Director of College
2 Discussion with ELTO on Certificado structure
3 First meeting with counterparts, two full-time members of staff
4 Observe two classes (Methodology, year 2)
5 Meet Year 2 students
6 Discussions with ELTO

Wednesday

1 Discussion with ELTO (focus on counterparts)
2 Follow-up discussion with counterpart (course review)
3 Meet Year 2 students
4 Observe reading skills class

Thursday

1 Review course materials
2 Visit classes in local secondary school
3 Follow up discussion with counterpart (course review)
4 Administer language tests and interview a sample of Year 2 students

Friday

1 Discussion with ELTO (review course materials)
2 Follow-up discussion with counterpart (study skills)
3 Informal discussions with staff and ELTO

Early closure of College due to heavy rain.

Saturday

1   Review course materials and draft syllabus
2   Prepare draft discussion paper

Week 2

Monday

1   Review course materials and draft syllabus with ELTO
2   Discussions with members of staff on counterpart needs
3   Teach class on Achievement Testing (Yrs 1+2 students)
4   Complete draft discussion paper

Tuesday

1   Discussions with Cultural Attaché, Aid Officer
2   Visit Ministry of Education with College Director
3   First meeting with part-time staff (skills courses)
4   Meeting on draft discussion paper with ELTO and full-time staff
5   Teach class on Achievement Testing (Years 1 and 2)

Wednesday

1   Discussions with ELTO
2   Feedback on programme from Year 1 students

Thursday

1   Meetings with Embassy staff
2   Farewell lunch hosted by evaluator for ELTO, Director, and all counterparts
3   Discussions with ELTO (conclusions, requests of ODA)
4   Return materials, collect documents

Friday

1   Final discussions with ELTO

Departure

5.2 Sample certificado timetables: Examples from two different semesters

First semester

Mon	Tues	Wed	Thurs	Fri
LI[a]	**LI**	Pschol	Doc Gen	TTI
LI	**LI**	Pschol	Doc Gen	TTI
LI	**LI**	Pschol	Doc Gen	**LI**
SS	**Lit**	**SS**	Filos	**LI**
SS	**Lit**	**SS**	Filos	**LI**

Special subjects (in bold)

Course	Classes[b]		Staff	Texts etc.
	Per week	Per semester		
LI (Lengua Inglesa)	8	120	X	Meridien 1
SS (Study Skills)	4	60	Y	Yorkey (chs 2, 3; O'Brien and Jordan ch. 1, 3)
Lit (Literature)	3	45	Z	Graded readers and worksheets
	15	225		

General subjects

Course	Classes	
	Per week	Per semester
Pschol (Psychology)	3	45
Doc Gen (Docencia general)	3	45
Filos (Philosophy of Education)	2	30
TTI: Tecnicas de trabajo y investigation (Study skills)	2	30
	10	150

Fourth semester

Mon	Tues	Wed	Thur	Fri
Gram	**Meth**	Prac Doc	**Meth**	Pedag
Gram	**Meth**	Prac Doc	**Meth**	Pedag
Ling	**Ling**	Orient	Orient	Orient
Skills	**Skills**	**Skills**	**Skills**	Ed Admin
Skills	**Skills**	**Skills**	**Skills**	Ed Admin

Special subjects (in bold)

Course	Classes		Staff	Texts
	Per week	Per semester		
Ling (Linguistics)	2	30	Z	Littlewood, *Foreign and Second Language Learning* and worksheets
Gram (Grammar workshop)	2	30	Z	Various
Meth (Methodology)	4	60	Z	Various
Skills				
Writing	2	16	A	Various
Listening	2	16	B	
Reading	2	16	C	
Speaking	2	16	D	
	16	184		

General subjects

Course	Classes	
	Per week	Per semester
Orient (Orientation)	3	45
Prac Doc (Teaching Practice)	2	30
Ed Admin (Educational Administration)	2	30
Pedag (Pedagogy)	2	30
	9	135

[a] Items in bold represent 'special subjects', the rest being general subjects shared with other specializations.
[b] The numbers refer to '*horas catedraticas*' – a 45-minute teaching period.

III.1 The evaluation methods paradigms debate summary of emphases: Theses, antitheses, syntheses

	Theses: Originally dominant 'scientific' paradigm	*Antitheses: Originally competing alternative paradigm*	*Syntheses: Utilization-focused evaluation, a paradigm of choices*
Purpose	Summative	Formative	Intended use for intended users
Measurement	Quantitative data	Qualitative data	Appropriate, credible, useful data
Design	Experimental designs	Naturalistic inquiry	Creative, practical, situationally responsive designs
Researcher stance	Objectivity	Subjectivity	Fairness and balance
Inquiry mode	Deduction	Induction	Either or both
Conceptualization	Independent and dependent variables	Holistic interdependent system	Stakeholder questions and issues
Relationships	Distance, detachment	Closeness, involvement	Collaboration, consultative
Approach to study of change	Pre-post measures, time series, static portrayals at discrete points in time	Process-oriented, evolving, capturing ongoing dynamism	Developmental, action-oriented: What needs to be known to get program from where it is to where it wants to be?
Relationship to prior knowledge	Confirmatory, hypothesis testing	Exploratory, hypothesis generating	Either or both
Sampling	Random, probabilistic	Purposeful, key informants	Combinations, depending on what information is needed
Primary approach to variations	Quantitative differences on uniform, standardized variables	Qualitative differences, uniquenesses	Flexible: Focus on comparisons most relevant to intended users and evaluation questions
Analysis	Descriptive and inferential statistics	Case studies, content and pattern analysis	Answers to stakeholders' questions
Types of statements	Generalizations	Context-bound	Extrapolations
Contribution to theory	Validating theoretical propositions from scientific literature	Grounded theory	Describing, exploring, and testing stakeholders' and program's theory of action
Goals	Truth, scientific acceptance	Understanding, perspective	Utility, relevance: Acceptance by intended users

Source: Patton 1986: 216–17

6.1 Data arrays

6.1.1 Subject totals of new overseas entrants to the university sector at undergraduate and postgraduate level in the three most populated disciplines

	Undergraduates						Postgraduates					
	76–77	77–78	78–79	79–80	80–81	81–82	76–77	77–78	78–79	79–80	80–81	81–82
Area 3 Engineering and technology												
Aeronautical engineering	96	79	89	48	55	47	17	22	24	24	16	10
Chemical engineering	183	197	136	112	85	80	238	227	236	220	123	105
Civil engineering	549	591	632	534	511	545	354	354	381	403	363	349
Electrical/Electronic engineering	611	676	580	495	417	438	524	494	507	510	364	309
Mechanical engineering	660	591	429	365	304	286	315	271	268	260	193	187
Production engineering	94	71	44	44	44	47	97	115	115	97	53	46
Mining	33	40	28	31	31	40	32	38	31	44	30	23
Metallurgy	26	56	34	24	20	19	96	89	97	114	69	80
Other general and combined engineering subjects	202	270	204	199	122	106	82	86	106	125	73	57
Surveying	23	25	37	30	37	46	13	17	24	18	15	16
Other technology and combinations of engineering and technology	110	105	94	83	110	94	502	551	519	477	454	346
Area 5 Science												
Biology	64	72	76	62	37	46	177	166	147	139	118	109
Botany	9	4	9	3	0	5	75	77	66	60	55	41

Zoology	20	14	12	14	5	3	50	57	70	53	47	39
Physiology and/or anatomy	13	13	24	13	7	10	23	16	17	17	13	18
Biochemistry	60	80	87	59	33	42	96	81	71	66	50	54
Other general and combined biological sciences	34	47	52	32	18	9	8	13	35	22	43	38
Mathematics	370	407	471	463	369	372	588	543	580	464	342	337
Mathematics/Physics	13	8	14	20	9	6	–	–	–	2	4	2
Physics	65	110	133	141	102	64	262	248	251	215	151	139
Chemistry	178	175	160	153	116	89	501	431	403	391	261	222
Geology	11	19	26	15	7	19	109	120	121	103	81	78
Other environmental sciences	7	14	15	14	8	11	63	41	33	25	36	29
Other general and combined physical sciences	27	39	23	40	17	20	12	10	5	5	4	2
Combinations of biological and physical sciences	216	224	288	221	205	185	9	22	12	14	5	2

Area 6 Social, administrative and business studies

Business management studies	113	102	152	134	109	119	513	588	570	504	589	676
Economics	190	189	217	161	120	149	619	636	640	627	561	522
Geography	19	13	14	17	6	4	85	98	73	87	72	52
Accountancy	43	58	66	88	98	90	71	73	70	50	95	96
Government and public administration	100	81	64	60	34	28	349	404	404	377	429	440
Law	152	151	179	176	219	258	352	392	427	410	394	348
Psychology	63	61	50	41	32	18	72	99	83	65	43	38
Sociology	78	83	80	78	47	28	313	331	341	270	164	163
Social anthropology	16	15	9	10	4	4	65	69	90	74	56	50

Source: Figures supplied by the Universities' Statistical Record

6.1.2 Number of overseas students enrolled on courses in universities, polytechnics, and further education colleges[a]

	Education	Medicine/Dentistry and Health	Engineering and Technology	Agriculture, Forestry and Veterinary Science	Science	Social, Administrative and Business Studies	Architecture and other professional and vocational subjects	Language, Literature and Area Studies	Arts, other than Languages	Totals
Universities (Undergraduate)										
1976–77	151	1004	6621	113	2499	2986	216	963	1154	15 707
1977–78	241	1120	7399	112	2920	3248	221	1000	1075	17 336
1978–79	286	1158	7334	99	3393	3391	249	1086	1229	18 225
1979–80	289	1160	6820	90	3489	3411	288	1022	1042	17 611
1980–81	342	1098	6029	68	3018	3238	335	621	655	15 404
1981–82	412	1130	5184	78	2569	3023	359	468	509	13 755
Universities (Postgraduate)										
1976–77	1246	1316	4069	620	4211	3766	565	1257	912	17 962
1977–78	1354	1427	3971	606	4103	4021	569	1184	923	18 158
1978–79	1421	1534	4165	624	4069	4072	643	1165	919	18 612
1979–80	1357	1595	3962	617	3773	3763	587	1074	838	17 566
1980–81	1263	1531	3491	584	3230	3698	512	919	643	15 871
1981–82	1372	1461	2918	596	2840	3467	536	816	604	14 610
Polytechnics										
1976–77	298	281	5903	–	2083	3977	860	310	562	14 274
1977–78	243	250	6353	–	2169	4203	954	167	456	14 796
1978–79	234	182	6106	–	2085	3934	937	209	528	14 215
1979–80	289	195	5654	–	2078	3336	830	168	489	13 039
1980–81	195	177	5172	1	1914	3301	962	136	382	12 240
FE colleges[b]										
1976–77	131	257	7359	144	644	6415	1636	1299	1641	19 526
1977–78	1092	251	7134	174	790	5298	1529	201	1507	17 976
1978–79	1184	261	7725	154	899	4907	1560	280	1585	18 555
1979–80	1209	232	7462	168	954	4667	1732	218	1525	18 167
1980–81	1071	278	6797	149	794	3919	1406	281	1191	15 886

[a] From 1977–78 onwards figures include certain higher education establishments as well as further education.
[b] Excluding students studying for GCE or CSE examinations.
Sources: Figures for universities were supplied by the Universities' Statistical Record and for polytechnics and FE colleges by the British Council (1978a, 1979, 1980a, 1981a, 1982).

6.1.3 Total numbers of overseas students enrolled on courses in the three largest discipline areas

	Engineering and technology 3	Science 5	Social, administrative and business studies 6
1976–77	23 652 (35%)	9 437 (14%)	17 144 (25%)
1977–78	24 402 (37%)	9 948 (15%)	16 430 (25%)
1978–79	25 330 (36%)	10 446 (15%)	16 304 (23%)
1979–80	25 058 (37%)	10 294 (16%)	15 177 (23%)
1980–81	21 489 (36%)	8 956 (15%)	14 156 (24%)

6.1.4 Total numbers of overseas students in universities as against other sectors in tertiary education

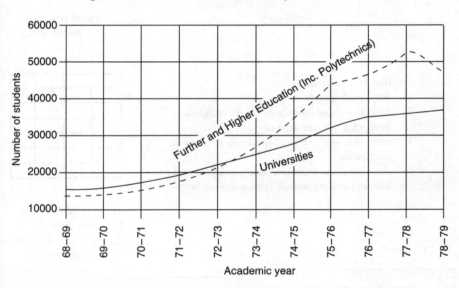

Source: British Council 1980a: 3

6.1.5   Student self-assessment

A4.   Please indicate how much difficulty you have found in each of the following:

Please tick the
appropriate box

H   M   L   N

1. Understanding spoken description or narrative
2. Understanding spoken instructions
3. Understanding informal language
4. Understanding the subject matter of the talk
   (i.e. understanding *what* is being talked about)
5. Any other general difficulties in understanding
   spoken English (please specify below)

A5.   Please indicate how much difficulty you have in understanding your teachers or other students when:

Please tick the
appropriate box

H   M   L   N

1. they talk very fast
2. they speak quietly
3. their accents or pronunciation are different
   from what you are used to
4. more than one person is speaking, as in group
   discussions
5. there are other problems which interfere with
   listening comprehension (please specify below)

H: a lot of difficulty
M: some difficulty
L: very little difficulty
N: no difficulty

			STUDENTS									
	OVERSEAS						BRITISH					
	No.	H	M	L	N	Staff	No.	H	M	L	N	Staff
Eng. U	173	12.1	43.4	33.5	11.0		153	2.0	17.0	*37.9	42.5	0.7
Eng. P	58	20.7	27.6	36.2	13.8	1.7	27	0.0	11.1	*33.3	55.6	
Sci. U	44	6.8	47.7	34.1	11.4		64	6.3	25.0	*28.1	40.6	
Sci. P	33	30.3	39.4	12.1	15.2	3.0	22	4.5	9.1	*31.8	54.5	
Sci. A	441	19.3	37.2	27.0	15.9	0.7	187	3.2	12.8	*32.1	51.9	
S.Sci U	151	27.2	27.2	31.8	13.9		71	9.9	14.1	*28.2	47.9	
S.Sci P	40	2.5	35.0	20.0	42.5		9	0.0	11.1	*22.2	66.7	

Figure A 3

6.1.6 Totals of returns to questionnaire

Summary of returns to the student questionnaire concerning the amount of difficulty they had in understanding teachers and other students when they QuA5/1: talk very fast; QuA5/2: speak quietly; QuA5/3: have different accents or pronunciation than they are used to; QuA5/4: are talking in a group

	QuA5/1				QuA5/2				QuA5/3				QuA5/4			
	H	M	L	N	H	M	L	N	H	M	L	N	H	M	L	N
Eng. U		φφ	φ Δ	ΔΔ	φ Δ	φ Δ	φ Δ		φφ	φ ΔΔ	Δ			φ	φφ ΔΔ	ΔΔ
Eng. P	φ	φ	φ Δ	ΔΔ		φ Δ	φ	φφ ΔΔ	φ	φ Δ	φ Δ	Δ		φ Δ	φφ	ΔΔ
Sci. U		φφ Δ	φ Δ	ΔΔ		φ Δ	φ Δ	φ Δ	φφ	φ Δ	Δ	Δ		φφ	φ ΔΔ	ΔΔ
Sci. P	φ	φ	Δ	ΔΔ		φ Δ	φ Δ	φ ΔΔ	φ	φφ	ΔΔ	ΔΔ		φφ	φ	Δ⁄ΔΔ
Sci. A	φ	φ	φ Δ	ΔΔ		φ	φ Δ	φ ΔΔ	φφ	φ Δ	Δ	Δ		φ	φ Δ	ΔΔ
S. Sci. U	φ	φ	φ Δ	ΔΔ		φ Δ	φφ Δ	Δ	φ	φ Δ	Δ	Δ		φ	φ Δ	Δ⁄ΔΔ
S. Sci. P		φ	φ Δ	φφ Δ⁄ΔΔ		φ ΔΔ	φφ ΔΔ		φ	φ Δ	φ	Δ⁄ΔΔ		φ	φφ ΔΔ	ΔΔ

Key

Overseas students' replies:
  φ means 20–39%
  φφ means 40–59%
  φ⁄φφ means 60–79%
  φφ⁄φφ means 80–100%

British students' replies:
  Δ means 20–39%
  ΔΔ means 40–59%
  Δ⁄ΔΔ means 60–79%
  ΔΔ⁄ΔΔ means 80–100%

H: a lot of difficulty; M: some difficulty; L: very little difficulty; N: no difficulty

Source: Weir 1983

6.1.7 Problems encountered by overseas students in listening comprehension, ranked in order of the amount of difficulty they claim to have experienced with each

HM	H	N	Qu		H %	M %	L %	N %
1	1	2	A5/1	Teachers and other students talk very fast	18.4	36.6	29.0	15.4
2	2	1	A5/3	Their accents or pronunciation are different from what they are used to	14.0	38.7	32.3	13.9
3	3	4	A7/2	Writing down quickly and clearly all the notes they want to	11.9	29.6	34.0	24.1
4	5	3	A5/4	More than one person is speaking as in group discussion	10.0	31.1	36.9	20.7
5	4	5	A4/3	Understanding informal language	10.1	28.5	33.2	26.6
6	7	6	A7/3	Thinking of and using suitable abbreviations	7.0	26.9	38.0	27.7
7	11	7	A4/1	Understanding spoken description or narrative	3.3	27.7	40.1	28.3
8	9	8	A6/1	Recognizing individual words in what is being said	5.1	25.7	40.3	28.5
9	6	12	A5/2	People speak quietly	7.3	22.0	32.0	37.9
10	8	9	A7/1	Recognizing what is important and worth noting	5.9	22.1	39.7	31.8
11	13	10	A6/3	Understanding completely what the speaker is saying and linking this to what he has said earlier	2.1	21.5	40.4	35.6
12	12	11	A4/2	Understanding spoken instructions	2.2	18.9	40.7	37.4
13	10	14	A7/4	Organizing the notes they take down so that they can understand them when they read them later	3.4	14.8	38.1	42.7
14	15	13	A4/4	Understanding the subject matter of the talk	1.5	16.6	40.3	39.9
15	14	15	A6/2	Recognizing where sentences end and begin	1.6	8.3	27.7	62.2

HM: ranked according to the combined totals for 'a lot of difficulty' and 'some difficulty' columns; H: ranked according to 'a lot of difficulty' column; N: ranked according to 'no difficulty' column; Qu: question number

H: 'a lot of difficulty'; M: 'some difficulty'; L: 'very little difficulty'; N: 'no difficulty'

Source: Weir 1983

6.1.8 Problems encountered by British students in listening comprehension, ranked in order of the amount of difficulty they claim to have experienced with each

HM	H	N	Qu		H %	M %	L %	N %
1	1	1	A7/2	Writing down quickly and clearly all the notes they want to	7.5	25.1	34.5	32.5
2	5	5	A5/2	People speak quietly	3.4	23.6	32.5	40.3
3	2	2	A5/3	Their accents or pronunciation are different from what they are used to	4.3	20.8	41.7	33.0
4	4	3	A7/1	Recognizing what is important and worth noting	3.6	18.6	42.8	34.9
5	3	7	A5/1	Teachers and other students talk very fast	3.9	15.4	32.6	47.8
6	6	6	A7/4	Organizing the notes they take down	3.2	15.8	34.3	46.5
7	9	4	A4/4	Understanding the subject matter of the talk	0.6	16.9	41.5	39.6
8	7	8	A5/4	More than one person is speaking as in group discussion	2.1	12.6	32.8	52.0
9	8	8	A7/3	Thinking of and using suitable abbreviations	1.5	10.7	35.3	52.0
10	10	10	A6/3	Understanding completely what the speaker is saying and linking this to what he has said earlier	0.6	10.1	36.2	52.7
11	14	11	A4/1	Understanding spoken description or narrative	0.0	4.7	26.3	68.5
12	12	13	A6/1	Recognizing individual words in what is being said	0.2	4.3	22.5	72.8
13	13	11	A4/2	Understanding spoken instructions	0.2	1.9	28.9	68.5
13	11	15	A6/2	Recognizing where sentences end and begin	0.4	1.7	14.8	82.9
15	15	14	A4/3	Understanding informal language	0.0	1.7	15.0	82.6

HM: ranked according to the combined totals for 'a lot of difficulty' and 'some difficulty' columns; H: ranked according to 'a lot of difficulty' column; N: ranked according to 'no difficulty' column; Qu: question number

H: 'a lot of difficulty'; M: 'some difficulty'; L: 'very little difficulty'; N: 'no difficulty'

Source: Weir 1983

6.1.9 Comparison of problems encountered by British and overseas students in listening comprehension

LISTENING	Difficulty				Frequency (Based on highest returns (N and O) for all classes)													
	Col. 1 OS	Col. 2 OS-BR	Col. 3 Staff OS	Col. 4 Staff OS-BR	Eng. U		Eng. P		Sci. U		Sci. P		Sci. A		S. Sci. U		S. Sci. P	
					N	O	N	O	N	O	N	O	N	O	N	O	N	O
(1) Understanding teachers and other students when they talk very fast	(1) 55.0% (2)	35.7%	—	—														
(2) Understanding when their accents or pronunciation are different from what one is used to	(2) 52.7% (3)	27.6%	—	—														
(3) Writing down quickly and clearly all the notes one wants to	(3) 41.5% (10)	8.9%	—	—														
(4) Understanding when more than one person is speaking as in group discussion	(4) 41.1% (4)	26.4%	—	—														
(5) Understanding informal language	(5) 38.6% (1)	36.9% (3)	52.5% (1)	47.5%														

Thinking of and using suitable abbreviations	(6) 33.9%	(7) 21.7%	–	–				++
Understanding spoken description or narrative	(7) 31.0%	(6") 26.3%	(2) 53.2%	(2) 41.9%				++
Recognizing individual words in what is being said	(8) 30.8%	(6) 26.3%	–	–				++
Understanding when people speak quietly	(9) 29.3%	(13) 2.3%	–	–				++ ××
Recognizing what is important and worth noting	(10) 28.0%	(12) 5.8%	–	–				+
Understanding completely what the speaker is saying and linking this to what he has said earlier	(11) 23.6%	(9) 12.9%	–	–			×	
Understanding spoken instructions	(12) 21.1%	(8) 19.0%	(4) 44.1%	(3) 35.3%	×	+	++ ++	
Organizing the notes one takes down so that one can understand them when one reads them later	(13) 18.2%	(15) -0.8%	–	–				
Understanding the subject matter of the talk	(14) 18.1%	(14) 0.6%	(1) 66.2%	(5) 11.4%				++
Recognizing where sentences end and begin	(15) 9.9%	(11) 7.8%	–	–				+
Making notes	–	(5) 40.2%	(4) 17.6%		××	++	++ ++	++

OS: overseas; BR: British. *Source:* Weir 1983

6.2.1 *Students' final questionnaire: Undergraduate/postgraduate*

STUDENTS' QUESTIONNAIRE

In this questionnaire, you will find reference to different kinds of classes. To help you in answering it, a short description of each type of class is given below.

a) *Lecture*

The teaching period is mostly occupied with continuous talk by the teacher. There may be some opportunity for questions during this type of class, but students mainly listen and take notes.

b) *Seminars and Tutorials*

These differ from a lecture in giving much more opportunity for the participation of students, e.g. there may be reading and study of a paper by a student; discussion of topics after a short introduction by students or teachers; a teacher may go through written work or questions prepared by student(s); there may be discussion of any matters or problems on the initiative of students or teacher; the students may work through problems set by the teacher.

c) *Practical class*

In this, students do exercises under the supervision of a teacher, which involve the handling of equipment, instruments, or specimens of some kind, e.g. scientific experiments; learning to use calculating machines; drawing plans; using industrial machinery.

Several questions are asked about what you do SPECIFICALLY in lectures, seminars and tutorials, or practical classes. You may not have certain of these e.g. you may not have any practical classes in your subject. If you do not have a particular type of class, please ✓ the 'Not applicable' box whenever a question is asked about it, thus

	Never	Sometimes	Often	Not applicable
(c) practical classes?	☐	☐	☐	☐

Please answer every other question on the basis of what happens in ALL of the classes that you are taking.

Start here

1) Please indicate (where applicable) how many hours a week you attend:

Number of
hours

    (a)   lectures ☐

    (b)   seminars and tutorials ☐

    (c)   practical classes ☐

2) Title of Degree course

3) Department

4) Country of Origin

5) First Language

SECTION A

LISTENING TO AND UNDERSTANDING SPOKEN ENGLISH

A1. How often do your teachers give you instructions to look at certain things, e.g. books, notes, diagrams or scientific and other equipment, in order to get further information, to make facts or principles clearer or to help solve problems, etc., during:

Please tick:

	Never	Sometimes	Often	Not applicable
(a) lectures?	☐	☐	☐	☐
(b) seminars and tutorials?	☐	☐	☐	☐
(c) practical classes?	☐	☐	☐	☐

A2. How often do your teachers provide you with duplicated notes, e.g. photocopies, printed notes, etc., in each of the following:

Please tick:

	Never	Sometimes	Often	Not applicable
(a) lectures?	☐	☐	☐	☐
(b) seminars and tutorials?	☐	☐	☐	☐
(c) practical classes?	☐	☐	☐	☐

A3.   How often do you take notes in your classes by each of the following methods:

Please tick:

	Never	Sometimes	Often
(a) copying diagrams, charts, graphs, written notes, etc. from the blackboard?		☐	☐ ☐
	Never	Sometimes	Often
(b) taking down notes dictated to you by the teacher?	☐	☐	☐
	Never	Sometimes	Often
(c) taking down the main points from what the teacher is saying at normal lecturing speed?	☐	☐	☐

A4.   Please indicate how much difficulty you have found in each of the following:

H: a lot of difficulty
M: some difficulty
L: very little difficulty
N: no difficulty

Please tick the appropriate box

	H	M	L	N
1. Understanding spoken description or narrative	☐	☐	☐	☐
2. Understanding spoken instructions	☐	☐	☐	☐
3. Understanding informal language	☐	☐	☐	☐
4. Understanding the subject matter of the talk (i.e. understanding what is being talked about)	☐	☐	☐	☐
5. Any other general difficulties in understanding spoken English (please specify below)	☐	☐	☐	☐

A5.   Please indicate how much difficulty you have in understanding your teachers or other students when:

Please tick the appropriate box

	H	M	L	N
1. They talk very fast	☐	☐	☐	☐
2. They speak very quietly	☐	☐	☐	☐
3. Their accents or pronunciation are different from what you are used to	☐	☐	☐	☐
4. More than one person is speaking, as in group discussions	☐	☐	☐	☐
5. There are other problems which interfere with listening comprehension (please specify below)	☐	☐	☐	☐

A6. Please indicate how much difficulty you have in each of the following:

<table>
<tr><td></td><td></td><td colspan="4">Please tick the
appropriate box</td></tr>
<tr><td></td><td></td><td>H</td><td>M</td><td>L</td><td>N</td></tr>
<tr><td>1.</td><td>Recognising individual words in what is being said</td><td>□</td><td>□</td><td>□</td><td>□</td></tr>
<tr><td>2.</td><td>Recognising where sentences end and begin</td><td>□</td><td>□</td><td>□</td><td>□</td></tr>
<tr><td>3.</td><td>Understanding completely what the speaker is saying and linking this to what he has said earlier</td><td>□</td><td>□</td><td>□</td><td>□</td></tr>
</table>

A7. Please indicate how much difficulty you have in each of the following aspects of note taking.

<table>
<tr><td></td><td></td><td colspan="4">Please tick the
appropriate box</td></tr>
<tr><td></td><td></td><td>H</td><td>M</td><td>L</td><td>N</td></tr>
<tr><td>1.</td><td>Recognising what is important and worth noting</td><td>□</td><td>□</td><td>□</td><td>□</td></tr>
<tr><td>2.</td><td>Being able to write down, quickly and clearly, all you want to</td><td>□</td><td>□</td><td>□</td><td>□</td></tr>
<tr><td>3.</td><td>Thinking of and using suitable abbreviation</td><td>□</td><td>□</td><td>□</td><td>□</td></tr>
<tr><td>4.</td><td>Organising the notes you take down, so that you can understand them when you read them later</td><td>□</td><td>□</td><td>□</td><td>□</td></tr>
<tr><td>5.</td><td>Any other difficulties in note taking (please specify below)</td><td>□</td><td>□</td><td>□</td><td>□</td></tr>
</table>

SECTION B

READING AND SUMMARISING WRITTEN MATERIAL

B1. Please indicate how often you read for the following purposes:

1) Reading carefully for comprehension of all the information in each of the following:

<table>
<tr><td></td><td colspan="3">Please tick:</td></tr>
<tr><td></td><td>Never</td><td>Sometimes</td><td>Often</td></tr>
<tr><td>1.1 duplicated notes given to you by the teacher e.g. photocopies, printed notes, etc.</td><td>□</td><td>□</td><td>□</td></tr>
<tr><td>1.2 written questions done either in class or at home</td><td>□</td><td>□</td><td>□</td></tr>
<tr><td>1.3 laboratory worksheets</td><td>□</td><td>□</td><td>□</td></tr>
<tr><td>1.4 examination questions</td><td>□</td><td>□</td><td>□</td></tr>
<tr><td>1.5 some textbooks: whole or part</td><td>□</td><td>□</td><td>□</td></tr>
<tr><td>1.6 any other (please specify below)</td><td>□</td><td>□</td><td>□</td></tr>
<tr><td></td><td>Never</td><td>Sometimes</td><td>Often</td></tr>
<tr><td>2) Reading to get a general idea of the main information about a topic, e.g. general background reading, as follow up to lectures or in preparation for seminars, etc.</td><td>□</td><td>□</td><td>□</td></tr>
</table>

	Never	Sometimes	Often
3) Search reading to get information specifically required for particular written assignments, e.g. for homework tasks, project work, etc.	☐	☐	☐
4) Critical reading to establish and evaluate the author's position on a particular topic	☐	☐	☐
5) Reading to check sources of new information such as articles in recent journals, new books etc, to see how useful they are to your course of study	☐	☐	☐
6) Reading quickly to find out how useful it would be to study a particular text more intensively	☐	☐	☐
7) Any other type of reading (please specify below)	☐	☐	☐
B2. How often do you make notes from textbooks	☐	☐	☐

B3.   Please indicate how much difficulty you have in each of the following (where applicable):

Please tick the
appropriate box

	H	M	L	N
1. Reading carefully to understand all the information in a text	☐	☐	☐	☐
2. Reading to get the main information from a text	☐	☐	☐	☐
3. Search reading to get information specifically required for assignments	☐	☐	☐	☐
4. Critical reading to establish and evaluate the author's position on a particular topic	☐	☐	☐	☐
5. Reading quickly	☐	☐	☐	☐
6. Making notes from textbooks	☐	☐	☐	☐
7. Reading texts where the subject matter is very complicated	☐	☐	☐	☐
8. Any other reading difficulties (please specify below)	☐	☐	☐	☐

H: a lot of difficulty
M: some difficulty
L: very little difficulty
N: no difficulty

SECTION C

WRITING ABILITY

C1. Please indicate how often you do each of the following:

1. Write short introductions to, or connecting sentences in, numerical calculations or mathematics arguments during:

Please tick:

	Never	Sometimes	Often
(a) Coursework	☐	☐	☐
(b) Examinations	☐	☐	☐

2. Write short connected answers to questions asking for a limited response (i.e. not more than a paragraph in length) in:

Please tick:

	Never	Sometimes	Often
(a) Coursework	☐	☐	☐
(b) Examinations	☐	☐	☐

3. Produce longer pieces of writing (i.e. continuous connected writing longer than a single paragraph) in:

Please tick:

	Never	Sometimes	Often
(a) Coursework	☐	☐	☐
(b) Examinations	☐	☐	☐

4. Produce other types of written work (please specify below)

C2. Please indicate how much difficulty you have with each of the following in your written work:

Please tick the appropriate box

	H	M	L	N
1. Writing grammatically correct sentences	☐	☐	☐	☐
2. Using a variety of grammatical structures	☐	☐	☐	☐
3. Using appropriate grammatical structures	☐	☐	☐	☐
4. Using appropriate vocabulary	☐	☐	☐	☐
5. Using a wide and varied range of vocabulary	☐	☐	☐	☐
6. The subject matter	☐	☐	☐	☐
7. Expressing what you want to say clearly	☐	☐	☐	☐
8. Arranging and developing your written work	☐	☐	☐	☐
9. Spelling	☐	☐	☐	☐
10. Punctuation	☐	☐	☐	☐
11. Handwriting	☐	☐	☐	☐
12. Tidiness	☐	☐	☐	☐

13.   Any other problems in written work
(please specify below)   ☐   ☐   ☐   ☐

H: a lot of difficulty
M: some difficulty
L: very little difficult
N: no difficulty

SECTION D

SPEAKING ABILITY

Please tick:

	Never	Sometimes	Often
D1. How often do you have to give oral reports or short talks during your course?	☐	☐	☐
D2. How often do you work together with other students, using English as a means of communication during:	☐	☐	☐

	Never	Sometimes	Often	Not applicable
(a) lectures?	☐	☐	☐	☐
(b) seminars and tutorials?	☐	☐	☐	☐
(c) practical classes?	☐	☐	☐	☐

D3.   How often do you actively take part in discussion involving the class as a whole and the teacher during:

Please tick:

	Never	Sometimes	Often	Not applicable
(a) lectures?	☐	☐	☐	☐
(b) seminars and tutorials?	☐	☐	☐	☐
(c) practical classes?	☐	☐	☐	☐

D4.   How often do you ask the teacher questions in:

Please tick:

	Never	Sometimes	Often	Not applicable
(a) lectures?	☐	☐	☐	☐
				Not

		Never	Sometimes	Often	Not applicable
(b)	seminars and tutorials?	☐	☐	☐	☐
(c)	practical classes?	☐	☐	☐	☐

D5. How often does the teacher ask the class questions in:

Please tick:

		Never	Sometimes	Often	Not applicable
(a)	lectures?	☐	☐	☐	☐
(b)	seminars and tutorials?	☐	☐	☐	☐
(c)	practical classes?	☐	☐	☐	☐

D6. Please indicate how much difficulty you have because of language in each of the skills listed below:

Please tick the appropriate box

		H	M	L	N
1.	Giving oral reports or short talks	☐	☐	☐	☐
2.	Asking teachers questions	☐	☐	☐	☐
3.	Asking other students questions	☐	☐	☐	☐
4.	Answering questions asked by teachers	☐	☐	☐	☐
5.	Answering questions asked by other students	☐	☐	☐	☐
6.	Working with other students using English to communicate	☐	☐	☐	☐
7.	Expressing your own opinions in discussions	☐	☐	☐	☐
8.	Explaining your opinions when they are not immediately understood in discussions	☐	☐	☐	☐
9.	Expressing counter-arguments to points raised by other students in discussions	☐	☐	☐	☐
10.	Expressing counter-arguments to points raised by teachers in discussions	☐	☐	☐	☐
11.	Any other general difficulties in spoken English (please specify below)	☐	☐	☐	☐

H: a lot of difficulty
M: some difficulty
L: very little difficulty
N: no difficulty

D7.   Please indicate how often you have the following problems:

Please tick:

	Never	Sometimes	Often
1. Thinking out how to say what you want to say quickly enough	☐	☐	☐
	Never	Sometimes	Often
2. Worrying about saying something in case you make a mistake in your English	☐	☐	☐
	Never	Sometimes	Often
3. Not knowing how to say something in English	☐	☐	☐
	Never	Sometimes	Often
4. Not knowing the best way to say something in English	☐	☐	☐
	Never	Sometimes	Often
5. Not knowing the subject well enough to answer questions	☐	☐	☐
6. Finding it hard to enter the discussion	☐	☐	☐
7. Any other problems (please specify below)	☐	☐	☐

THANK YOU VERY MUCH FOR YOUR COOPERATION

Source: Weir 1983

6.2.2 Teacher assessment of students' language proficiency

Student's Name: _____

Institution: _____

_____

Dear Colleague

We would like to get your opinion on specific aspects of the language ability of each student taking the Test in English for Academic Purposes (T.E.A.P.).

Please answer the following questions by putting a tick in the appropriate box.

Tick   – the H (high difficulty) box if the student has a lot of difficulty,
        – the M (medium difficulty) box if the student has some difficulty,
        – the L (low difficulty) box if the student has very little difficulty,
        – the N (no difficulty) box if the student has no difficulty,
        – the DK (don't know) box if you are not sure.

This information will be treated in the strictest confidence.

1. Please indicate how much difficulty the student has in each of the following:

Please tick the
appropriate box

		H	M	L	N	DK
(a)	Reading carefully to understand *all* the information in a text.	☐	☐	☐	☐	☐
(b)	Reading to get the *main* information from a text.	☐	☐	☐	☐	☐
(c)	Reading to get *specific* pieces of information from a text.	☐	☐	☐	☐	☐
(d)	Reading quickly	☐	☐	☐	☐	☐
(e)	Making notes from written sources.	☐	☐	☐	☐	☐

2. Please indicate how much difficulty the student has in each of the following:

Please tick the
appropriate box

		H	M	L	N	DK
(a)	Understanding spoken description, narrative or instructions, when one person is talking.	☐	☐	☐	☐	☐
(b)	Understanding people when they talk quickly.	☐	☐	☐	☐	☐
(c)	Understanding people when they talk informally.	☐	☐	☐	☐	☐
(d)	Understanding people when their accents or pronunciation are different from what he/she is used to.	☐	☐	☐	☐	☐
(e)	Understanding why more than one person is speaking, as in group discussions.	☐	☐	☐	☐	☐
(f)	Making notes from spoken language.	☐	☐	☐	☐	☐

3. Please indicate how much difficulty the student has in each of the following in written work:

Please tick the
appropriate box

		H	M	L	N	DK
(a)	Organising the content.	☐	☐	☐	☐	☐
(b)	Expressing clearly what they want to say.	☐	☐	☐	☐	☐
(c)	Using the appropriate language.	☐	☐	☐	☐	☐
(d)	Writing grammatically correct sentences.	☐	☐	☐	☐	☐
(e)	Spelling correctly all the words they want to use.	☐	☐	☐	☐	☐
(f)	Punctuating correctly what they have written.	☐	☐	☐	☐	☐

Thank you.

TEACHER'S GLOBAL ASSESSMENT (TG)

OVERALL RATING OF STUDENT'S ENGLISH LANGUAGE ABILITY

We would also like your opinion of the student's general ability in the skills of reading, listening, speaking and writing. Please read the following band descriptors and then indicate in the boxes below your estimate of the student's ability.

Band III: Proficiency in this area almost equal to his/her native speaker contemporaries, though perhaps with minor faults, none of which would handicap him/her in English medium study.

Band II: Reasonable proficiency, some weaknesses which could handicap him/her in English medium study. A higher standard is desirable. Could benefit from remedial instruction in this area.

Band I: A large number of weaknesses which could seriously hamper him/her in English medium study. A higher standard is *necessary*, needs remedial language tuition in this area.

Band 0: Very limited ability in this area, well below a satisfactory standard. Could not cope with an academic course of study, needs a long term language course in this area.

Put X in appropriate box for each skill area.

	Band III	Band II	Band I	Band 0
Ability to understand spoken English	☐	☐	☐	☐
Ability to speak English	☐	☐	☐	☐
Ability to understand written English	☐	☐	☐	☐
Ability to write English	☐	☐	☐	☐

Other comments on the student's ability to cope with the language demands that will be placed on him/her in following an academic course of study:

SUBJECT TUTOR'S (PREDICTIVE VALIDITY) ASSESSMENT

Dear Colleague

We would like to assess the effectiveness of the language screening tests administered to overseas students at the start of their courses. It would be most helpful if you could complete and return this pro forma as soon as possible to:

Title of Course _____

Name of Student _____ Candidate Number _____

Tutor/Specialist _____ Centre Number _____

1. How would you rate the academic progress of this student in the first two terms of his/ her course?

Please tick the appropriate box

			Below	Totally
Very good ☐	Good ☐	Average ☐	Average ☐	Inadequate ☐

2. How would you rate the student's ability to cope with the language demands the course makes on him/her in terms of reading, listening, writing and speaking?

Please tick the appropriate box

	No difficulty	Very little difficulty	Some difficulty	A lot of difficulty	Don't know
Reading	☐	☐	☐	☐	☐
Listening	☐	☐	☐	☐	☐
Writing	☐	☐	☐	☐	☐
Speaking	☐	☐	☐	☐	☐

3. Is this student likely to pass the course he/she is enrolling on without any extension beyond the time normally taken by British students?

Please tick the appropriate box

Yes ☐   No ☐   Don't ☐
know

If 'no', how far do you feel this is due to deficiencies in his/her English?

A lot ☐   To some extent ☐   Very little ☐   Not at all ☐

ALL INFORMATION WILL BE TREATED IN THE
STRICTEST CONFIDENCE
THANK YOU FOR YOUR HELP

6.3 Sample structured interview

Two sets of structured interviews were administered, one to subject teachers and the other to the undergraduates taught.

STRUCTURED INTERVIEW   Ref. ID/basic Info/75

Professor's Version   Faculty
          Subject
          Professor's name

1 What proportion of the required reading for this course is available in Spanish?
   None ☐   0–24% ☐   25–49% ☐   50–74% ☐   75% or more ☐

2 Are texts in a language other than Spanish recommended reading material for this course?

                                                     Yes ☐   No ☐

(If YES:
In what language(s) is the recommended reading material published?
                                           most important_____

                                           2nd most important_____)

3 In your opinion, is it *necessary* for your students to know a foreign language in order to pass this course?

                                                     Yes ☐   No ☐

(If YES:
What language(s) is/are *necessary*? (in order of importance) For what purpose(s)?)

4 Do you consider it necessary to know a foreign language in order to graduate in veterinary medicine?

                                                     Yes ☐   No ☐

(If YES:
What language(s) is/are necessary? (in order of importance))
(If NO:
Do you think that your students could gain any benefit from knowing a foreign language?

                                                     Yes ☐   No ☐)

(If YES:
What language(s)? (in order of importance)
What benefits could they get?)

5 Do you find it necessary to read in a foreign language/languages in order to prepare your classes in this subject?

                                                     Yes ☐   No ☐

(If YES:
What language(s)? (in order of importance)
How frequently do you read in that/those language(s)?
Daily ☐   Weekly ☐   Monthly ☐   Occasionally ☐
With what facility do you read in that language/those languages?
What do you read in order to prepare your classes?)

6 Have you done postgraduate work?

                                                     Yes ☐   No ☐

(If YES:
Where did you do it?/specify institution and country)

7 What do you recommend your students to read in this course?
Please specify:
Which of these do you consider indispensable for the student to PASS this course?

8 How would you describe the usefulness of ENGLISH for graduating as a well-qualified professional in this field?
                        Necessary ☐   Convenient ☐   Unnecessary ☐

STRUCTURED INTERVIEW   Ref. ID/Basic Info/75
Student Version   Faculty
                              Subject
Student's name: Professor in Charge

1 What proportion of the required reading for this course is available in Spanish?
   None ☐   0–24% ☐   25–49% ☐   50–74% ☐   75% or more ☐
                                                                    43

2 Are texts in a language other than Spanish recommended reading material for this course?

                                                        Yes ☐   No ☐
   (In what language(s) is/are the recommended material published?
                                    most important_____

                                    2nd most important_____)

3 In your opinion, is it NECESSARY to know a foreign language(s) in order to PASS this course?

                                                        Yes ☐   No ☐
   (What language(s) is/are necessary?)

4 Do you consider it NECESSARY to know a foreign language in order to GRADUATE in this field?

                                                        Yes ☐   No ☐
   a) What language(s) is/are necessary?_____
      (in order of importance)
   b) Why is it/are they needed? _____

5 Can you read in a foreign language?

                                                        Yes ☐   No ☐
   (If affirmative, a) In what languages(s)?
                b) How frequently do you read in that/these languages?
                Daily ☐   Weekly ☐   Monthly ☐   Occasionally ☐
                c) How do you read?   fluently ☐
                                                           little difficulty ☐
                                                           some difficulty ☐
                                                           great difficulty ☐
                d) What do you read?   basic texts ☐
                                                     professional journals ☐
                                                       theses/dissertations ☐
                                                     other (please specify) ☐)

   (If negative)
   Would knowing a foreign language help you in your studies?
                                                        Yes ☐   No ☐)
   (If affirmative, what language(s)?

Why?)

6   What texts does your professor recommend you read in this course?

Author _____ Title _____

Which of these do you consider of greatest help in your studies?

7   How would you describe the usefulness of ENGLISH for graduating as a well-qualified professional in this field?

Necessary ☐   Convenient ☐   Unnecessary ☐

Source: Mckay and Mountford (eds) 1978: 24–7

7.1   Formative observation – Sample instruments

Linder (1991) reports a collaborative action research project into mixed-ability teaching of English at secondary school level. The participating teachers developed a range of instruments: for self-evaluation, to observe students and to be observed by colleagues. Their purpose was to enhance their self-monitoring, self-evaluation, and reporting of lesson events. These instruments are one example of the way 'insiders' can develop their own observation methods for formative use. This work is also reported in Roberts (1993). Further ideas on self-monitoring methods are provided in Altrichter et al. (1993), Kemmis and McTaggart (1982), McNiff (1988), Nunan (1989), and Open University (1980).

Chart for evaluating classroom behaviour.

Checklist items	Comment	How do I know
The pupils: They listened to each other more readily.		
They employed self-check devices to a greater extent		
The work they handed in was more carefully executed.		
The talk was in English to a greater extent.		
They managed to divide the work in the group more effectively.		
There was greater evidence of cooperation.		
They learned to select from options.		
They learned to accept variety rather than uniformity in assignments.		
There is more evidence of learning.		
They are participating in classroom management functions.		
There is evidence that they are working more independently and turning to each other for guidance.		
The teacher: I am able to do less of the work.		
I am able to step aside and observe what is going on.		
I can attend to individual pupils more readily.		
I have been able to relinquish some of the classroom management responsibilities.		
The proportion of teacher–pupil talk has changed.		
Materials are being exploited more effectively.		
My voice is more often at a lower pitch.		
I am ready to have learners prepare materials.		
Language is being used for a greater variety of contents.		

Observation in your class during a group work task

TASK: Plan a group work task of any kind for one of your lessons.

1. How did you introduce the activity? _____

_____

_____

2. What were the pupils' reactions? _____

_____

3. How did the pupils get into groups? _____

_____

4. How long did it take the pupils to form their groups? _____

_____

5. Describe the group work task. _____

_____

_____

_____

6. If you had entered the classroom midway through this activity, how would you have

described what was going on (the classroom atmosphere etc.)? _____

_____

_____

7. What did you do during the activity? Did you:
   - listen to the students?
   - watch students?
   - help students who were confused?
   - correct students' errors?
   - participate in the activity with any group?

Did you find it difficult to:
- divide students into groups?
- get the activity started?
- guide the activity?
- terminate the activity?

If you encountered difficulties, how did you overcome them? _____

_____

How might you overcome them next time? _____

_____

8.   Choose one group. Observe them for *five* minutes and fill out the following table. Indicate the degree in which the pupils contributed to the group work task according to the following scale:

5 = outstanding
4 = above average
3 = average
2 = below average
1 = unsatisfactory

Pupil:	A	B	C	D	E
1. Participates in the discussion					
2. Asks for help					
3. Gives help					
4. Asks questions					
5. Gives personal opinion					
6. Listens to others in group					
7. Contributes factual information					
8. Looks at others in group					
9. Corrects mistakes					
10. Other _____					

9.   Evaluate your lesson:
     How did the lesson go? _____

_____

Would you do a similar group activity like the one you did again? _____

Why?/Why not? _____

_____

_____

Teacher's self-evaluation form of the lesson

During and after the lesson, think about some of the following and record your responses.

1   Evidence that the lesson was: successful; unsuccessful; went smoothly; was poorly organized; was interesting; boring.
2   Think of a student who seemed not involved in the lesson. What do you think the reason was?
3   What would you have liked to improve/have done better in the lesson?
4   What have you learnt?
5   How would you like to improve/change/develop you teaching in the future?
6   What subject/issue would you like to discuss in the next staff in-service session?
7   What evidence was there that the pupils were interested/not interested?
8   What will you do next as a follow-up to this lesson?
9   Which of your/your pupils' aims were achieved? Were their other unplanned-for achievements?
10   How do feel about the lesson?
11   What are your feelings about the class that you were teaching?
12   How suitable was the material?
13   Looking back, what might you have done differently?
14   What areas do you think you should work on, on yourself? with the pupils?
15   What are you going to do when you teach this class again?
16   Were there any smiles/laughter during the lesson?

During the lesson

Try to observe your class. Are the pupils involved? If not, why not?

Stand aside for a few minutes while they are working and observe them. See what you can learn.

Is the seating arrangement appropriate?

Listen to what some of the pupils are saying. Write down one or two of the things that were said. What can you learn from them?

After the lesson

Think carefully about your lesson and respond to the following:

1 Which part/s went well? Why?
2 Which part/s went badly? Why?
3 What changes are you planning for the coming lessons?
4 What aspects of your teaching would you like to work on?
5 Is there any technique/approach/arrangement you would like to try out with your class?
6 If you were disappointed with some attempt as change, would you like to give it another try?
7 Would you like the project leader to observe another lesson? If so, when?
8 Any other thoughts?

Description of a group work activity

The class is divided into groups of four people. Each member of the group will get a different part of an article. Each member of the group will report about his part of the article to the rest of the group.

1 What is your opinion of the above preparation for the activity?
2 What are the possible difficulties that might arise?
3 Would you change anything? Why?
4 Do you think 'learning' will be going on?

_____

_____

_____

_____

_____

_____

_____

_____

_____

_____

_____

_____

_____

_____

_____

7.2 Criteria for assessing observation systems

Checklist	Comments
1 For what purpose was the system developed? Does the stated purpose match your goal?	
2 Are the conditions for observer reliability met? a Behaviours to be viewed are sufficiently specified so as to be: Mutually exclusive (do not overlap each other). Exhaustive (all behaviours of concern for the given problem can be classified). b Categories are sufficiently narrow so that two or more observers will place an observed behaviour into the same category. c Is observer interpretation necessary or not?	
3 What type of system is employed? a Category system: every unit of behaviour observed is categorized into one of the categories specified. b Sign system: selected behavioural units, listed beforehand, may or may not actually be observed during a period of time.	
4 Are appropriate sampling procedures employed? a The procedure for sampling behaviours is systematic: Time sampling: occurrence or non-occurrence of behaviours within specified uniform time units. Event sampling: event recorded each time it occurs. b Is the procedure feasible? How do you sample individuals to be observed? In what period of time? Is the desired detail possible given the number of individuals and time units? c What is the coding system like? Do tallies or codes require memorization? If coding required, is code indicated on the record form? d Are the behaviours to be viewed representative? How many behaviours are to be viewed? Over what period of time? Using how many subjects?	
5 Are the conditions for validity met? Are the behaviours you observe relevant to the inferences you make? Have sources of observer bias been eliminated?	

Source: Boehm and Weinberg 1977

7.3   A sample of ELT teacher assessment criteria

The following instrument, essentially a checklist of criteria for flexible use by observers, is used in RSA/UCLES Diploma in TEFLA assessments.

RSA/UCLES Diploma in TEFL – Categories for Comment

Personal Qualities

1.1   Personality, presence, general style
1.2   Voice – audibility, ability to project, modulation
1.3   Voice – speed, clarity of diction
1.4   Ability to establish/maintain rapport
1.5   Self-awareness
1.6   Experience

Preparation and Lesson Plan

2.1   General shape and balance of activities
2.2   Patterns of learner–teacher interaction
2.3   Timing
2.4   Clarity, limitation and specification of aims/objectives
2.5   Clarity of specification of procedures
2.6   Suitability of aids, materials and methods for the class and its level
2.7   Suitability of materials and methods for teaching what is to be taught
2.8   Anticipation of learners' difficulties

EXECUTION

General Class Management and Direction

3.1   organisation of physical resources
3.2   giving of instructions
3.3   indication of stages of the lesson
3.4   achievement of changes of activity and pace
3.5   achievement of changes of grouping

Introduction and Presentation Techniques

4.1   use of appropriate techniques to introduce new material
4.2   use of appropriate techniques to review previously learned/encountered material
4.3   contextualisation of language items
4.4   motivation and involvement of students in these phases of the lesson
4.5   giving of explanation/clarification, where appropriate, to aid learning

4.6   sequencing and relating of bits of material to one another/the context
4.7   checking of students' grasp of concept (see also 15.3)

Questioning Techniques

5.1   grading of questions to suit the level of the learners
5.2   appropriate distribution of questions among the learners
5.3   formulation of questions which are authentic to the context
5.4   formulation of questions to elicit the answers required
5.5   development of sequences of questions to aid learning
5.6   ensuring that learners ask as well as answer questions
5.7   acceptance of answers

Controlled and Semi-Controlled Practice Techniques

6.1   sufficient variety in techniques
6.2   provision of meaningful practice
6.3   appropriate balancing of teacher–learner, and learner–learner interaction
6.4   appropriate balancing of class/group/pair/individual practice
6.5   appropriate sequencing of controlled and less controlled activities

Communicative Interaction Techniques

7.1   preparation for communicative interaction activities e.g. group work, games, role play, simulation
7.2   organisation/setting up of communicative interaction etc.
7.3   judgement of proper balance between fluency and accuracy

Skills

8.1   Ability to foster better listening
8.2   Ability to foster better speaking
8.3   Ability to foster better reading
8.4   Ability to foster better writing
8.5   Ability to handle complex integration of the four skills

The Use of Teaching Aids

9.1   The use/adaptation of textbook material
9.2   Work sheets — design, rubrics, etc.
9.3   Blackboard work, writing, lay-out, drawing, spelling, etc.
9.4   Magazine pictures, cut outs, figurines, wall charts, deskstands, flip charts etc.
9.5   Realia, models, puppets
9.6   Overhead projectors
9.7   Tape recorder
9.8   Flash cards/cue cards
9.9   Video
9.10 Computer

Sensitivity to Learners

10.1 Control of language to level of class
10.2 Taking account of and responding appropriately to learners' linguistic/conceptual difficulties
10.3 Taking account of and responding appropriately to factors which may affect learners' motivation and learning – e.g. cultural factors, learners' expectations
10.5 Encouragement of learners
10.6 Involvement of and attention to individuals
10.7 Courtesy to learners

Error

11.1 Awareness of learners' errors
11.2 Appropriate treatment of learners' errors

Flow

12.1 Pace
12.2 Variation
12.3 Timing
12.4 Development
12.5 Orderliness

Ability to Adapt and Extemporise

13.1 Ability to match material prepared to time and class being taught
13.2 Ability to deal appropriately with the unexpected

Language

Knowledge of and ability to handle formal linguistic matters relevant to TESOL

14.1 phonology – segmental, rhythmic, intonation
14.2 grammar – at sentence, clause, group, and morpheme level, structural meaning
14.3 lexis – sets, fields, semantic relations, etc.
14.4 functions
14.5 selection, grading, sequencing and simplification
14.6 discourse, cohesion, coherence
14.7 language variation – dialect, register

Achievement of Aims/Objectives

15.1 Extent to which specified aims or sub-aims are achieved
15.2 Relation between implicit and explicit aims
15.3 Checking of learning – formal/casual

Conformity to Regulations

16.1   two lessons of same level offered
16.2   insufficient range of techniques demonstrated
16.3   lesson too long/short
16.4   two lessons too similar to one another

8.1   Some needs identification and prioritizing activities

In 8.1.1 and 8.1.2, both techniques are used to elicit, record and prioritize perceived needs and concerns. Their aim is to be open and democratic while also communicating the perceptions of individuals to the whole group. Nominal group technique is best suited to relatively small groups, while Delphi is used when informants cannot meet face to face. 'GRIDS' (Guidelines for the Review and Internal Development of Schools) is a step-by-step procedure for internal school review and development led by senior staff which has been extensively trialled in English schools. It is appropriate to a system which devolves considerable freedom of action to school management. It is based upon principle of ownership and development of the whole staff along broadly agreed lines rather than on uncoordinated individual agendas. The diagram below is a mere summary of the procedure. A full account can be found in McMahon et al. (1986).

8.1.1   Nominal group technique

The procedure

1. *Clarification of the task*
The task is presented on a blackboard or overhead projector (e.g. 'What aspects of the curriculum do we need to discuss?') in order that all participants fully understand the question, time is spent in group discussion about the nature of the task.

2. *Silent nominations*
Individuals are given a fixed period to list their own private responses. This should not be hurried. They are then asked to rank their own list in order to establish felt priorities.

3. *Master list*
The group leader compiles a master list on the blackboard or OHP taking *only* one item from each group member in rotation. No editing of the material is allowed and no evaluative comments are to be made at this stage. It is helpful to number the items.

4. *Item clarification*
During this phase each item is discussed until all members know what it means. Clarification only is allowed. If a member of the group now feels that their item is already covered by someone else, they may request its withdrawal. No pressure should be applied to any individual to have items withdrawn or incorporated in another.

5. *Evaluation*

It is now necessary to decide the relative importance of items in the eyes of the group. Each person is allowed five weighted votes (i.e. five points for the item that is felt to be most important, four points for the next, and so on). A simple voting procedure allows the consensus to emerge.

Once the composite picture has emerged, it provides an agenda for normal group discussions to proceed.

Reminders to group leaders

1 Do not reinterpret a person's ideas.
2 Use the participants own wording.
3 Do not interject your own ideas – YOU ARE NOT PARTICIPATING.
4 Give people time to think.
5 This is *not* a debate – do not allow participants to challenge each other or attempt to persuade each other.
6 Do not try to interpret results – do not look for patterns.

A method for obtaining group responses to questions or problems which:

(i)   ensures that everybody contributes;
(ii) avoids the dominance of the group by a few people with strong ideas;
(iii) avoids too narrow an interpretation of the task;
(iv) ensures a wide variety of responses; and
(v)   allows a systematic ordering of priorities.

Example: Phonology review

We used the nominal groups technique to elicit an account of your perceived needs, and the priorities. 'We want . . .

Votes
10   watch more video films concerning articulation
16   have some practice listening to intonation
16   know my weak points in my pronunciation
10   have more diphthong practice
9   practice listening to vernacular language (no notes)
9   practice correct English rhythm i.e. stress and intonation
9   have a focus on the problems in phonetics for Arabic teachers and pupils
9   practice word stress, with noun/verb and to have a list of such words
7   listen to native speakers so as to be able to take notes

Source: Middleton (n.d.)

8.1.2 The use of Delphi technique for needs assessment

Delphi technique is a method of establishing consensus in a group without necessarily bringing its members together for a meeting. It offers individuals feedback on what others think without putting pressure on them to express conforming views, and it enables a record of divergent opinions to be preserved. The basic method, which is very simple, can be pursued in a situation where members of the group are together but can equally well be conducted by post (the main disadvantage being that that takes a longer time).

1 Individual staff are asked to write down a list of their in-service training needs. The enquiry may relate to INSET needs in general or in relation to a specific theme (e.g. the uses of microtechnology in schools). The scope of the enquiry should be made explicit on the enquiry form, which will simply be a single sheet with numbered lines and space for the respondent's name and address.
2 All the responses that have been received are listed, and a summary is circulated to the respondents.
3 Each individual rates the needs on that list according to their personal priorities and returns the list to the organiser. It is helpful to set a clear deadline for this, as for other stages in the Delphi process.
4 These ratings are again summarised, and a new list is circulated. This time the lists are individualised, showing both the group rating and that of the individual respondant.
5 Individuals are then asked to reconsider their ratings. If they decide to diverge from the group consensus, they are invited to explain their reasons. (A form giving more space for comments is required for this.)
6 A third report is circulated. Normally this will be sufficient for the purposes of INSET needs assessment. But in principle one can continue the process through repeating stages 4 and 5 until a broad consensus on all important points is apparent.

Attached to this paper are a set of questionnaire sheets used for assessing in-service training needs in relation to special educational needs in one county's secondary schools. They may provide a model of how the sheets for a Delphi exercise can be designed.

A key element in the Delphi method is the influence brought to bear on individuals to modify their views in the light of what they perceive the group consensus to be. Frederick Cyphert and Walter Gant demonstrated this process vividly during a study in which they were investigating views on what prime targets the State of Virginia School of Education 'should concentrate its energies and resources in the next decade'. After the first round they took an item which had initially been rated below average in importance – 'emphasizing the production of doctoral graduates who can improve the programs in schools of medicine, law, nursing and engineering'. They distributed the feedback giving it a high rating. The participants then rated the item considerably above average although it was not among the ten highest-ranked targets.' Not a recommended strategy!

8.1.3 Guidelines for review and internal development of school (GRIDS)

STAGE 1. GETTING STARTED

1. Decide whether the GRIDS method is appropriate for your school.
2. Consult the staff.
3. Decide how to manage the review and development.

STAGE 5. OVERVIEW AND RE–START

1. Plan the overview.
2. Decide whether the changes introduced at the development stage should be made permanent.
3. Decide whether this approach to internal review and development should be continued or adapted.
4. Re-start the cycle.
5. Decide if you wish to inform anyone else about what happened in the first cycle.

STAGE 2. INITIAL REVIEW

1. Plan the initial review.
2. Prepare and distribute basic information.
3. Survey staff opinion.
4. Agree upon priorities for specific review and development.

STAGE 4. ACTION FOR DEVELOPMENT

1. Plan the development work.
2. Consider how best to meet the various in-service needs of the teachers involved in the development.
3. Move into action.
4. Assess the effectiveness of the development work.

STAGE 3. SPECIFIC REVIEW

1. Plan the specific review.
2. Find out what is the school's present policy/ practice on the specific review topic.
3. Decide how effective present policy/practice actually is.
4. Agree conclusions and recommendations arising from the specific review.

Index